Language Intervention Series
Volume V

EMERGING LANGUAGE
IN
AUTISTIC CHILDREN

EMERGING LANGUAGE IN AUTISTIC CHILDREN, by Warren H. Fay, Ph.D., and Adriana Luce Schuler, Ph.D., is the fifth volume in the **Language Intervention Series**—Richard L. Schiefelbusch, series editor. Other volumes in this series include:

Published:

Volume I **BASES OF LANGUAGE INTERVENTION** edited by *Richard L. Schiefelbusch*

Volume II **LANGUAGE INTERVENTION STRATEGIES** edited by *Richard L. Schiefelbusch*

Volume III **LANGUAGE INTERVENTION FROM APE TO CHILD** edited by *Richard L. Schiefelbusch and John H. Hollis*

Volume IV **NONSPEECH LANGUAGE AND COMMUNICATION** **Analysis and Intervention** edited by *Richard L. Schiefelbusch*

In preparation:

EARLY LANGUAGE INTERVENTION edited by *Richard L. Schiefelbusch and Diane D. Bricker*

DEVELOPMENTAL LANGUAGE INTERVENTION Psycholinguistic **Applications** edited by *Kenneth F. Ruder and Michael D. Smith*

COMMUNICATIVE COMPETENCE Acquisition and Intervention edited by *Richard L. Schiefelbusch and Joanne Pickar*

Language Intervention Series
Volume V

EMERGING LANGUAGE IN AUTISTIC CHILDREN

by
Warren H. Fay, Ph.D.
Crippled Children's Division
University of Oregon Health Sciences Center

and

Adriana Luce Schuler, Ph.D.
Department of Special Education
San Francisco State University

Series Editor
Richard L. Schiefelbusch

Technical Editors
Marilyn Barket
Robert Hoyt

University Park Press
Baltimore

UNIVERSITY PARK PRESS
International Publishers in Science, Medicine, and Education
233 East Redwood Street
Baltimore, Maryland 21202

Typeset by American Graphic Arts Corporation.
Manufactured in the United States of America by The Maple Press Company.

Library of Congress Cataloging in Publication Data
Fay, Warren H.
Emerging language in autistic children.

(Language intervention series; v. 5)
Includes index.
1. Autistic children—Language.   2. Speech
disorders in children.   I. Schuler, Adriana Luce, joint
author.   II. Title.   III. Series. [DNLM: 1. Autism
—In infancy and childhood.   2. Language development.
W1 LA616s v. 5 / WM203.5 F282e]
RJ506.A9F39   618.92′8982   80-13564
ISBN 0-8391-1586-5

contents

Foreword.   vii
Preface.   xi
Acknowledgments.   xiii

chapter 1 **Autism** Introduction.   1

chapter 2 **Aspects of Speech**.   19

chapter 3 **Aspects of Language**.   51

chapter 4 **Aspects of Communication**.   87

chapter 5 **Aspects of Cognition**.   113

chapter 6 **A Review of Intervention Techniques**.   137

chapter 7 **Guidelines for Intervention**.   165

Index.   211

As explained by the authors, the term *autism* denotes a problem of heartbreaking developmental complexity. The problem is perceived by parents early in the life of the child. Until recently the parents faced a double jeopardy. They were overwhelmed by the episodic events precipitated by their child, and they were also automatically blamed as the cause of the problem. Thus, the dramatic daily events, the uncertain causal factors, and the nagging guilt surrounding their own parenting roles combined to make autism a parental nightmare. Parents also had to face several years of indecisive treatments for their child, leaving them uncertain and confused about their child's future.

Fay and Schuler have carefully documented the most relevant information about the language and communication of autistic children. They have stripped away the prejudices and have exposed the tendency of earlier writers to oversimplify the disorder. They have provided an especially valuable perspective on the cognitive/language dimensions of the problem. In their analysis, the behaviors of autistic and autistic-like children can be improved through appropriate individualized training. Their analysis and their suggestions provide a measure of hope and also a realistic caution that progress will usually be slow and often limited in nature.

Chapter 1 provides both a historical and a current overview of the state of the art in speech, language, communication, and cognition. The autistic child is benefiting from the improving state of knowledge, and the child, in turn, is contributing further to our understanding of acquisition and intervention as we struggle to find the keys to improved language functions.

> His characteristically delayed and prolonged development, coupled with his unique linguistic anomalies, allows for what might be termed a *time lapse analysis* of the normal gone awry. His subsequent communicative failures expose our social dependence upon behaviors—verbal and nonverbal—not formally appreciated (p. 18).

Chapter 2 provides an intensive analysis of articulation in echolalic speech of both autistic and non-autistic children. Interestingly, the autistic child seems to have better articulation than one would expect from the child's general development of speech and language. In contrast, intonational variation is limited, and in general, the child is prosodically maldeveloped. Perhaps we can agree with the author's speculation that echolalic speech is keyed to a memory system independent of the phonological rule system. Thus, the autistic child seems to learn the echoic material in a parrot-like manner, but does not learn the rules that permit him to generate new word combinations. This issue may provide a major clue as to why speech as a delivery system for language is ineffectively taught to many autistic children.

Chapters 3 and 4 examine the speaking behavior of autistic children to emphasize why it is so often devoid of meaning and communicative intent. Even the object-naming functions of language may be merely the assignment of concrete labels rather than rule-linked conceptual units. "The memorized words denote but fail to connote" (p. 84). Even more apparent is the autistic child's difficulty in shifting referents according to the demands of the speaking situations at the moment. Thus, the pragmatic features of language may be especially difficult for the autistic child. In fact, the autistic child may provide a dramatic illustration of the importance of "intent" in social communication. It becomes apparent in designing modes of communication—verbal or nonverbal—that intent can be communicated in various ways if the relationships and the codes are perceived by the communicant.

In Chapters 4 and 5 the suggestion is made that autistic children apparently do better when presented with nontransient stimuli that are coded in space rather than in time. This issue may be relevant to the selection of alternatives when speech does not seem to be feasible. Nevertheless, the time variables, that is, the auditory and visual tracking of speaking agents, the sequences in human actions and relations, and the rates and rhythms of social events, cannot be avoided in communication activities. The authors point out that the autistic child's early tendency to relate to objects rather than people may account, at least in part, for the limited way the child uses symbols, after they are attained, to engage in conversational "give and take."

This perspective suggests that language training for autistic children must aim for viable symbol modes that can be learned and used in many social contexts. The latter undertaking is likely to be more difficult than the former.

In Chapter 5 the author assumes the bold initiative of discussing the *interaction* of cognitive, linguistic, and social development. She points out that it is difficult to support theories of autism that focus on a single aspect of development. However, efforts to strike a true synthesis of these important areas are limited to a few effective studies. For instance, studies by Bruner (1975) and Snyder (1974) provide some examples of a joint focus on cognitive/linguistic as well as communicative aspects of development.

The first five chapters of the book may be taken as a unit and used as a statement of the current state of knowledge about emerging language in autistic children. A theoretical framework for the study and analysis of speech, language, communication, and cognition in childhood autism is presented. The final two chapters then may serve the reader as a guide to emerging practices in language and communication training. Major historical developments with regard to the teaching of language skills to autistic children are reviewed and discussed, and guidelines for designing language-teaching programs are provided.

Chapter 6 includes a review of behavioral procedures in language teaching. One is impressed with the short history and with the changing nature of this work. Initially, the emphasis was upon imitation of speech sounds or upon the establishment and expansion of a functional repertoire of verbal behavior. This technique has probably reached its most advanced stage in the work of Lovaas (1977). His procedures have been used to teach "abstract terms" that define simple relationships in time and space as well as relationships among people, objects, and events. However, there is doubt about the generalization of the language responses to other contexts as appropriate speech acts. The generalization problem raises a special question for language intervention specialists. Is the instructional problem due to the behavioral procedures used in training, as the authors imply, or because of the speech mode used in the instruction? Schaeffer (1980), who was one of Lovaas's clinicians during his experimental work with autistic children, has suggested that a principal issue is spontaneous speech. He finds that spontaneous speech acts can be increased by using signed speech and subsequently fading the signs as the range of communication increases. This suggests that the mode of responding may be an important variable in language training of autistic children.

This issue is examined under the heading of "Alternative Systems of Communication." The possibility that signing can be a prominent aspect of the communication teaching program with autistic children is strongly indicated.

However, there is apparent need for further research on spontaneous signing and the possible effects of signing on speech.

An interesting question can be posed relative to language and communication training of autistic children: What can be taught that is valuable for social purposes? A second closely related question might be: Does language and communication training serve to increase the social exchanges of autistic children? These questions are not answered in the material presented by Fay and Schuler but the answer may logically be *yes*—but not to the degree desired. Perhaps, then, the point should be: How can language and communication training be designed to enhance the social exchange objective?

Some direction is provided for this training in specifying objectives leading to the giving of instructions and messages, asking questions, making phone calls, going shopping, role playing, and playing games. However, even though the authors endorse the directions that the recent approaches to instruction are going it still seems apparent that the results are indeed limited.

The content of this book provides an honest appraisal of the current state of the art. Language teaching methods have progressed remarkably in recent years, but we still have far to go. Probably the special problems of autistic children expose the weaknesses of current instructional procedures. We may assume that we are better at teaching referential naming skills to autistic children than we are at teaching the language that goes with social functions. I submit that this analysis applies to all children for whom a functional language must be taught. It remains to be seen, of course, whether we shall achieve remarkable successes with autistic children as our functional language teaching skills improve.

Richard L. Schiefelbusch, Ph.D.

Bruner, J. S. 1975. The ontogenesis of speech acts. J. Child Lang. 2:1–19.

Lovaas, O. I. 1977. The Autistic Child: Language Development through Behavior Modification. Irvington, New York.

Schaeffer, B. 1980. Spontaneous language through signed speech. *In* R. L. Schiefelbusch (ed.), Nonspeech Language and Communication: Analysis and Intervention, pp. 421–446. University Park Press, Baltimore.

Snyder, L. 1975. Pragmatics in language delayed children: Their prelinguistic and early verbal performatives and presuppositions. Unpublished doctoral dissertation, University of Colorado, Boulder.

Do the limitations of the autistic child's world define the limitations of his language, or does his language define the limits of his world? The intimate relationship between reality and the symbol system we use to describe it disallows an adequate answer to this question. Nevertheless, the aspects of speech, language, communication, and cognition have been discussed separately in this volume. This approach not only provides a means of organization (and clarification) but also serves to underscore the intricate interrelationships between these various aspects. Autism, we must recognize, should not be viewed as merely a speech impediment, a language disability, a cognitive deficit, or an interrelational disorder.

One of our principal reasons for writing this book, therefore, was to emphasize that social, linguistic, and cognitive development closely interact, and that autistic patterns of behavior should be considered in the light of this interaction if they are to be delineated from normal or non-autistic patterns of behavior. With this perspective in mind, we hope that this volume will serve to 1) improve insight into the world of the autistic child as it is shaped by his disabilities in verbal as well as nonverbal behavior, and 2) provide a rationale for language/communication intervention that is capable of expanding the limits both of the autistic child's communication and of his world. In an attempt to accommodate this double objective, the text has been arranged to highlight these two major emphases. The first five chapters address theoretical issues, while Chapters 6 and 7, more practically oriented, explore ways in which the insights gained in the first section can be applied to the intervention work with autistic and autistic-like children.

This volume evolved from the authors' incidental discussions and arguments at professional conferences, which were followed by a lively correspondence on issues as diverse as the biological basis of vocal mimicry and the schedule of plane connections between Portland and Santa Barbara. While we were able to overcome our geographical separation for purposes of planning, the actual writing of the chapters was undertaken separately. The first three chapters were written in Portland by Warren, while the last four were written near Santa Barbara by Luce.

A variety of fields, including psychiatry, experimental and developmental psychology, neuropsychology, psycholinguistics, speech pathology and audiology, linguistics, special education, and aphasiology, provided a wealth of material for our work. To a synthesis of this literature we added reports from our own clinical, tutorial, and experimental undertakings with both autistic and non-autistic children exhibiting some autistic-like behaviors. Given this broad orientation, we hope that this volume will be useful to people from various backgrounds and with diverse concerns. We recommend *Emerging Language in Autistic Children* as a primary text for undergraduate and graduate courses in language disorders, autism, and developmental disabilities, as well as for supplemental use in courses that focus on child development, in general, and on exceptional children, in particular. In addition, we hope that the materials gathered will be useful to professionals in the fields of speech pathology, special education, and child psychiatry and psychology, and to therapists in psychiatric clinics and centers for retarded persons. Finally, it is hoped that our writing will be of value to parents of autistic and autistic-like children, and will help them to understand the nature of, and cope more effectively with, their child's communication difficulties.

acknowledgments

First, I wish to acknowledge the support of the Crippled Children's Division of the University of Oregon Health Sciences Center, its able director, Victor Menashe, and its director of the Section of Speech Pathology and Audiology, Robert Blakeley. They have been most generous with their encouragement and assistance. I owe a special thanks to C. Donald Nelson, of the Crippled Children's Division, for his comments and criticisms of the manuscript. Most of the research for the initial chapters of this book was conducted while I was affiliated with the Oregon Unit of the Collaborative Perinatal Study, which was supported by PHS Grant No. NB02370 and PHS Contract No. PH-43-NINDS-68-10. It is with sincere appreciation that I acknowledge this support and the help of the study staff. The person perhaps most responsible for continued pursuit of my research efforts is William Clark, Jr., Project Director of the Collaborative Perinatal Study. I feel the deepest gratitude to him, not only for his official support, but also for his personal encouragement and advice.

We are indebted to Dr. Richard L. Schiefelbusch and his excellent staff for their expert advice and editorial assistance.

The contributions of my wife Carol have been particular and pervasive. Our daughter Betsy provided much inspiration for my interest in emerging child language.

Finally, I owe a debt to my many autistic and post-autistic friends and their parents, particularly Jack Dewey and his parents Margaret and Horace. We all should be grateful for what the thousands of autistic children have taught us and have yet to teach us. Thanks.

W.H.F.
Portland, Oregon

First, I want to thank Warren Fay and Anne Donnellan for encouraging me to write my contributions, and for getting me started. Further, I thank my mentors and friends for keeping me going. Most of all, I feel indebted to all those individuals described as autistic, psychotic, schizophrenic, or otherwise atypical, their parents and their teachers, who raised and sustained my interest in this subject matter. Without them my contribution could never have been completed. In particular I want to thank my co-workers at the Santa Barbara County Autism Dissemination Project and at Camarillo State Hospital, who were always ready to share their experiences and knowledge and to raise new questions and challenge old beliefs.

Special words of thanks should be expressed to Christiane Bormann, Andrea Thompson, Pam Cote, Cheryl Fletcher, Jaydene Davis-Welsh, Carol Prutting, Carey LaVigna, and James Underwood for criticisms and comments that proved most helpful in preparing my contributions.

A.L.S.
San Francisco

Language Intervention Series
Volume V

EMERGING LANGUAGE
IN
AUTISTIC CHILDREN

chapter 1

Autism

Introduction

Warren H. Fay

Crippled Children's Division
University of Oregon Health Sciences Center
Portland, Oregon

contents

EARLY INFANTILE AUTISM 3
EARLY INTERPRETATIONS 7
THE SYNDROME REVISITED 9
LANGUAGE AND DIAGNOSIS 13
SUMMARY AND CONCLUSIONS 17

Thirty-five years have passed since child psychiatrist Leo Kanner (1943) described children he had encountered over the years who seemed to have certain unusual characteristics in common. Perhaps the most common of these characteristics was language deficit. Few authorities since that time have failed to observe this most striking feature, nor have many been without ready explanations for the language symptoms. Goethe wrote, "It is only when we know very little about a subject that we are quite sure; and with knowledge doubt arises and grows." The brief history of the attitudes toward the autistic language symptoms has been one of increasing doubt about causes. This introductory chapter examines the development of some of the literature that nurtured these doubts, and addresses current attitudes toward the symptoms and toward diagnostic and prognostic concerns. (For a more comprehensive review of the literature, see Bryson and Hingtgen, 1971, and Ornitz and Ritvo, 1976.)

EARLY INFANTILE AUTISM

Kanner (1943) gave the name *early infantile autism* to a disorder he characterized as the earliest possible manifestation of childhood schizophrenia. He emphasized, nevertheless, that it was not the schizophrenia of children and adults—a departure from an initially present relationship—but rather an extreme autistic aloneness from the start. The common characteristics noted by Kanner were profound withdrawal, an obsessive desire for preservation of sameness, a skillful and even affectionate relation to objects, an intelligent and pensive physiognomy, and either mutism or the kind of language that does not serve interpersonal communication. Kanner believed the autistic child was the product of a "parent type," characterized as cold, intellectual, ego-oriented, driving, and ambitious. "My search for autistic children of unsophisticated parents has remained unsuccessful to date.... One is struck again and again by what I should like to call a mechanism of human relationships" (1949, p. 421).

Kanner (1946) subsequently described the clinical features of the language of 23 children whom he studied at The Johns Hopkins Hospital, Baltimore, Maryland. He noted that eight were mute but might utter a complete sentence in an emergency situation. Other characteristics were echolalia (immediate and delayed); metaphorical substitution; transfer of meaning through substitute analogy—through generalization (the whole for the part) and through restriction (the part for the whole); literalness; simple verbal negation used as a means of protection against unpleasant occurrences; affirmation by repetition; and pronominal reversals—the child referring to himself as "you" and to the person spoken to as "I." This last feature Kanner regarded as "typical, almost pathognomonic" of the condition. He concluded that there was no fundamental difference between the speaking and mute children as far as communication through speech was concerned.

3

Also noted was excellent rote memory coupled with the inability to use language in any other way. This combination often led parents to "stuff" the children with more and more verses, zoological and botanical names, titles and composers of recorded pieces, and so on. Such "stuffing" methods were not universally successful. In one case study (Kanner, 1951), the parents of Frederick W. reportedly spent hours each day "teaching" him to talk. They begged him to repeat words after them. He remained mute, except for two words ("Daddy" and "Dora") that he had never been taught to say. But one day, at about 2½ years of age, he spoke up and said, "overalls," a word which was decidedly not a part of his teaching repertoire. Similar case reports including unusual "first words" permeate the early literature and, when coupled with tutorial failures, create a strong suggestion of elective mutism. One 5-year-old who had never been heard to pronounce one articulate word in his life, became distressed when a prune skin stuck to his palate. He exclaimed distinctly, "Take it out of there!" and then resumed his muteness (Kanner, 1949).

Further evidence militating for an "elective" component to the mutism came from parental reports. One mother remarked in her notes:

> I can't be sure just when he stopped the imitation of word sounds. It seems that he has gone backward mentally gradually for the last two years. We have thought it was because he did not disclose what was in his head, that it was there all right. . . .

Further insights were forthcoming:

> Now that he is making so many sounds, it is disconcerting because it is now evident that he can't talk. Before, I thought he could if he only would. He gave the impression of silent wisdom to me. . . . One puzzling and discouraging thing is the great difficulty one has in getting his attention! (Kanner, 1943, p. 225).

When sentences are finally formed, according to Kanner, they remain for a long time merely "parrot-like" repetitions of word combinations previously heard. Sometimes these are echoed immediately and at other times they are retained and uttered later. Kanner referred to the latter behavior as "delayed echolalia."

It is particularly noteworthy how Kanner accounted for the difficulty with personal pronouns. In his book *Child Psychiatry* (1948), he noted that the absence of spontaneous sentence formation and the echolalia-type of reproduction give rise to a peculiar grammatical phenomenon:

> Personal pronouns are repeated just as heard, with no change to suit the altered situation. The child, once told by his mother, "Now I will give you

your milk," expresses this desire for milk in exactly the same words. Consequently he came to speak of himself always as "you," and the person addressed as "I." Not only the wording, but even the intonation is retained (p. 718).

Between the ages of 5 and 6 years, echolalic children "gradually abandon the echolalia and learn spontaneously to use personal pronouns with adequate reference" (Kanner, 1946, p. 246). Kanner did not elaborate on his choice of the terms "abandon" and "learn spontaneously." He indicated that these anomalies were replaced by more communicative language in the sense of a question-and-answer excercise, and then in the sense of greater spontaneity of sentence formation. After his review of 55 patients, he concluded that "Those who eventually begin to talk give evidence that during the silent period they have accumulated a considerable store of readily available linguistic material" (Kanner, 1949, p. 418).

Eight of Kanner's original 11 children acquired the ability to speak either at the usual age or after some delay. All but one of the speaking children did so with clear articulation and phonation.

Among the post-echoic peculiarities of Kanner's concern were excessive "literalness" and difficulties in acquiring the concept of yes. In lieu of answering with a yes, children were often found to indicate affirmation by repetition. (Such an interpretation tends to differentiate echolalia in its more automatic manifestations from a more communicative form. See Chapter 3.)

One child described by Kanner (1949) learned to say yes when his father told him that he would put him on his shoulders if he did so; this word then came to "mean" only the desire to be put on his father's shoulders. This type of literalness was also illustrated with prepositions. When Alfred was asked, "What is this picture *about*?" he replied: "People are moving *about*." And John F. corrected his father's statement about pictures on the wall with a declaration that the pictures were "*near*" the wall. Donald T., when requested to put something down, promptly put it on the floor. Kanner concluded that the meaning of a word apparently cannot be used with any but the originally acquired connotation. Kanner's observations are of particular interest in light of contemporary views on the limited abilities in the areas of generalization (see Chapter 5).

An example of "metaphoric language" was offered by Kanner (1948, p. 521) in the case of Jay S., who referred to himself as "Blum" whenever his veracity was questioned. An explanation for this finally became clear when Jay, who could read fluently, one day pointed to a furniture firm's advertisement which said in large letters, "Blum Tells the Truth." Since Jay told the truth, he *was* Blum. Kanner explained this as being an analogy not unlike the designation of Romeo as a lover, but in cases such as this the autistic child has his private, original references, the meaning of which is transferable only to the extent to which any listener can trace the source of the analogy.

Between the ages of 6 and 8 years, reading skill is acquired quickly, according to Kanner's (1943) earliest observations, but the children read monotonously, and a story or a moving picture is experienced in unrelated portions rather than in its coherent totality. Also, many become preoccupied with the spelling of words.

Intellectually, Kanner reported that the children of his early cases all related well with objects. Binet or similar testing could not be carried out because of limited accessibility, but the subjects did well with the Sequin Form Board (Kanner, 1948, p. 720). Elsewhere he noted that in early infantile autism and related syndromes the patients appear feebleminded because of emotional interference with the unfolding of cognitive personalities (Kanner, 1948, p. 96).

The preceding descriptions are a sampling of the original—the Kannerian—picture of the autistic language symptoms. Not only did Kanner identify and label the syndrome, thereby opening the doors for clinical and experimental exploration, but he also provided a remarkably descriptive (and durable) account of the verbal peculiarities encountered in autism.

Despite Kanner's acknowledged contributions, an important "minority report" was filed. Shortly after the first papers describing the syndrome became available, Scheerer, Rothmann, and Goldstein (1945) published a monograph on personality organization using a case of "Idiot Savant" as their point of departure. In this work they compared Kanner's autistic language and that of their idiot savant. In both instances they interpreted the major deficiency as an impairment of abstract capacity. They wondered whether the fact that the children did not grasp the meaning of language in the normal way might not be the key to their heightened responsiveness to, and their tenaciously obsessive reproduction of, sound patterns. They regarded the problem as the result of a concrete level of thinking in which the child cannot detach the words from their experienced "belongingness" in the actual situation and reverse this belonging in terms of a relational symbol. The autistic child and the idiot savant, they suggested, have done all that they could with language: repeat it rather than understand it. In a later paper, Goldstein (1959) challenged the traditional explanations of why the autistic child reacts against the pin rather than the one who pricked him with it: "Is it not simpler and more understandable to assume, as I do, that with his primitive reaction types the child reacts to 'stimuli' and not to whole persons?" (p. 545).

EARLY INTERPRETATIONS

Unfortunately, despite the stage set by Kanner and by Scheerer et al. for a potential language-oriented interpretation of language symptoms, these concerns were to be largely ignored, subverted, or relegated to ancillary status in the years that followed. Etiological speculations permeated the literature with primary focus on such causative factors as social withdrawal, extreme introversion, and schizophrenic variation. Language symptoms tended to be interpreted in light of the clinician's or theorist's own views as to the psychogenetic nature of the disorder.

A prime example of how language anomalies were reinterpreted or overinterpreted occurred in the formal discussion period following delivery of Kanner's (1946) paper, "Irrelevant and Metaphoric Language in Early Infantile Autism," at the meeting of the American Psychiatric Association. In that discussion J. Louise Despert presented this expanded interpretation of Kanner's explanation of pronominal reversals:

> It is highly significant, for instance, that the "I not I" distinction is not established in the autistic child, as it is early in the development of language in the normal child, and Dr. Kanner pointedly selects the pronominal reversal as an almost pathognomonic sign of infantile autism. Since the appearance of the first-person pronoun in language development shortly follows that stage of individuation which corresponds to the child's consciousness as one, whole, and apart from others, the importance of this sign cannot be over-emphasized (Despert, 1946, p. 246).

That the importance of the sign could be overemphasized was evident in the explanations of pronoun acquisition in a context of anal function (Mahler, Furer, and Settlage, 1959; Bettelheim, 1967). According to this view, there is in elimination a separation of the self from the nonself and a separation of the "I" out of the undifferentiated "you."

Echolalia received much the same treatment. Psychotic echolalia was variously described as "serving an autoerotic function," as "autoerotic and autoaggressive motoric discharge of basic drives," as "hostility dressed in the unique manner of imitation," and as "echolalia that serves to mock." Regarding the remarkable rote memories of verbal material by autistic youngsters, Bettelheim (1967) noted, "Far from indicating that the child can only memorize but does not understand the more complex functions of language, it suggests to me that these children understand them very well indeed" (p. 429).

For those concerned with the language aspects of the syndrome, the landmark of the 1950s was the publication by Eisenberg (1956) of the results of a follow-up of 63 diagnosed cases of early infantile autism seen at the Children's Psychiatric Service of The Johns Hopkins Hospital in Baltimore. Median age at follow-up was 15 years. Of the 63, three were said to have achieved good adjustment (functioning well at academic, social, and community levels and accepted by their peers). Fourteen achieved a fair adjustment (attended regular school classes at a level commensurate with age and had meaningful contacts with other people, but exhibited schizoid peculiarities of personality sufficient to single them out as deviant and to cause interference with function). Forty-six children were classed as having made poor adjustment (not emerging from autism to any extent and exhibiting markedly maladaptive functioning, characterized by apparent feeblemindedness and/or grossly disturbed behavior, whether maintained at home or in an institution).

Using as a line of demarcation useful speech at the age of 5, the study group was divided into 32 "speaking" and 31 "nonspeaking" children (unable to communicate verbally with others—including mutism, echolalia only, and use of private words). The first group of 32 classified as "good" in 3, "fair" in 13, and "poor" in 16 instances. Of the 31 nonspeaking children, one was classified as "fair" and 30 rated "poor." Thus, 16 of the 32 children with useful speech at 5 years of age had been able to achieve a "fair" to "good" social adjustment, whereas only one of 31 nonspeaking children could be so classified. Eisenberg (1956) concluded:

> Clinically, the degree of disturbance in language function emerges clearly as an important guide to prognosis. In effect we have an index of the extent of autistic isolation for the development of language obviously bespeaks a meaningful interchange with other people. In the absence of speech, the probability of emergence is vanishingly small, apparently without regard to which of the currently available treatment methods is employed (p. 610).

Language thus gained status (albeit secondary) as a prognostic factor, and in doing so inflated the potential value of language-oriented therapy.

Meanwhile, the popular press reflected none of these findings. The cover story of the February, 1960, issue of *Harpers* magazine reported the successful therapy of an autistic child, "The Rebirth of Johnny." At age 8 he was reported to have cried when hurt, laughed when happy, loved, and evoked love in others. Also mentioned, almost parenthetically, was the fact that he still did not talk, although he once said "Go to hell" and "I can't."

In an April 15, 1960, syndicated doctors' advice column (Frances L. Ilg, M.D., and Louise Bates Ames, Ph.D.), the parents inquired about their 4-year-old Otto who was diagnosed autistic. They were concerned about his very limited receptive vocabulary and his failure to talk despite improvements in relating, self-care, and a few other areas. The doctors' reply included the notation that these children show themselves to worst advantage the first 5 years. "It seems quite conceivable that you have a boy who is just naturally slow in speech in addition to being of somewhat autistic temperament. Actually it is the relation to others, and the warmth to parents which is apt to come in most slowly—so you can at least congratulate yourself on those scores."

THE SYNDROME REVISITED

Neglect of attitudes about language features, which typified the 1950s, was to change in the decade that followed. Cunningham and Dixon (1961) observed an autistic boy (age 7) over a period of 6 months during which time they analyzed his speech both quantitatively and qualitatively. They found that in terms of length of utterance and variety of words used his speech resembled that of a normal 24–30-month-old child. Qualitatively, however, it was at a much lower level of development as reflected in its monotony, the rarity with which questions were asked and information given, and the frequency of incomplete sentences. Egocentric speech was more frequently used than in the language of a normal 24–30-month-old child. In the course of 6 months the boy did, nevertheless, show some progress in relation to developmental norms for language acquisition.

The first systematic study of the language of a group of autistic children was the work of Wolff and Chess (1965). They compared the language of 14 autistic children under 8 years of age with regard to total number of words, number of different words, average length of utterance, number of nonverbal utterances, number of immediate and delayed non-communicative repetitions, number of communicative repetitions, and number of original communicative utterances in a language sample. No formal comparisons were made with normal or non-autistic youngsters, but Wolff and Chess regarded stereotyped repetitions of utterances appropriate to an earlier developmental level or to a previous environmental context as the "most striking abnormalities." They further postulated that repetition rather than failure to communicate may be the more basic abnormality. It is also noteworthy that 9 of the 14 children had reportedly acquired reading skills without particular efforts having been made to teach them to read. Five of these began to read before the age of 5, at a time when they had rarely been observed to speak.

Concurrent with these early explorations of language behavior was the publication of *Infantile Autism* (Rimland, 1964), which was selected for the first Century Psychology Series Award in 1962. Rimland's "working paper" theorized that the autistic child suffers from an inability to relate present sensation to past experience. The author said this basic dysfunction was the course for the child's inability to understand relationships or to think abstractly. Being thus unable to integrate his sensations into a comprehensive whole, Rimland contended that the autistic child cannot perceive himself as an organized and unitary entity.

What had been traditionally presumed to be part of the affective component of the disorder was now viewed as the consequences of the child's inability to associate the biological rewards given by the mother with the social relationship in which they were presented. Rimland proposed a rather speculative account of the etiology of the child's cognitive deficiency on the basis of malfunctioning of the brain stem reticular formation, which normally seems to monitor attentional behavior as well as status of consciousness in the process. His firm genetic-cognitive orientation brought about a shift of thinking on the part of the clinical and scientific community; in effect, a psychogenic approach made way for one more biologically oriented. This shift served as an invitation for new behaviorally and biologically oriented research.

The involvement of the professional disciplines of speech pathology and special education dates from 1966 with the publication of "A Longitudinal Study of the Speech Behavior and Language Comprehension of Fourteen Children Diagnosed Atypical or Autistic" in *Exceptional Children* (Pronovost, Wakstein, and Wakstein, 1966). This case study approach of eight "vocalizers" and six talking children evolved from Pronovost's (1961) earlier clinical observations which raised several questions concerning the interrelationships among speech behavior, language comprehension, and other aspects of the child's physical and psychological status. Among other findings, Pronovost noted wide variations in pitch, intensity, duration, and quality of the autistic children's speech. Echolalia was reported to be characteristic of the talking group with a trend for the echoed phrases to be monotonous in terms of pitch, intensity, and rhythm rather than faithful imitations of the patterns of the adult stimuli. The children in both groups were found to be seriously impaired in their capacity to comprehend language, despite psychiatric reports that assumed intelligence to be basically within normal limits. Such studies led inevitably to more concentrated analyses of the aberrant behaviors per se. For example, preliminary findings of an intensive study of echolalia in delayed and neuropathological conditions of childhood, as well as in cases of childhood psychosis, have been reported (Fay, 1966).

Systematic experimental studies into the psychological functioning of autistic children were also well underway in the latter half of the decade. Outstanding examples of this line of research were the investigations of Hermelin, O'Connor, Frith, and others of the Developmental Psychology Unit of the Medical Research Council, London (Hermelin and O'Connor, 1970). Although their studies did not specifically address language symptomatology, considerable attention was given to linguistic coding, perceptual-motor tasks, ordering, immediate memory, and the interdependence of IQ and language development. These studies were of particular value because to a large extent they were based on the comparisons of the performances of autistic youngsters with control groups of mentally subnormal as well as normal children. One of their findings was the relatively greater impairment by the autistic group in the appreciation of syntactic and meaningful verbal structures. The autistic children were reported to have immediate auditory rote memories that were superior to those of subnormals and as good as, or better than, those of normal children of similar mental age. However, when syntactic and meaningfully related material was presented, the recall capacity of the control groups improved significantly more than did that of the autistic children. Hermelin and O'Connor concluded from their numerous investigations that the inability of autistic children to interpret stimuli meaningfully constituted their basic cognitive deficit (1970, p. 129).

The most extensive investigations of the autistic syndrome during this period were follow-up studies carried out in England (Rutter, Greenfeld, and Lockyer, 1967; Rutter and Lockyer, 1967; Lockyer and Rutter, 1969, 1970) and in the United States (DeMyer et al., 1973). The Rutter group conducted a 5- to 15-year follow-up of 63 autistic youngsters together with matched controls. The latter group was said to have typically exhibited some degree of mental subnormality and retardation of speech. They found that 7 children among the 63 gained speech after 5 years of age and made "fair progress." Of 37 speaking children, 19 showed pronominal reversals, and, with one possible exception, they were also echolalic. In a subsequent summary of their cognitive and linguistic findings, Rutter and Bartak (1971) concluded that autistic children exhibited a central disorder of language involving both the comprehension of language and the use of language or conceptual skills in thinking. It was suggested that *this disorder constituted the basic handicap to which the other autistic behaviors were only secondary.* They claimed support for the view from research reported by Hermelin and O'Connor (1970), but acknowledged also that these studies revealed the cognitive defect to be more widespread than originally suggested.

DeMyer et al. (1973) evaluated 85 autistic boys and 35 autistic girls at 5 1/2 years of age and in follow-up ranging from 2 to 16 years. A control group of nonpsychotic subnormal children was also followed. Autistic children were classed either as *high autistic, middle autistic,* or *low autistic* according to criteria of emotional withdrawal, noncommunicative speech or muteness, and nonfunctional object use. At initial evaluation, 40 children had communicative speech so minimal that it was considered to be nonuseful, and 46 children were mute. Of those 86, 30 developed some useful speech by follow-up time and 15 developed their useful speech after 5 years of age. No child whose communicative speech developed after 5 was found to be normal or nearly normal at follow-up. Presence of communicative words at initial evaluation proved to be a more favorable prognostic sign for the development of useful speech than muteness or echolalia without communicative value. Of the children whose speech consisted of only a few communicative words, 43% gained conversational speech characterized as more complex than expressing immediate needs, while only 29.1% of the echolalic and 10.8% of the mute gained such speech. About 65% of the mute children remained mute, and only 19% gained useful speech. This outcome was reversed for echolalic children, 20% of whom were mute on follow-up, while 62% gained some useful speech. With reference to IQ scores, 5% to 10% had IQs within normal range and 12% to 20% within the mildly retarded range, while 43% to 68% were moderately to profoundly retarded. Also, 73.4% of the autistic group were "far outside the range of normal" in signs of brain dysfunction as determined by neurological evaluation. DeMyer concluded that the learning disorder hinders the acquisition of language, and that the social isolation is a logical end product of closed communication (verbal and nonverbal) channels with the child's parents. She suggested that the language disorder is organically based and, in conjunction with a perceptual-motor disorder, interferes with both verbal and nonverbal communication skills.

One further event of the 1960s had a major impact on the management of autistic language behavior. This was the publication by Lovaas et al. (1966) of initial successes in the establishment of speech through the use of operant learning techniques.

And so, within a decade, the formerly regarded ancillary character of the autistic child's speech and language symptoms became the paramount concern of those studying and treating the syndrome. To many, the "autistic aloneness" became the ancillary symptom to a severe cognitive/language disorder. Prognostic hope through resolution of a severe emotional disorder was gradually shifting to prognostic hope through education. Imputed aggression was giving way to more solid evidence of linguistic incompetence. But this strange malady was to continue to generate far more questions than answers in terms of etiology, nosology, prognosis, and intervention strategies. More than 400 articles and six books were published between 1964, the year Rimland's book appeared, and 1969 (Bryson and Hingtgen, 1971). As the relative importance of the language disorder increased, so did the literature and the questions concerning how normal language was to be acquired and, if acquired, how such acquisition might enhance the outlook. But it remains to be shown that any rationale or specific treatment has altered the natural history of the disease (Ornitz and Ritvo, 1976).

Finally, recent studies have exonerated parents from playing a causative role in the syndrome. Cox et al. (1975), for example, compared the parents of autistic children with parents of children having developmental receptive language disorders. The autistic group was found to have a larger proportion of middle-class families, but no differences between the groups were found with respect to parental warmth, emotional demonstrativeness/responsiveness or sociability, or parental psychiatric disorder, or with respect to early stress of any kind. They concluded that it is unlikely that autism develops as a consequence of parental personality attributes.

LANGUAGE AND DIAGNOSIS

Not uncommonly, speech and language pathologists or audiologists are among the earliest to be consulted by parents of an autistic child. Concerns about possible hearing impairment and failure to develop speech on schedule are frequently the presenting complaints. The child's seeming nonresponsiveness to many sounds, particularly speech, is often reported with a contradictory history for low tolerance to some environmental sounds such as vacuum cleaners and lawn mowers. Complete failure to talk or failure to speak after a period of reportedly normal speech development until around 18 months of age are typical.

Rarely does the speech pathologist or language specialist diagnose childhood autism, although his observations and assessments may contribute to the ultimate diagnosis. As the focus has shifted through the years toward cognitive/linguistic psychopathology, the relative contributions of psychology, speech-language pathology, and special education have increased. Succeeding chapters of this volume, however, show that the nature and extent of language and communicative behaviors in autism remain poorly understood. Standardized tests, such as the Peabody Picture Vocabulary Test (PPVT), the Illinois Test of Psycholinguistic Abilities (ITPA), and the Northwestern Syntax Screening Test (NSST), are of questionable value for assessing the abilities of autistic children. Those tests were not specifically designed to be used with a population with such aberrant language. For example, the imitative tasks commonly employed are meaningless because of the excellent imitating skills that are so often exhibited by autistic children. In addition, the behaviors sampled often require higher verbal skills than can be expected in childhood autism. Finally, accurate psychometric or linguistic testing of these children may be compromised by their abnormal attending and relating behaviors.

Nevertheless, an understanding of the behaviors, their relative significance, and their evolution can contribute to both initial diagnosis and the ongoing diagnostic process during intervention. For these reasons this section offers a current description of the syndrome and its differential diagnosis with emphasis on delayed and deviant language development.

Apparent in the earlier sections of this chapter was a tendency for investigators and clinicians to use interchangeably the terms *early infantile autism, autism, childhood autism, primary autism,* and *autistic children* in variance somewhat from Kanner's syndrome as originally defined. Even *childhood schizophrenia* and *childhood psychosis* are employed as synonyms for the disorder. Kanner himself has deplored "the dilution of the notion of early infantile autism," and observed that "the diagnosis has been made much too prodigiously" (Kanner, 1958, p. 108).

Rimland (1971), acknowledging the need for an objective method of diagnosing early infantile autism and for isolating other previously undifferentiated syndromes in the population of psychotic children, developed a checklist method of diagnosis. This Diagnostic Form E-2 was completed by parents for 2,218 autistic and autistic-like children. These lists were then analyzed with respect to criteria defined by Kanner. Information on such symptoms as avoidance of people, gazing into space, fascination with mechanical objects, and insistence on sameness were components of the "behavior score." A "speech score" included items such as delayed echolalia, pronominal reversal, metaphorical usage, extreme literalness, and other characteristics identified by Kanner. The higher the score, the more likely the child was a "true autistic." The behavioral demarcation was +20; +7 was needed in speech to meet criterion. (Symptoms counterindicating the diagnosis were subtracted, thus creating a range of −33 to +37 on the behavioral scale and −9 to +13 on the speech scale.) Among the 126 children who scored +20 or higher on the behavior items, 52 (41%) met the speech criterion. Rimland regarded this as a "high degree of association between the two criteria." The way in which mute children were handled proved particularly troublesome, however. Rimland noted that about one-half of the children with the classical syndrome are mute. The mutes were assigned to the 0 to +6 speech category, thus failing to make the speech criterion. But also included in this category were talking children who accumulated some (but not enough) speech symptoms. This strange mixture comprised 62% (1,379) of the sample. Of these 0 to +6 children, 1,309 were declared non-autistic on the basis of their sub-autistic behavior scores. An additional 234 were declared non-autistic on the basis of the behavior scores, even though they met or exceeded the +7 on speech. Of these, 88 fell into the behavioral category of 0 to −33. From these data Rimland concluded that, although speech symptoms are closely correlated with the diagnosis of early infantile autism, their pattern is not unique to the disorder. He further suggested that it is easy to misdiagnose a child as "autistic" if only his speech is taken into account.

It is questionable whether these results, with the heavily weighted behavioral scale, and contamination of almost two-thirds of the sample by mixing mutes with subcriterion speech scores, have reflected the role of speech symptoms either in the classical sense or in the neoclassical sense of the past decade. Moreover, there is a strong suggestion that many autistic children could not accumulate such verbal symptoms as literalness and metaphoric language, for example, until perhaps as late as the preadolescent years. Yet examination of the Form E-2 reveals that questions referring to language are in all but a few instances qualified as either "before age 5" or "age 3–5." Questions not age qualified related to initial onset of speech. Thus, a mute child could not acquire a +7 criterion because he had no speech to be deviant. A talking child would have to meet criterion between speech onset and chronological age (CA) 5. A good deal would seem to depend on the age of the child at the time the E-2 was completed and on the developmental rate of additive symptoms once speech began.

An alternative and more functional approach to the diagnostic issue has been offered by Colby and Smith (1970):

> To call a child autistic is to place him in a class of psychiatric disorder characterized by a syndrome, i.e., a cluster of properties which tend to appear together. . . . Commonly a class is defined by a property or conjunction of properties, possession of which is necessary and sufficient (by stipulation) for membership in the class. In contrast to this type of class, there are polythetic classes (*poly* = many, *thetos* = arrangement) which are defined as follows: (a) each individual in the class possesses a large (unspecified) number of properties, (b) each property is possessed by a large number of individuals, and (c) no property is possessed by every individual in the class (p. 1).

Colby and Smith consider autism representative of such a polythetic class defined by certain behavioral properties.

The most recent listing of the behavioral properties defining the syndrome is the report submitted by Ritvo and Freeman (1977) to the National Society for Autistic Children and to the American Psychiatric Association. The syndrome of autism, according to this report, is a developmental disability that is defined and diagnosed behaviorally. (Throughout this volume the use of the terms *autism* and *autistic* will be understood in the context of the definition below, unless otherwise indicated.) The essential features are manifested prior to 30 months of age and indicate disturbances in each of the following areas:

1. Developmental rates and sequences: Normal coordination of the three developmental pathways (i.e., motor, social/adaptive, language/cognitive) is disrupted by delays, arrests and regressions.
2. Responses to sensory stimuli: There may be generalized over- or underreactivity or alternations of these two states. One or more sensory systems are involved.
3. Development of speech, language/cognition, and nonverbal communication: Symptoms include: a) speech—mutism, delayed onset, and immature syntax and articulation, modulated by immature inflections; b) language/cognition—absent or limited symbolic capacity, specific cognitive capacities present (for example, intact rote memory and visual spatial relations), failure to develop the use of abstract terms and reasoning, echolalia, nonlogical use of concepts, and neologisms; c) nonverbal communication—absence or delayed development of appropriate gestures, dissociation of gestures and language, and failure to assign symbolic meaning to gestures.
4. Relationships to people and objects: These are manifested by the failure to develop normal responsivity to people and to use objects appropriately.

Other conclusions from the Ritvo and Freeman report include an etiology based on an underlying physical dysfunction, the exact nature of which is as yet unknown. It occurs alone or in association with mental retardation and other disorders known to affect the brain. Recent work by DeMyer (1975) has revealed that the intelligence of autistic children can be measured reliably and validly, that the IQ has good predictive power, that most autistic children have subnormal intelligence, and that in only a few children does the verbal IQ reach normal levels—no matter how intense the treatment and education.

Ritvo and Freeman report an incidence of approximately four or five per 10,000 births and a likelihood of four to five times more common occurrence in males.

Regarding differential diagnosis, the report emphasizes the differentiating generalized delays in the case of mental retardation. Also, responses to sensory inputs, responses to people and objects, and speech and language development are appropriate to the overall developmental level of cognitive functioning in mental retardation. Similarly, in cases of deafness and blindness the ability to relate to people and objects is usually appropriate to developmental level. (There is a subpopulation of the blind, nevertheless, that closely resembles childhood autism. This condition is discussed in Chapter 2.) Sequelae of physical and psychological trauma, such as hospitalization and maternal deprivation, are differentiated from autism in that symptoms of these conditions generally respond to specific therapies if instituted before permanent changes have resulted. Childhood schizophrenia is characterized as a thought disorder. Certain patients with autism also may fit the criteria of childhood schizophrenia, particularly at a later age (ages 5 to 12). For additional criteria on the differential diagnosis of childhood schizophrenia and childhood autism see the discussion by Rutter (1968).

Differentiating autism from "Congenital, Developmental, and Acquired Disorders of Central Processing of Language (Aphasias)" was presented in the Ritvo and Freeman (1977) report as follows:

> Here (in aphasic conditions) disturbances in language development and central processing are not accompanied by disturbances of responses to sensory inputs, dissociation of other developmental courses (motor, social), relatedness to people and objects. The patients imitate and use gestures and other means to communicate symbolic intent.

For other information on this most important differentiation of autism from developmental aphasia see Churchill (1972), Bartak, Rutter, and Cox (1975), Cox et al. (1975), and Baker et al. (1976).

SUMMARY AND CONCLUSIONS

Childhood autism is a male-dominated developmental disability representative of a polythetic class defined and diagnosed behaviorally. It is likely the result of an as yet unspecified structural, chemical, or physiological entity. More than a quarter century of observation and study has been characterized by efforts to try to fit the "syndrome" into known diagnostic and remedial classifications. But autism simply will not fit. Even latter day recognition and general acceptance that language/cognition is a primary (if not *the* primary) consideration for diagnosis, prognosis, and—by extension—remediation has changed little. The patholinguistic fit has been little better than the psychogenic fit in providing a rationale for better understanding and treatment. Attempts to fit the autistic picture into a frame of developmental delay or of mental retardation accounted for some of the aberrant verbal behaviors. But, here again, the rubric *retardation* is inadequate and off target. Whatever its basis, there is something decidedly language-specific in addition to (causing? resulting from?) the cognitive, emotional, and social shortfalls characteristic of the condition.

Such realizations serve only to underscore our ignorance of the complex relationships of language (verbal and nonverbal) to speech, to communication, to cognition, and to the development of the unimpaired personality. A better understanding of how these relationships develop in the normal child is essential for customizing a fit for autism. It is, moreover, a necessary precursor to intelligent intervention aimed at ameliorating the autistic language deficits.

The extent to which informed language intervention can alter the course of childhood autism is not known at this time, but the relative success evident in the follow-up studies for those youngsters who acquired communicative language by age 5 or 6 constitutes a mandate to try. Perhaps even this successful minority could have reached higher levels of performance with less intervening trauma had they had available to them therapy based on applied knowledge, a knowledge of the ways in which language serves the interaction of one individual with another through its linkage with human motivation.

And so, with this disorder that has so successfully resisted categorization, we, as language specialists, are in a position to make a difference. We may be able to ease human suffering insofar as the wisdom of action increases with depth of knowledge. Knowledge, in this instance, is knowing all that we can about the abnormal processes. That is why we must consult the still incomplete understanding of those who are attempting to solve the mysteries of normal language acquisition. Wisdom of action depends on the application of this knowledge to therapeutic philosophy and strategy.

Not only is the autistic child a potential benefactor of this applied knowledge, but he is also a prime provider. From careful observation of his idiosyncratic patterns of language development we can gain knowledge applicable not only to other language disorders but also, most importantly, to the normal developmental course of language and communication. His characteristically delayed and prolonged development, coupled with his unique linguistic anomalies, allows for what might be termed *time lapse analysis* of the normal gone awry. His subsequent communicative failures expose our social dependence upon behaviors—verbal and nonverbal—not formerly appreciated. Jakobson (1968) has stressed the instructiveness of the acquisition and dissolution of language to those who are concerned with the fully developed structure of language. The autistic child with his rare combination of anomalous development and deviance is potentially even more instructive. Or, in the words of John Wing (1966):

> Autistic children do have a fascination which lies partly in the feeling that somewhere there must be a key which will unlock hidden treasure. The skilled searcher will indeed find treasure . . . but the currency will be everyday and human, not fair gold. In return for our attention, these children may give us the key to human language, which is the key to humanity itself (p. 14).

chapter 2

Aspects of Speech

Warren H. Fay

Crippled Children's Division
University of Oregon Health Sciences Center
Portland, Oregon

contents

MUTENESS 21
ECHOLALIA.. 25
   Developmental Echoing 26
   Non-autistic Echolalia 31
   Autistic Echolalia 34
VOCAL DELIVERY 41
   Voice Quality and Intonation 42
   Characteristics of Articulation 47
SUMMARY 49

Linguist Otto Jesperson (1964) has written that to the child and adult alike, the outer phonetic element of a word and its meaning are "indissolubly connected" (p. 113). In the case of the autistic child, however, as postulated in this and succeeding chapters, the word and the word's meaning are very often completely disconnected. For this reason the components of communication are dealt with in separate chapters in this volume, while the somewhat arbitrary nature of this separation is acknowledged.

This chapter is concerned with speech behavior. It focuses on those sounds (produced and modified by the vocal tract) that are *normally* used to code communicative intent and meaning. While elaborate speech is sometimes produced by autistic children, that speech often fails entirely as a vehicle for conveying meaning. Instead, it appears to be an automatic phenomenon or a goal in itself. In the latter case it is similar to and often coexistent with other forms of self-stimulatory behaviors such as body rocking and various repetitive motility patterns with fingers and hands. Such forms of nonintentional vocalization fail to meet the criteria to be classified as "language" or "verbal communication."

Dichotomizing speech and language in this fashion is not without precedent. Arguments for their separation have been advanced from a theoretical as well as a clinical perspective. Sapir (1921) said that the mere phonetic framework of speech does not constitute the inner fact of language. And in the area of acquired aphasias, Alajouanine and Lhermitte (1963) and Denny-Brown (1963) concluded that there must exist an audiovocal system that is essential for the evocation of the phonemic units but that is independent of (or divorceable from) those cerebral functions that supply the semantic values of language.

The function and nonfunction (muteness) of this audiovocal system as inferred from the behaviors of autistic children are the subjects of the following sections.

MUTENESS

Muteness or mutism includes a range of behavior from total silence to the emission of inarticulate vocalizations bearing little resemblance to human speech. Schuler (1976) has specified three levels of muteness: 1) *total*, absence of both communicative and noncommunicative vocalizations, 2) *functional*, vocalizations generally used for self-stimulation and sound play void of meaning, and 3) *semi-mute*, found in children who show a limited repertoire of words and word approximations used in a functional manner to express immediate desires or dislikes. (The semi-mute condition is more typical of other childhood language disorders than autism.) Schuler further postulates a parallel hierarchy of deficient receptive skills ranging from "probably minimal" in the case of total muteness to "probably poor" in functional muteness to "somewhat better developed" in the case of the semi-mute.

21

Incidence of muteness reported in various studies ranges from 28% (Wolff and Chess, 1965; Lotter, 1967) to 61% (Fish, Shapiro, and Campbell, 1966). Some of this variability can be accounted for by limitations placed on the definition of the term, by sample size, and by the ages and level of autistic involvement of the children at the time of observation.

Such statistics do little to help us understand the mute condition as exhibited by the autistic child. And there is a paucity of research to help us. What studies have appeared are retrospective, usually relying on parental reports. It seems that we are geared to scientific observation and manipulation of behavior, but remarkably unresourceful when it comes to accounting for the absence of behavior. As a consequence, speculations and inference dominate our thinking. These, in turn, are confounded by an emotional climate that can best be defined as a developmental hope countered by fear.

Although we all enter this world as mutes, the usual period of verbal silence is short-lived. "It is clear that man is born to talk," wrote Hebb, Lambert, and Tucker (1971), "innately provided both with the capacity and with the motivation, almost a *need*, to learn, at least in the case of the native language" (p. 213).

If the period of muteness is unduly prolonged, it is a common practice to consider deafness the etiology. Such is frequently the case with autistic muteness. Approximately 80% of the autistic children in one study (Bartak and Rutter, 1976) were said to be deaf at one time. Such a notion is often nurtured by frustrations born of inattention to tutorial efforts as well as to sounds in general. Even when there is some recognition that the child does react to certain sounds, the more general pattern of seeming unawareness is sufficient to impute the hearing mechanism and suggest the need for professional intervention. (For a comprehensive account of audiological considerations in the assessment of autistic children believed to be deaf, see Koegel and Schreibman, 1976, and Lowell, 1976).

Paradoxically, concerns about a baby's deafness are often accompanied by a history of agitation or panic resulting from unexpected or loud sounds to which he had been completely oblivious on other occasions. Ornitz (1973) has related this inconsistency to changes observed in other modalities. Illumination, the feel of certain fabrics or food textures, and proprioceptive and vestibular sensations induced by change in position may also evoke distress. Bartak and Rutter (1976) addressed the noise hypersensitivity question in their comparison of 17 autistic children with nonverbal IQs below 70 (mean: 45.7) with 19 autistic children having IQs above 70 (mean: 93.6). Ninety percent of the high group showed "extreme noise sensitivity" as compared to 54% of the retarded autistic children.

If the autistic child hears, does he babble? Babbling—defined as a diversity of sounds, repetitions, and adult-like intonational patterns (Siegel, 1969)—is generally regarded as an important stage through which the child must pass, although the function of the behavior continues to raise questions (Rees, 1972). Rutter, Bartak, and Newman (1971), in a study of 14 autistic children and 11 children having developmental receptive speech problems, noted that the parents reported either diminution in amount or deviation in the quality of babble in about half the former group and in the majority of the latter group. Ricks (1975a) reported that the parents he interviewed recalled no normal conversational babble in their autistic children's first year. However, Ricks did record vocalizations of some babbling autistic children ages 3 to 5 years. He observed that their babble was monotonous, somewhat similar to a normal child falling asleep. Ricks also found that, whereas normal babies and preverbal children with Down's syndrome (ages 3 to 6 years) paid little attention to their own babble recorded and played back to them, autistic children behaved differently. If the autistic child responded, he did so by precisely imitating his own vocalizations. However, autistic children ignored recordings of other autistic children and taped imitations of their own babble made by a normal child. It is possible that the desire to "preserve sameness" played a role in their selective imitations. In conclusion, it is with caution that it is suggested that deviations in onset, quantity, and quality of babbling *may* reflect a cause or effect relationship to the period of extended muteness. Data are needed to define the limits of normal babbling behavior in infants before the prognostic or diagnostic significance of its developmental variations can be interpreted.

At some period during the extended silence of their autistic children, it occurs to many parents that the muteness is intentional. The typically intelligent, handsome face coupled with normal or nearly normal developmental milestones (e.g., sitting up, walking, use of hands) must kindle this hope. In the vein of the early literature on the subject (Chapter 1), one is tempted to postulate elective mutism. The argument holds that during the long silence an anatomically normal brain has been stoically developing speech, language, and information about the world—perhaps at a normal rate. Underlying this belief is the optimism that if the right treatment approach could be found, the reservoir of stored verbal skills could be undammed, thus eventually exposing an unrealized potential. Parents might come to take considerable comfort in the notion that "he could talk, if only he wanted to." But, as noted in Chapter 1, the elective mute and the autistic mute are entirely different individuals with different symptoms and different etiologies.

Some children reportedly remain mute all of their lives. About 65% of the children who were mute at age 5 in the study by DeMyer et al.

(1973) were still mute when reevaluated several years later. Some severely retarded mutes are excluded from studies designed to follow developmental milestones and language onset. Bartak and Rutter (1976), for example, drew their sample from special and regular schools in the community. The severely retarded and handicapped autistic children generally found in residential institutions were specifically excluded.

When their silence is eventually broken, the lingering hopes of a quiet but capable child storing information and skills (perhaps spitefully) receive impetus in some cases. It is not uncommon that the initial utterances will be fully intelligible words or phrases that have never been "taught" in the parents' tutorial efforts. Early case studies reported such first utterances as "You go there," "Put the foot in the bed," "Beethoven," "American flag," "Chocolate," "Want to go home," and "Mama." With the exception of "Mama," these are clearly not typical initial attempts at English. But with the aid of hindsight we can now appreciate that such articulate ejaculations rarely if ever reflect linguistic competence. Most are probably attributable to delayed echolalia, which is discussed in Chapter 3. In any event, to the extent that these first words denote the emergence from muteness—even if only temporarily—they are generally regarded as positive signs.

In rare cases words might be observed prior to 16 or 22 months only to vanish suddenly. A long period of muteness supplants ostensibly normal, albeit truncated, vocabulary development. This history is suggestive of cerebral insult, such as virus infection or auto-immune reaction, but these hypotheses remain unconfirmed (Colby, 1973; Stubbs, 1976).

Many variables, such as the severity of the autistic process per se (Clancy and McBride, 1969) and overall level of intellectual functioning, define the upper limits of the mute period. In Bartak and Rutter's (1976) comparative study of autistic children having IQs above and below 70, it was found that all were late in speaking. In addition, all showed a marked impairment in imagination or pretend (representational) play in childhood. Such defects are suggestive of deficient "inner language" (Wing et al., 1977). For the lower IQ group the mean age of first use of single words was 4 years, 7 months. For the high IQ group the mean age of onset was 2 years, 6 months. The mean age of first phrases to communicate was 6 years, 5 months for the low group and 4 years, 8 months for the high IQ classification. Differences between groups were statistically significant for both words and phrases.

We may conclude that delayed onset of speech is characteristic of the autistic child. And because silence tends to isolate the individual from the talking world it has the potential of exacerbating the symptom of "autistic aloneness." Prognosis for children not speaking before age 5 or 6 is considerably more guarded than for those who commence before 5

(Eisenberg, 1956; Rutter and Lockyer, 1967; DeMyer et al., 1973). The prolonged mute period is more likely a product of receptive and cognitive malfunctioning than of throttled oral expressive skills. Nevertheless, aberrations of expression (discussed later in this chapter) suggest that matters are more complex, sometimes involving motor speech output. Much more research is needed on the nature of the silent period before we can generalize causes and effects.

ECHOLALIA

> One day the youth (Narcissus), being separated from his companions, shouted aloud, "Who's here?" Echo replied, "Here," Narcissus looked around, but seeing no one called out, "Come." Echo answered, "Come." As no one came, Narcissus called again, "Why do you shun me?" Echo asked the same question. "Let us join one another," said the youth. The maid answered with all her heart in the same words, and hastened to the spot, ready to throw her arms about his neck. He started back, "Hands off! I would rather die than you should have me!" "Have me," she said; but it was all in vain. (Translation from Ovid and Virgil, Bulfinch, 1947, pp. 101–102.)

Echo's tragic breakdown in communication was, according to the myth, the result of her excessive talking and her fondness for always having the last word. For her transgression Echo was punished by Juno: "You shall still have the last word," the goddess said in sentencing Echo, "but no power to speak the first."

Today we can only speculate about the model that served the mythologists in creating Echo's verbal behavior. She may have been anthropomorphized from the reverberating sound waves of the Grecian hills where, according to the myth, her bones were changed into rocks with nothing left of her but her voice. And yet her confrontation with Narcissus bears such a striking resemblance to human echoic behavior that one cannot avoid euhemeristic speculation. One modern psychoanalytic interpretation of the myth holds that schizophrenic children are both Narcissus and Echo. Like Narcissus they cannot distinguish between themselves and others, and, like Echo, they do not distinguish whether words belong to them or to others (Rodique, 1957, p. 178).

Beyond the issue of her creation is the paradox of Echo's plight. She employed a human—and, it would seem, a nymphal—communicative speech mode to the total detriment of communication. Why? Or, alternatively, why did she not stop the behavior that was destroying her relationship with Narcissus? Would not silence or gesture have been the tactic of choice when speech communication was serving her purposes so poorly? Apparently she could not stop doing what she was doing.

Echolalia is generally defined as the meaningless repetition of a word or word group just spoken by another person. Dictionary definitions may include such additional qualifiers as *involuntary* or *unmotivated* for describing the repetitions. Its greatest practitioners are the very young and the mentally afflicted of all ages. Yet whether ontogenetic or pathologic, its occurrence is generally short-lived, uncomplicated, and uncomplicating. It is a passing phase, typically a successor to muteness. And, as in Echo's plight, power to speak the first word is commonly diminished.

Accordingly, the terse question "Why bother?" seems equally applicable to both the echoer and to those who would study the phenomenon. And it is probably because the echoer *does* bother that we cannot avoid wondering why.

In this section echolalia is dealt with as an audiovocal behavior void of language and communicative intent. Sometimes what has been termed *delayed echolalia* is equally sterile as communication, but the discussion in this section is limited to the more commonly observed and reported immediate echolalia.

Developmental Echoing

Clinical echolalia cannot be understood unless its relationship to normal language development is clarified. In 1959, child psychiatrist Stella Chess (1959, p. 134) cautioned her fellow clinicians against reliance on the observations of echolalia as a differentiating criterion for diagnosis of schizophrenia. She contended that echolalia is a normal way of learning speech, and that it is therefore not unexpected in a retardate who is mastering speech.

Chess's approach to the behavior is at variance with Piaget (1926), who dismissed normal echolalia as useless: "The part played by echolalia is simply that of a game; the child enjoys repeating the words for their own sake, for the pleasure they give him, without any external adaptation and without an audience" (p. 34). Piaget was, of course, looking at the behavior only in terms of cognitive development, not as audiovocal behavior nor possible clinical analogs thereof. But he was neither the first nor the last to emphasize the otiose character of the phenomenon. Jason Brown (1975), for example, wrote that echolalia is related neither to normal repetition nor to childhood imitation, but is a pathological condition. In a similar vein, N. Simon (1975) stated simply that echolalia does not represent retarded or arrested development because it "does not represent any of the intermediate stages of normal language development" (p. 1441).

It is tempting to try to resolve the polarity of views expressed by Chess and by Simon through recourse to terminological confusion. The dual employment of "echolalia" to describe a normal as well a pathological behavior is but one source of conflict. (Defining "imitation" is another.) But while it is true that some clarification of terminology is overdue, the problems lie much deeper. And they cannot be resolved by simply denying the existence of a normal behavior on the basis of clinical observations. Only through careful study of the behavior can its existence as a developmental entity be established or refuted.

In order to accomplish such a study it is necessary to consult the reported observations of previous authorities. Echolalia is not a single, stable behavior clearly delimited by developmental landmarks. It is a continuum of behavioral change from the more automatic to the less automatic; from the mechanical to the quasi-volitional. Keeping this *echoic continuum* in mind, the following points are examined: 1) the characteristics of echolalia as interpreted by the early observers, 2) the more recent issues of echolalia's theorized "transitional role," and its upper limits of developmental occurrence, 3) imitation studies in which the automatic condition persists into the upper extensions of the echoic continuum, and 4) the issue of non-universality among able and disabled persons.

Wyllie (1894) long ago described how the child's articulative exercises at about 14 months of age assume an imitative character and develop into "echolalia." Such words, according to Wyllie's account, are produced in parrot fashion without the "slightest inkling" of their meaning and without apparent effort to understand them. This mechanical repetition was regarded as an important preliminary exercise in the development of true speech. "In the 23rd month," Wyllie wrote, "it is noted that if the child hears someone speak he often repeats the last syllable of the sentence just finished, if the accent be on it; as in 'What said the *man*?' when he says *man;* or in 'Who is there?' when he says *there*" (p. 100). While Wyllie's time specifications of 14 and 23 months were a bit precise for generalization, his 19th century observations—particularly of noncomprehension and accentuation—were remarkable.

In this century, Fröschels (1932, p. 84) added to Wyllie's contributions. Defining echolalia as the imitation of uncomprehended words, Fröschels emphasized the dynamic relationship between motor speech impulse and comprehension of meaning. He contended that those children who understand precociously much of what they hear will imitate less than others. He indicated that there are no inhibitions that "would prevent overflow of acoustic excitation" from passing into the motor sphere. Fröschel's theoretical contribution was what we might term an "echo ratio"—the reciprocal relationship between echoing and comprehension.

Discussions of the early echolalic period often underscore the transitional character of the behavior from the prelinguistic state to the linguistic (Myklebust, 1957; C. T. Simon, 1957). In the Russian literature, also, *ékholaliya* is regarded as a transitional stage in the formation of the Pavlovian second signal system (Porshnev, 1964). Pavlov stated that the direct impressions of objects and phenomena of the external world are the first signals of reality and that the verbal symbols or verbal designations of these impressions are the second signals of reality (Bridger, 1960). Porshnev wrote that echolalia lies to no small degree at the level of the first signal system where the communication function is still not a function of communicating anything.

As a subject for formal research, developmental echolalia has received little attention. This is largely due to the cloudy differentiation of the behavior from the less mechanical forms of verbal imitation. Zipf (1949), in defining echolalia as the automatic and purposeless repetition of words spoken by others or self, analyzed written recordings of the speech of preschool children. He found, among other things, that as the child grows older the proportion of echolalia in his total speech tends to decrease. Although still present at 29 months of age, Zipf's data indicated that echolalia is no longer a statistically significant component of the child's verbal output beyond that age. Zipf's work has been recently improved upon in a longitudinal study of 10 Japanese children (ages 1 to 3 years) by Nakanishi and Owada (1973). These investigators studied *echoic utterances*, noting that they developed along with vocabulary up to approximately 2 to 2½ years of age. After this age, echoing gradually disappeared and was followed by a further growth of vocabulary.

Here is a behavior that has essentially abated in the normal child prior to age 3. It progresses from a more automatic repetition to a less automatic variety; from a general level of noncomprehension to a level of comprehension; from a nonsymbolic (prelinguistic) stage of development to a symbolic (linguistic) stage. During any specific observation a given child may be functioning along these continua toward echo abatement. He may or may not be consistent within himself or in comparison with his peers. Some of the inconsistencies may be attributable to the fact that individual grammatical competence develops only gradually, in one aspect of performance at a time (DeVilliers and DeVilliers, 1974).

Results from research on verbal imitation need to be considered at this point, taking into consideration the notion of a continuum from the more to the less automatic. Such a continuum is not effectively dichotomized by any currently accepted referential properties of the terms *echolalia* and *imitation*. In this regard Ruth Clark (1977) has noted with concern that many discussions of imitation have been too categorical, assuming that it must either be a purely mechanical perceptual-motor process, or entirely a matter of interpretation and reconstruction. Clark has written:

What the child already knows about the material which is presented to him is bound to determine what he can extract from it, as is his interpretation of the context. But this does not mean that there is no mechanical element whatever in imitation, or that nothing a child includes in his rendering is beyond his current competence (p. 355).

Fraser, Bellugi, and Brown (1963) found that 3-year-olds' *elicited imitation* of grammatical contrasts surpassed their verbal comprehension, which in turn was superior to their freely generated speech. For example, the children would choose the correct action picture, or repeat "The sheep are jumping," more often than they could speak the correct name when a picture was pointed out. One of the authors' main conclusions was that imitation is a perceptual-motor skill that does not work through the meaning system. At least three replications of the study (Lovell and Dixon, 1967; Turner and Rommetveit, 1967; Nurss and Day, 1971) have been reported, and all obtained similar results. However, the methodology and results have been challenged by Baird (1972) and Fernald (1972). A replication by Fernald using a different scoring procedure nevertheless confirmed the earlier finding that imitation scores were higher than the comprehension and production scores. No consistent relationship between comprehension and production was demonstrated.

Four additional studies of imitation have provided new insights into the meaning of the behavior and, by deduction, the meaning of echolalia. Shipley, Smith, and Gleitman (1969) observed that young children were more likely to repeat a command that included a nonsense word (e.g., "Gor me the ball") than a command composed of all-English forms. In fact only when the stimulus contained nonsense were the more mature subjects triggered to repetition as frequently as the less mature children. The authors concluded *that children seem to repeat what is just a little beyond them, what is just a little bit odd*. Similarly, Bloom, Hood, and Lightbown (1974), in their study of spontaneous linguistic imitation, concluded that their young subjects who imitated did so on *words that they did not yet know*. Ramer (1976) studied developmental imitations of seven children following adult requests and commands. Analysis of the triggering utterances revealed one or both of these phenomena: 1) at least one lexical item in the adult's utterance had never been observed to occur in the collected corpora for the child and thus may not have been known, and/or 2) the structure of the adult's string involved a complex syntactic construction never observed in the collected corpora for the child and thus was possibly not comprehended. And finally, Moerk (1977) confirmed Bloom et al. (1974) on a number of points including the temporal sequence in which specific constructions appear in imitative and spontaneous speech. They are in most instances first employed in imitation, then are produced both in imitation and spontaneously, and finally, once mastered, are no longer imitated.

This limited digest of selected studies of imitation fails to do justice to the aim or scope of the investigations that were more concerned with the relationship of imitation to grammar than with audiovocal mechanics. (For comprehensive discussions of the role of imitation in language development, see Rees, 1975; Prutting and Connolly, 1976; R. Clark, 1977.) We have simply tried to point out the repeated observations that mechanical repetition is not easily divorced from what is seemingly a much higher form of behavior, but what is more likely a distantly removed behavior on the echoic continuum. Repetitive acts seem to be triggered by new or difficult auditory material which is, as yet, unknown. By extension it could be assumed that a child having more extensive problems with the symbol system might well exhibit greater amounts of echoic output both in numbers of utterances and in length of echoes. The former would define in part the extent of difficulties with comprehension, whereas the latter would reflect increments in short term memory with physiological maturation and increased exposure to verbal stimulation.

All of this would be more acceptable if overt echoic behavior were universally observed. It is not. Some closely followed children are never observed in the act of overt imitation (e.g., Bloom, Hood, and Lightbown, 1974; Ramer, 1976). Leopold (1949/1970) found no evidence of echolalia in the detailed linguistic study of his daughter's language development, but observed it strikingly in another normal child (p. 648).

It seems somewhat illogical that extensive behavior can be observed in a normal child and not observed at all in another. Our image of the normal distribution curve contravenes such a notion. But it is conceivable that the curve for language development is different. For example, some children may do overtly that which others do covertly, i.e., audible versus inaudible repetitions. On the other hand, there may be different varieties of persons. Day (1973a, 1973b) has postulated that some are clearly "stimulus-bound" whereas others are "language-bound." Her studies employed a number of verbal tasks with adult subjects. Included were digit span memory, phonological fusion, and dichotic listening. Results showed clear differences between the two groups. Stimulus-bound subjects are able to track the "speech" end, that is, the actual performance aspects of an utterance. Language-bound subjects perceive an utterance through "language," that is, through the abstract structure of their language. Perhaps this dichotomy is even observable in the prelinguistic stage, with the echo-imitative group representing a subpopulation of stimulus-bound children. It may also be that some non-echoers have become very early abaters by reason of inhibitory control over the overt, externalized product. Yet the mere disappearance of the audible echoic response on the basis of inhibition via linguistic growth fails to explain the mechanisms underlying the behavior when generated in the first place.

We must not overlook yet another group of non-echoers. These youngsters, included among the severely subnormal, have not learned even the low level audiovocal skills needed to reach a stage of mechanical repetition. Let us examine the nature of the learning that eventuates in echolalia. As posited by Hebb, Lambert, and Tucker (1971), this learning is the gradual building of motor connections from the child hearing his own vocalizations, at first in random babbling and then later in more organized combinations of phonemes. That this process leads to imitation is demonstrated by the fact that the childs ends up with the vocabulary, accent, and other speech mannerisms of his social group. The imitation itself, the overt speech, *depends on the prior perceptual learning*, according to Hebb et al. "In this sense, the child can imitate only what is already within his competence; *in the early stages at least the imitation is more a product of learning than a mechanism of learning*" (p. 218).

Further insights into the nature of the type of learning requisite for echoing come from the comprehensive case report by Geschwind, Quadfasel, and Segarra (1968) concerning an adult manifestation of echolalia. The young lady involved suffered from an episode of carbon-monoxide poisoning and became quadriplegic, incontinent, confused, and disoriented. Her spontaneous speech was limited to a few stereotyped phrases. Over 9 years of observation she never uttered a sentence of propositional speech and showed essentially no evidence of ever comprehending anything said to her. By contrast she exhibited marked echolalic repetition with excellent articulation. She retained the ability to sing and to learn new popular songs, i.e., songs released subsequent to her trauma. When new song recordings were played to her, after a few repetitions, she learned some lines correctly.

It seems reasonable to assume that if some normal youngsters demonstrate this product of learning at a prelinguistic transitional stage, so, too, might some of their impaired peers. At that point of transition the normal children move on to symbolic behavior (the second signal system). The less fortunate may find that next developmental step particularly difficult and thus reach a plateau at their highest level of performance.

Non-autistic Echolalia

The multiple manifestations of echolalia have been enumerated and described in the literature for many years (see, for example, Schneider, 1938; Stengel, 1947; Porshnev, 1964). A sampling of associated illnesses includes a number of psychoses such as schizophrenia of both children and adults, so-called "transcortical" and "frontal dynamic" aphasias, degenerative brain disease (e.g., Pick's cerebral atrophy), post-epileptic states, conditions of clouded consciousness, Gilles de la Tourette syndrome, childhood "aphasia," childhood autism, and severe mental retardation. In addition, echolalia appears in regional manifestations as part of conditions known variously as latah (Malaya), myriachit (parts of Russia), Jumping Frenchmen (Maine, New Hampshire, northern Michigan, and parts of Canada), and arctic hysteria (extreme northern hemisphere).

Adult symptoms—whether neurological or psychotic in etiology—are generally attributed to a primordial manifestation of an earlier period in which young children returned questions and other verbal stimuli echoically. Hughlings Jackson is credited with originating the regression theory and he, in turn, credited Spencer with the concept of dissolution, i.e., the reduction to a more automatic condition (Taylor, 1958). Extreme suggestibility and identification with the host speaker are often regarded as integral parts of the psychodynamics. It was Stengel (1947, 1964) whose clinical assessment of the many manifestations of echo-reactions, including echopraxia (Dromard, 1906; Fay and Hatch, 1965) and echographia (Pick, 1924), led him to the conclusion that all instances of echolalia reflected difficulty in communication because of impairment or lack of understanding coupled with an attempt at overcoming this difficulty through identification with the interlocutor (Stengel, 1964, p. 287). The term *identification* here is a Freudian expression referring to "the assimilation of one ego to another one, as a result of which the first ego behaves like the second in certain respects, imitates it and in a sense takes it up into itself" (Freud, 1965, p. 63).

The principal concern here is with the echolalia of children who are past the age of developmental echoic behavior but who are not autistic. The autistic child's behavior can be appreciated better when compared with a more conventional developmental lag. Moreover, as part of a transitional phase, echolalia gives evidence of both normal and abnormal verbal processes. The speaking autistic child, after all, is displaying normal as well as abnormal behaviors, and any program of effective remediation should consider these differences.

In the 1960s there was an unusual opportunity to work with severe echoing subjects 36 months or older. In the routine administration of the 36-month Speech, Language, and Hearing Examination of the National Collaborative Perinatal Study (NINDS, PHS) (Lassman et al., 1980), most of the 3,465 children registered to the Oregon unit were examined. The initial pilot sample of late-abating echoers was made up of 12 children from the lower socioeconomic population who echoed 20% or more of 50 consecutive speech-evoking stimuli (Fay, 1966). A standardized interview protocol was developed and tape-recorded with the qualifying subjects in individual follow-up sessions. On the basis of this pilot effort 24 3-year-olds, together with 24 non-echoic matched controls, were obtained, and an additional group of 13 youngsters of various diagnoses was drawn from clinical referrals. This clinical group ranged in age from 36 to 104 months and had a mean age of 60.4 months. The late-abating group was reinterviewed with the same protocol when they returned at 48 months of age (± 2 months) for psychological assessment.

Results of the study (Fay, 1967a) showed that the 3-year-olds echoed 40.9% of the stimuli, whereas the clinical group echoed 40.5% and the 3-year-old control group tallied 1.3%. At age 4 years (mean: 48.4 months), the late-abaters' echo rate had diminished to 6.1%, a comparable performance to that registered 1 year earlier by the control group.

Why did the two echoic groups show echolalia on 40% of the stimuli and not on the remaining 60%? Both late-abating and clinical echoers were approximately 45% non-echoic and the remainder (13%) silent. Of the non-echoic responses, 41% and 62% were judged "appropriate" for the two groups, respectively, and 32% and 24% "inappropriate." The remainder was classed "unintelligible." At age 4 the percentage of appropriate responses had risen to 64.

In an effort to determine why some stimuli were responded to echoically and others appropriately, 22 of the 3-year interviews were analyzed according to types of questions asked (Fay, 1975). Most of the 1,509 questions addressed to the children fell into three classifications: yes/no, nominal, and locative. The pooled echo rate for locative probes (e.g., "Where is the dog?" or "Where do you sleep?") was almost twice as great as that obtained for the other two types: yes/no, 32.4%; nominal, 31.1%; and locative, 57.6%. It seems clear that the more elaborate the probe in its grammar (Brown, 1968; Ervin-Tripp, 1970) or in the complexity of its response demand (Williams and Naremore, 1969), the greater the likelihood of echo generation. This issue is pursued in greater detail, particularly as it relates to Wh-questions, in Chapter 3.

Two additional studies addressed the developmental dichotomy of speech and language systems as demonstrated by young echoers. One study (Fay and Butler, 1968) compared two groups of subjects according to 1) their 3-year language performances (the verbal comprehension, verbal expression, and object-naming subtest results), and 2) their 3-year speech performances (articulation of initial consonants, final consonants, and vowels/diphthongs). The experimental group was composed of 22 late-abating echoers. A control group was obtained by matching each of the 22 with another child according to race, sex, age, and 48-month Stanford-Binet IQ. The mean IQs and IQ ranges for the echoers and controls were 83.59 (53–109) and 83.86 (54–109), respectively. Results showed statistically significant differences between the two groups on each language measure, with the control subjects performing markedly better on each measure. But the differences between the two groups in "speech" were virtually zero and insignificant for each articulation category. These data were viewed as further support for the thesis that in some children the audiovocal skills develop relatively independently from the syntactic-semantic system. Such was the case even though the groups were both depressed in average IQ.

Then, latencies between trigger and echo were examined (Saxman and Fay, 1970). Since the speed with which a response follows the stimulus presentation is known to reflect, among other things, the complexity of the response process (Woodworth and Schlosberg, 1954, p. 36), intervocal latencies were measured to deduce processing complexity. The children were not, for the most part, echolalic but were observed to echo an occasional stimulus picked up through routine tape-recording of the verbal comprehension subtest of the 36-month exam. Thus, 323 echoic responses were collected from 59 3-year-olds. The resultant response latency distribution, i.e., completion of stimulus to onset of echo, was skewed positively with mean and median latencies occurring at 0.88 and 0.78 seconds, respectively. Comparisons between average latency values of the three difficulty levels of conceptual complexity of the subtest (identification of familiar objects, understanding action words, and understanding space relationships) resulted in no significant differences. The average latencies with the context objects did not differ significantly from conversationally triggered echoes obtained without object involvement from 19 of the 59 subjects. The very brief latencies were interpreted as still further support for the postulate of an audiovocal response pattern apparently triggered by the meaning system of language, yet independent from it.

The next chapter is directed toward some "higher level" functions of echolalia. But, first, the autistic child's variations on a theme of echolalia is examined.

Autistic Echolalia

By far the most practiced of echoers is the young autistic child. In no other condition is one likely to see so many children echoing. In no other childhood condition is echolalia observed of such late onset, such prolonged duration, such consistent occurrence, such parasitic fidelity, and of such minimal benefit. Does this proficiency suggest that autistic manifestations are extraordinary, or simply the extreme end of the behavioral continuum?

To answer this question, a study with a repeated measure paradigm assessing verbal comprehension and echoic output of three young echoers was undertaken (Fay, 1969). The instrument was the Verbal Comprehension subtest of the 36-month Speech, Language, and Hearing (SLH) Examination (Lassman et al., 1980). The children were 1) a developmental echoer (W.A.), 30 months old, with an IQ of 102, 2) a belated echoer (P.B.), 36 months old, with an IQ of 75, and 3) an autistic echoer (L.C.), 58 months old, with an IQ of 53. Each child was tested with the same protocol at 2-month intervals. The sessions were tape-recorded and subsequently analyzed for number of test errors (error score), number of echoes (echo score), words-per-echo (WPE), and other qualitative variables. W.A. abated after one follow-up session in which he also achieved a zero error score. P.B. continued echoing for eight interviews during which his error score declined from 10 to 2, where it remained for the final sessions. L.C., the autistic echoer, continued in echolalia for a year. His error score was a remarkably consistent 9 of 16. His echo score began at 8, increased to 15, and then declined to 13 at the time the study was terminated. W.A. and P.B. had very similar tonal patterns with considerable variety. W.A. had a mean WPE of 2.01 compared to P.B.'s mean of 2.15 (range: 1.28 at 36 months to 2.29 at 44 months). L.C.'s mean WPE was 2.33, and his delivery was characterized by monotone void of any evident interest. He also seemed more "parasitic," as evidenced by a consistent tendency to return echoically his own name used in personal address as well as such remarks as "Sit down" and "That's right." L.C.'s recordings also revealed unique evidence of whispered echolalia, autoecholalia, delayed echolalia, and pronominal confusions.

Although the repeated measure study did not answer the question of "autistic uniqueness," it did confirm once again the relationship of echolalia to understanding. It also confirmed those additional aspects of autistic echolalia that seem to be widely recognized in the literature. Some of these, for example larger WPE, are attributable to older chronological age (CA) and the associated neurophysiological increments in short term retention. Other qualitative variables might well be the result of practice effects from years of echoing. Still other variables, such as monotonal delivery, are products of verbal output in general, not of echolalia per se. But, taken together, the amount and proficiency of echolalia as manifested by autistic children suggest that the comprehension problems are more severe, the communication systems more impaired, and the social consequences less self-evident than in other childhood conditions.

Studies of the 1970s supplied additional comparisons. Shapiro, Roberts, and Fish (1970) compared imitative responses of eight schizophrenic children near their 4th birthdays with control groups of 6-, 4-, 3-, and 2-year-olds without symptoms. The schizophrenic children spoke as often as the controls but were retarded in the length and expansiveness of their utterances. They also had a significantly greater proportion of imitations than the 3- and 4-year-old children but were not significantly different in this measure from the 2-year-old normal children. However, the schizophrenic children had a significantly greater number of rigidly congruent echoes (pure echolalia) than each of the control groups. Because imitations of the 2-year-olds were significantly less rigid than the schizophrenic children, the suggestion was strong that the latter group was deviant as well as immature.

Premack and Premack (1974) reported an earlier unpublished work by Metz and Premack using as subjects a heterogeneous group of eight children bearing such labels as "emotionally disturbed . . . institutionalized . . . and psychotic." An experimental group (15%–80% echolalic) was matched with a control group (0%–8% echolalic). These groups were first trained and later tested on a variety of activities involving nominative or associative responses. In one test, each object in the array was presented along with the question, "What goes with this?" (cup with cup handle, cup with saucer, shoe with lace, etc.). The child's array included the stimulus object, thus allowing for the visually mediated nonverbal response (cup with cup). Such imitation was the dominant response of both groups, but the more verbally imitative experimental group was also more imitative in nonverbal imitation.

In another study by Metz and Premack (Premack and Premack, 1974), the same two groups of children were assessed for language comprehension. The heavy echoers gave virtually no evidence of comprehension of either syntactic or morphological distinctions. It is of interest that pluralization and negation, which were failed in the comprehension mode by all echolalic children, were clearly marked in the speech of all of them. Here is further evidence of the need for caution when inferring competence in comprehension and grammar on the basis of certain speech samples. Overall, the tests suggested that the criterion (degree of echolalia) could divide the children into groups of profoundly different kinds of language function: one group, according to the authors, clearly understood language, while the other group clearly did not.

Stimulus variables in echolalia were studied in a series of replicated single-subject designs across six schizophrenic and five normal children (Carr, Schreibman, and Lovaas, 1975). In one experiment, neutral stimuli (no learned response) and discriminative stimuli (stimuli to which the child had learned a response) were used. The neutral stimuli were nonsensical (e.g., "min dar snick"), whereas the discriminative stimuli were questions and commands (e.g., "How are you?" and "Clap your hands"). When presented with the neutral stimuli, the psychotic children displayed marked echolalia. The discriminative stimuli triggered little echoing. Children in the control group typically echoed neither the neutral nor the discriminative stimuli. Their data led the investigators to the conclusion that an important determinant of echolalic speech of psychotic children centers on whether a given child has in the past learned a response to the stimulus presented to him. In a second experiment, appropriate responses were taught to three of the psychotic children for each of the neutral stimuli. The echoing to these stimuli generally abated after training, suggesting that the verbal incomprehensibility may be an important determinant of immediate echolalia. The authors also hypothesized that echolalia may not be so much a psychotic speech form as a speech pattern characteristic of an early stage in the development of normal language functioning.

As previously noted, there are a number of authorities who reject a "normal language basis" for autistic echolalia. The rationale for this rejection is most clearly advanced in a comprehensive paper entitled "Echolalic Speech in Childhood Autism—Consideration of Possible Loci of Brain Damage" (Simon, 1975). After rejecting the concept of echolalia in normal, retarded, or arrested development, Simon asserts that the predominant echoing of long phrases from the speech of others must be considered abnormal. Her argument continues that the echolalic autistic child appears to have missed the normal steps of development, and has, therefore, not acquired a normal grasp of grammar or the basic subunits required to put together unique sentences. Simon concludes that autism most likely results from diverse organic causes and that the occurrence of language handicaps in both autistic and retarded children calls attention to possible defects in auditory processing (and its underlying neural substrate in both groups). Simon's viewpoint is not totally at variance with that of the authors of this volume. However, she seems to be implying that the pathology causes abnormal echolalia and also causes abnormal language. Or, in other words, echolalia is the result of the presumed pathology. There is no empirical support for such a direct cause-and-effect relationship among either childhood or adult manifestations of echolalia. Although there are no pathological studies on brains of autistic individuals, post-mortem analyses of adult brains of echolalic subjects are remarkable in that they reveal the *intactness* of an isolated speech area (Geschwind, 1965; Geschwind, Quadfasel, and Segarra, 1968). Hughlings Jackson warned against attributing causes of utterances in aphasia to destruction of nervous tissue: "The utterances are effected during activity of nervous arrangements which have escaped injury" (Taylor, 1958, p. 189).

The effects of the pathology eventuating in autism are to be seen in the maldevelopment or retarded development of language—not of speech. Whereas normal children ascend developmentally to more symbolic forms of behavior (Pavlov's second signal system), the autistic child becomes plateaued at a level of persistent repetition. On the echoic continuum he would seem to have gained audiovocal competence but very little else. The consequence is a truncated transition—a developmental stagnation due to nonemergence of normal linguistic competence. The persistent echoing may be regarded as a maladaptive use of a normal mechanism because the options permit nothing else, save silence. Thus, the echolalia signals the pathology but is not itself a *direct result* of the condition. It may, however, be regarded as an indirect consequence if it extends in duration beyond the time of normal abatement. Extended echolalia points to a failure—at least for a time—in the development of linguistic competence. Non-abatement, coupled with impaired language comprehension and eventual abatement when linguistic competence emerges, is offered as evidence in support of such a postulation (Fay, 1967a, 1969, 1973; Fay and Butler, 1968). But in addition to pointing to the inadequacies of language development, echolalia also reflects integrity of the audiovocal system together with whatever learning has taken place in order to deal with the auditory patterns and articulatory features.

Philips and Dyer (1977), who strongly support the notion that autistic echolalia is a late-onset form of normal imitation functioning in young children, have argued, therefore, that the key to its progressive clinical elimination is in the condition itself.

Autistic children, having missed out at the *infant* echolalic stage, are further handicapped by late-onset speech at an equivalent point by not generally receiving the spontaneous help that the normal child would. What they receive from adults who use language appropriate to their physical development perseverates them in echolalia which blanks off from them potentialities of contextual meaning other than at a level of naming vocabulary (p. 55).

These authors present an intervention program that exploits the echolalia by using an interlocutor, a prompter (who feeds appropriate responses), and the child who echoes the prompter's responses rather than the interlocutor's stimuli. In this way—in a clinical or home environment—the echolalia becomes useful to the child and gives him access to an experience with the complexities of grammar. Such an approach seems decidedly more rational than one that treats echoic behavior as simply disruptive and therefore in need of eradication.

A separate subgroup of children who show a distinctive variety of echolalia that is remarkably similar to autistic echolalia is a subpopulation of the infant blind (Fay, 1973). The similarity of echolalic styles is important to the understanding of both autism and some forms of blindness. For example, successful intervention techniques employed with the autistic child may also be applicable to a child blinded by retrolental fibroplasia. As might be expected, similarities between autism and blindness in some children have not gone unrecognized. Keeler (1958) and Fraiberg (1971) reported on comparable samples of blind children which were in both instances obtained unexpectedly from larger groups of patients. Keeler, who was seeking a sample of autistic and schizophrenic youngsters, obtained in the process five blind preschoolers who "presented the most strikingly similar picture to infantile autism" (p. 64). All had been born prematurely, had received oxygen therapy, and during the ensuing 3 to 14 weeks had developed blindness resulting from retrolental fibroplasia. These children manifested numerous autistic patterns, including delayed language consisting of echolalia, repetitive use of apparently meaningless words, and referring to oneself in the third person. The mother of one of his patients (age 5) described her child's speech in these words:

> She is just like a parrot. She'll say any word in this world, just to say it, but it means nothing to her. If I say, "Betty, go and sit down like a good girl," she will say, "Betty, go and sit down like a good girl," and she'll do it, but she'll say it also.

Fraiberg's (1971) extensive longitudinal research of blind infants clearly delineated a subpopulation of "congenitally blind autistic." She described the group, constituting approximately one-quarter of the population that was totally blind since birth and had no known brain damage, as having gross abnormalities in ego development which she regarded as closely related to autism. Fraiberg followed 10 of these infants, whom she described as appearing to have no significant ties, no definition of body boundaries, and motor stereotypes of the trunk and hands. Their language, if present at all, was echolalic. She regarded the absence or failure of human connections to be the most morbid sign among this subpopulation and wondered whether echolalic speech was not testifying to the last failure in human connections.

An ambitious study to find "early infantile autism" among the blind was undertaken by Chase (1972). She studied 236 children handicapped by retrolental fibroplasia. Using Rimland's (1971) E-2 diagnostic checklist, she was unable to confirm the diagnosis. Whether this related to the adequacy of the E-2 or to extraneous variables such as the absence of vision is not known.

Among the congenitally blind children exhibiting "autistic echolalia" followed in Oregon was a 9-year-old functioning in the low trainable range of intelligence. Her echolalia was so marked and so rapid that her stimulus-echo latencies were studied to determine her capabilities in the transduction/reproduction of a verbal signal (Fay and Coleman, 1977). Because her echo-reactions were so rapid as to overlap the trigger occasionally, a two-channel tape recording system was used. Thus, her mother (the interlocuter) would provide the stimulus on one channel and the echo was recorded on a second channel. Mean offset-to-onset latencies of 270 milliseconds and onset-to-onset latencies of 792 milliseconds were obtained. These are comparable data to laboratory reaction times for syllable imitation. The child showed almost no evidence of verbal comprehension or non-echoic expression, and her echolalia appeared to be at a parrot level. Her sound reproduction skills were not limited to speech. For example, she reproduced an instantaneous echoic "double click" of a retractable ballpoint pen heard within her range. Thus, she seemed to be making no distinctions between relevant and irrelevant stimulation. This raises questions about the capabilities of a prephonological, psittacine level of reproduction that is nevertheless interpretable as human speech. But, as Studdert-Kennedy (1975) has noted, we have no clear concept of, and no terminology to describe, such a prephonological stage in the perceptual process.

The blind child who echoes tells us also something about the visuosocial dynamics of echolalia. Stengel (1947), Denny-Brown (1963), and Campbell and Grieve (1978) have stressed the importance of vision to the occurrence of echolalia. Denny-Brown (1963), writing from the perspective of echolalic aphasia, has noted:

> The visual cortex of this fundamental automatism is of particular importance to the understanding of mutism in association with states of impaired vision. Just as the parrot can be silenced by covering his cage, so the chattering of monkeys ceases when the striate cortex is bilaterally ablated (p. 49).

Large quantities of data on echolalia have been obtained from sighted, but blindfolded, children and from echoic children triggered while alone with a tape recorder. These occurrences and those of the blind would seem to be ample evidence that vision is not essential for the behavior to occur among some children.

While it is beyond the scope of the present work to consider why some, but not the majority, of congenital and neonatal blind exhibit autistic symptomatology including echolalia, a few speculations are difficult to resist. The common ground may be the similarity in the trauma to the language processes of the brain. A common "central" or "cortical" basis may underlie the conditions with the blindness being but an additional symptom, in certain cases due, perhaps, to more extensive tissue involvement. We know that visual defect per se does not add to the risk of autism (Chess, Korn, and Fernandez, 1971). DeMyer et al. (1973) have speculated that brain deficiencies in the autistic child would seem to be located in the pathways that connect word production with vision or with motor activities, thereby blocking the acquisition of abstract language concepts and symbolization of objects. Edelheit (1971) noted that,

although the audiovocal modality is the most important for the establishment of language, all other sensory modalities including visual imagery
enter into the structure of language symbolism. When one of the
modalities is cut off by pathology, such as blindness or deafness, there is
a tendency to compensate for the deficit by increased employment of the
others. Such a theory would seem to be typical of all blind children,
however, unless in some children it took the form of a sustained arousal
state for sound stimulation. Such an arousal state has been postulated by
Hermelin and O'Connor (1968, 1970) to account for many behaviors of
autistic children.

Additional research will bridge the two manifestations that seem to
share common language symptoms. The direction of such research is
likely to be that pioneered by Hermelin and O'Connor (O'Connor, 1976).
They presented verbal and cognitive tasks to groups of blindfolded
autistic children, blind children, deaf children, blindfolded normal
children, and sighted children. These efforts, discussed more fully in
Chapter 5, are based in part on Hebb's (1949) theory of learning. Hebb's
assumption is that learning is a successive but also a hierarchical process
insofar as the absence of certain links in the chain could result in a
developmental failure in the next higher phase of learning. Unabating
echolalia may well signal the failure of the next higher phase of learning.

VOCAL DELIVERY

Two categories of acoustic features underlie normal analyses of
continuous speech: the nonsegmental (including intonation, stress,
rhythm, speaking rate, duration, and voice), and the segmental (the distinctive sound features of vocal productions that constitute phoneme seg-
ments) (Crystal, 1969). Those nonsegmental features that have a grammatical function (e.g., question intonations or word stress) are sometimes
referred to as prosodic (Lyons, 1972). Those that serve to support and
color verbal forms of communication are sometimes referred to as paralinguistic, a category that also includes gestures and facial expressions
that accompany dialogue.

This section is concerned with paralinguistic features such as voice
quality and grammatically irrelevant pitch inflections as well as with such
prosodic features as intonation and word stress. Such distinctions,
however, are not religiously observed in the literature. Consequently, it is
not always clear in which way the term *intonation* is being used. It is
used here with reference to the melody of speech as it changes over time.

The following discussion includes voice quality per se and then pitch
and volume relationships over time. Some postulations about the basis
for intonational deficiencies in autistic children conclude the nonseg-

mental discussion. Finally, the characteristic patterns of articulation and the segmental features of vocal delivery are considered.

Voice Quality and Intonation

The voice quality, that is, the permanent background vocal invariable, of the autistic child has been recognized as "bizarre" for as long as the symptom has been recognized. The peculiarities are not confined to childhood, however, as evidenced by Kanner's (1971) follow-up report of Barbara, one of his original subjects. At age 36, Barbara was described as still parroting with a little girl's voice, while humming certain melodies in a bizarre, monotonous manner.

One frequently noted vocal characteristic is that of consistent high pitch, often described as "bird-like." Detailed descriptions (Goldfarb, Braunstein, and Lorge, 1956; Pronovost, Wakstein, and Wakstein, 1966; Goldfarb et al., 1972) have noted excessively high pitch levels with insufficient pitch changes. Pronovost and his associates analyzed by Sonograph one child's high pitched vocalization and determined a fundamental frequency of 2,500 Hz (Pronovost et al., 1966).

Some have speculated about possible organic bases of such high pitch levels, but no definite conclusions can as yet be drawn. Simon (1975) postulated that the high pitch levels that are found in some children may be due to failures in the perception of low frequency sounds. The present authors know of no evidence linking pitch anomalies to specific pathologies of the vocal apparatus, although individual instances may be thus attributed.

Other vocal idiosyncrasies that have been noted include hoarseness, harshness, and hypernasality (Pronovost et al., 1966). Again, it remains unclear whether organically based deficiencies may interfere with the production of adequate vocal quality. The Pronovost group noted marked deficiencies in the control of oral and respiratory musculature. They suggested that those children who had remained mute were deficient in those learned activities that require precise control of the breath stream. While poor vocal control may be partially attributable to some kind of dyspraxic condition, there is no evidence to suggest that such motor impairment should be regarded as a primary cause.

Idiosyncrasies have also been reported in regard to vocal volume: loudness levels have been noted to fluctuate as reflected by whispering, muttering, and occasional loud ejaculations (Goldfarb et al., 1956; Pronovost et al., 1966). More advanced echoers often seem to settle into a pattern of whispered echolalia, occasionally supplanted by audible echoes (Fay, 1969, 1973). This whispering might be viewed as an effort to inhibit echolalic responses. On the other hand, various alternative explanations could be offered, e.g., inconsistent auditory perception, some form of vocal rest, a need to reduce auditory feedback, or plain personal whim. In addition, poor volume control could be viewed as part of a broader inability to perceive and interpret social and contextual cues. This would result in a corresponding failure to monitor volume levels. Such an interpretation would be consistent with a more general pragmatic failure as discussed in Chapter 4.

Among the intonational peculiarities attributable to autism, *monotony* seems to be most widely recognized. The literature abounds with such descriptions as "mechanical," "hollow," "dull," "wooden," "arrhythmic," and so on. In apparent contrast to this large group are those who reportedly speak in a singsong manner. The fact is that persistent singsong patterns can also be characterized as monotonous because the same intonation pattern is being endlessly repeated.

Nevertheless, differences may exist between those children who speak in a completely flat, uninflected manner and those who speak with distinct—albeit stereotyped—intonation. The latter may be endowed with better skills in pitch-time relationships with the result of more melodic delivery. From a listener's perspective, however, this result is no less disturbing than the flat delivery.

These more melodic children may be those to whom musical abilities are often attributed. While the nature of such skills remains to be clarified, some interesting observations have been made. Pronovost et al. (1966) reported on a subject who would repeat the rhythm and melody of a musical phrase several times, and who would subsequently alter the musical key of the phrases upward or downward. After several repetitions he would pause for a period of time and then begin a new series of musical phrases having a different rhythm and melody.

Intonational peculiarities, particularly monotony, have traditionally been explained on the basis of presumed emotional disorders of the children and, in some instances, their parents. The term "flat affect" was introduced by Kanner (1943) with reference to monotonous speaking manners. Despert (1946) commented on the lack of "emotional tone" and the "failure to express personality." According to Bettelheim (1967), intonational idiosyncrasies are due to a lack of feeling and often represent an expression of anger. These interpretations would seem to be another example of efforts to fit observed behaviors (or symptoms) into presumptions about the nature of the autistic syndrome.

Intonational phenomena are easily attributed to emotional factors in the context of general beliefs about the emotional basis of intonation (cf. Moses, 1954). This may be illustrated by the fact that intonation has been largely excluded from the realm of linguistic investigations. But intonational phenomena are far too complex to be dismissed simply as by-products of personality type or emotional condition. Variations of pitch, loudness, and duration of vocalizing serve multiple functions. For example, pitch and loudness determine matters of word stress; raising pitch patterns mark questions; pausing and pitch inflections serve to clarify complex syntactic structures. Nonsegmentals are not restricted functionally to a structural level as noted previously. They are also of immediate relevance to the pragmatic aspects of communication. These features may thus be used by the speaker to draw the listener's attention to specific aspects of the message conveyed. Such use typically occurs when those items of information that are most relevant to the listener are foregrounded by emphatic marking ("Jimmy *is* missing" rather than "Jimmy is *miss*ing"). Here, the speaker must realize and appreciate the perspective of the listener. Correct use of nonsegmentals thus requires not only a grammatical ability but also an ability to attend to and interpret social cues. In addition, nonsegmentals pertain to a number of communicative roles at the level of emotional and individual expression, i.e., gestures, body postures, facial expressions, and so on. Once again, the autistic child has been characterized as strikingly deficient in the use and interpretation of these paralinguistic features. (For a more detailed discussion of these issues, see Chapter 4.)

Given the complexity of nonsegmental variation and its multiple functions, it is very important to determine which aspects are specifically critical in the case of autistic children. Unfortunately, this area remains largely uninvestigated, due in part to the complex methodological problems encountered. Similarly, little is known about the normal development of nonsegmentals. According to some, normal children appear to learn about intonation before they learn segmental features (Weir, 1962). It has been hypothesized that intonational contours may serve as a "mold" into which words and sentences "are formed" (Pike, 1967). If intonation indeed takes such a primal position, it is quite possible that intonational patterning is a residual of a primitive signaling system used to code communicative intent (see Malinowski, 1949, for a discussion).

Ricks (1975a, 1975b) investigated the way in which normal babies express meaning in their intoned vocalizations. When recordings of the 10 babies were played back to their parents, the parents accurately identified sounds conveying requesting, frustration, greeting, and pleasant surprise. They could not, however, pick out their own babies significantly better than chance. Ricks then studied eight autistic children (CA 3–5.11) and three retarded but non-autistic children (CA 5–8). None of the children had begun to use verbal labels. Again, recordings were made for the parents of the autistic children to identify requesting, frustration, greeting, and pleasant surprise after listening to tapes of their own child, two other autistic children, and one retarded non-autistic child. Unlike the results with the normal babies, parents of the autistic children could identify their own child with ease. They also had no problem in picking out the non-autistic child, whom they said "sounded normal." They understood the messages conveyed by their own child and the non-autistic child but not those of the other two autistic children. This suggested that the children's vocalizations served functions similar to those of normal children. But each did so in a personal, idiosyncratic way which, most interestingly, was described by Ricks as *articulated* rather than *intoned* as in the case of non-autistic babies.

The study of the acoustic correlates of intonational peculiarities has remained relatively inaccessible. However, Fletcher (1976) investigated the ability to imitate intonation patterns among six autistic adolescents and six preadolescents. She presented subjects with regular as well as idiosyncratic intonation patterns that were to be imitated. The obtained speech samples were then subjected to a computerized pitch analysis. It was found that non-autistic subjects did much better than autistic subjects in terms of accuracy of the imitations. Also, it was found that downward pitch inflections were much more prominent among the non-autistic subjects than among the autistic subjects. Generally, the autistic children exhibited an almost equal number of upward and downward inflections, which was not the case for the normal children. These acoustic analyses suggest that generalizations pertaining to presumed well developed mimicking skills of autistic children deserve some reconsideration.

Clearly, much more information is needed to fully understand the nature of autistic intonational deficiencies. For instance, we do not know to what extent perceptual-motor factors may be involved and, if so, whether these are a result or a cause of idiosyncratic development. If intonational contours do reflect a requisite rhythmic framework—a human variation of a developing bird's sub-song (Marler, 1970)—then it is plausible that the autistic child may lack sensitivity to those cues in his environment that would normally lead to conventionalization of these patterns. The resultant apparent "lack of affect" could therefore be explained alternatively as an unacquired (or poorly developed) appreciation of environmental cues rather than as a reflection of emotional states.

Much of the autistic child's nonsegmental maldevelopment could also by viewed as the result of how he perceives what he sees and hears in the speech of others. There is evidence from a recall study by Frith (1969) that the emphasis on stress may be recognized albeit unappreciated. Frith presented "stress" and "nonsense" messages to 32 autistic and normal children. Half of each message type was presented with stress placed on key words such as nouns and verbs (e.g., "Ŕead them the bóok" and "Shów us was hóuse"), while the remainder were read with stress on connecting words such as prepositions, articles, and adverbs (e.g., "Get óff his bed"). In overall performance, the autistic children were less able to take advantage of the stress cues than the normals, but the autistic children—like the normals—did remember stressed key words better than unstressed ones. Stress apparently did not help either group to recall connected words. Although Frith concluded from her data that autistic children are not impaired in their appreciation of "physical structure" variables such as stress, the generality appears considerably overstated. Stress, after all, is but one—probably the most easily appreciated—nonsegmental. Also, good auditory memory, a virtual hallmark of speaking autistics, can function (as in echolalia) quite independently of linguistic or paralinguistic parameters of the received signal. In this respect it may be of interest that the phenomenon of stimulus overselectivity has often been associated with autism (see discussion in Chapter 5).

It is still unclear how prelinguistic intonation interacts with syntax and semantics. Martin (1972) has maintained that a great deal of child language data that remains poorly understood would make sense if considered in terms of prosodic features. For example, it is not clear how such features may serve as an aid in learning how speech should be segmented into smaller units. If lacking in these skills, the autistic child may be crippled in his ability to perceive parts of speech as separable from longer strings of sounds, presumably an initial step in decoding meaning. The authors have considerable evidence from clinical observations of such a disability in the speech of older autistic children. Failure to appreciate syllable boundaries may reflect incorrect pitch and volume accents as in "towél" instead of "tówel" or "sandwích" instead of "sándwich." Multiple syllables in word combinations serve to compound the problems of accentuation with the result that word and phrase boundaries go unheeded. For example, in trying to differentiate for one young client a picture of a polar bear from one of a brown variety the latter was passed off as "just a bear." Thereafter the second picture was religiously labeled "justabear."

There is clinical evidence of a failure to appreciate word boundaries, phrase boundaries, and even breath groups in autistic echolalia (Fay, 1969). Rather than a facsimile of the interlocutor's word or syllable boundaries, the echoed sound package is typically better described as a single chunk of speech sound. This perhaps explains why the autistic child, as opposed to other young echoers, will return his name used in personal address as in "Show me the dog, John." The non-autistic echoer would likely echo "da dog," whereas the autistic child would more likely include the "John." Even when the echoer shows fidelity in mimicking pauses, accents, and other nonsegmental features, one cannot assume that he appreciates the implications of these for the decoding operation. Moreover, the extent to which an inability to segment and comprehend speech might be superimposed on a limited appreciation for nonsegmental cues still needs to be resolved.

Finally, a word about emphasis and the final word. As Wyllie (1894) noted in the last century, there is an increased likelihood of echoic return of the terminal word in an utterance "if the accent be on it." Autistic children have a marked tendency to recall the last words of a message (Hermelin and Frith, 1971). Does this mean that autistic youngsters are sensitive to terminal stress or accentuation? Possibly. However, the issue is far more complex than simply word position and stress. For imitation and echolalia also initiate with the terminal word. If but one word is echoed, it is rare that it will be other than the final word of the triggering utterance. Normal young children in the Brown and Fraser (1964) study of elicited imitation correctly imitated 96% of final morphemes compared with correct initial and middle imitation of 70% and 64%, respectively. Among the possible explanations for retention of the final element are—in addition to emphasis on material in the final position—limitations in memory span, recency effect, relative unpredictability of final words, high information content of final words in English (frequently nouns), and combinations of these. Aborn and Rubenstein (1956) have published evidence that, in six-word sentences, nouns are more frequent in the final position whereas function words tend to be most frequent in the fourth and fifth positions. Blasdell and Jensen (1970) found that children 28 to 39 months of age imitated significantly more often those syllables with primary stress and those occurring in the final position. These authors suggested that the normal child may learn content items of the language on the basis of intonational cues. So, too, might the autistic child. But the confounding of stress, recency, position, function, and memory underscores a need for caution when crediting a performance to a single parameter. Given his overall insensitivity to intonation, the odds would favor immediate auditory memory.

Characteristics of Articulation

Eisenberg (1956), reporting a follow-up study of Kanner's original 11 cases, noted a precocity of articulation in the eight children who developed speech. The trend in other studies (e.g., Rutter and Lockyer, 1967; Bartak, Rutter, and Cox, 1975) is toward the conclusion that those children who develop speech show, as a group, transient immaturities of articulation. One apparently critical variable in appreciating the quality of articulation is whether the speech samples are obtained from freely generated or echolalic utterances. Some observers (Pronovost, Wakstein, and Wakstein, 1966; Ricks and Wing, 1975) have noted a contrast between pronunciation in the two situations, spontaneous speech being less well articulated than echoed utterances.

Probably the most striking features about the relationship of articulation and echolalia are 1) the relative high quality of articulation as contrasted with the echoer's other verbal skills, and 2) the sustaining quality of the articulation in the absence of the model. This is not to suggest that we are dealing here with an island of prime performance in a sea of inferior verbal abilities. Nor is it to suggest that the echoer is as proficient on his own as he is with an interlocutor. Generally, however, echoers articulate satisfactorily, and the autistic echoer is no exception. Some of these children do make articulation errors, sometimes many, but they do not as a group seem to deviate markedly from the developmental patterns of the non-autistic. Moreover, the autistic child's articulation contrasts favorably with the motor speech patterns characteristic of children with severe delay, dyspraxia, dysarthria, and developmental "aphasia."

Boucher (1976) administered the Edinburg Articulation Test (EAT) (Anthony, et al., 1971) to 31 autistic children, to 31 controls matched by CA and Peabody Picture Vocabulary Test (PPVT) scores, and to 11 receptive dysphasic controls who were matched with an equal number of "more able" autistic youngsters. The autistic children's articulation was found to be significantly superior to that of both control groups. Boucher concluded that the articulation ability represents a peak in the language performance profile of groups of autistic children, whereas this is not the case with groups of predominantly subnormal or dysphasic controls. Voeltz (1977) has recently reported similar findings with regard to relative quality of articulation.

In yet another recent study on the subject, Bartolucci et al. (1976) compared phonological development of speaking autistics with a group of ideopathic mentally retarded subjects having the same mean mental age (MA). The EAT was used as the measure of articulation. The investigators first established that the phoneme distribution patterns of the two groups were similar to those of normal children and adults. Then the phonological errors made by the two groups were classified according to type: substitution, simplification, environment, and addition. There was no significant difference in the distribution of error types between groups. A further analysis in the percentage of one-feature substitutions showed that, again, the autistic group did not distinctly differ. In both groups the less frequently used phonemic classes—where the higher percentage of errors also occurs—are those acquired later in the process of speech sound development. The investigators concluded that verbal autistic children show a delayed but normal sequence of appearance of phonemes.

Taken as a whole, these studies make a convincing case that the autistic child's articulation stands in favorable contrast to his overall linguistic and communicative abilities. He may do less well than his normally developing peers in the rate of acquisition, but he apparently follows a similar sequential developmental pattern. Echoic articulation apparently surpasses the quality found in spontaneous utterances. This raises two interesting theoretical issues. One is the extent to which articulation can develop as sound-making behavior not under the jurisdiction of a phonological rule system. To what extent is the human capable of duplicating the skills of the parrot or myna bird in the replication of sounds identifiable as human speech? Can the young autistic child regard speech as more than yet another noise impinging on his consciousness (Creak, 1972)? The second theoretical issue concerns the upper limits of phonological development. How far can phonological development proceed detached from syntactic-semantic development? Perhaps the autistic child will ultimately provide answers to these and similar questions.

SUMMARY

In the case of the autistic child, it is not known what key restraint(s) militates against that which is for the normal baby an innate capacity and motivation to learn the native language. Given the potential number and range of anomalies evident in the communicative performances of speaking autistic children, it is remarkable that speech develops at all. Yet while it is true that many never acquire speech, it appears equally true that those who do so are typically delayed in onset and development of verbal behavior. Moreover, eventual acquisition is often limited to an audiovocal facsimile (echolalia) coexisting with and frequently triggered by verbal noncomprehension. Although such echoic behavior is not unique to children with autism or to those with certain types of congenital blindness, it reaches in them a maximum manifestation both in terms of rigid congruency and longevity. The longevity is seen as the result of developmental failure in supplementing the audiovocal output with linguistic and communicative operations. Thus, the vocal product, whether echoic or otherwise noncommunicative, continues unimpinged by the meaning system. If words, meanings, intonational patterns, gestures, and nuances of facial expression are perceived at all during this period of speech without language, they apparently go unappreciated. Consequently, with such an incapacity to receive and register incoming signals, it is hardly surprising that the child fails to incorporate them into his own vocal output. The typical product is rote, wooden, and either monotonous or erratic in tonal phrasing. Nevertheless, such speech is usually quite intelligible and characterized by articulation, which stands in dramatic contrast to the stillborn meaning system. As in the case of muteness, many youngsters do not progress beyond this sterile level of output. For others, symbol-manipulating skills gradually overlay the rote vocal routines, thereby signaling the belated emergence of language.

chapter

3

Aspects of
Language

Warren H. Fay

Crippled Children's Division
University of Oregon Health Sciences Center
Portland, Oregon

contents

ECHOLALIA AND COMMUNICATIVE INTENT 53
   Immediate and Delayed Echolalia 53
   Mitigated Echolalia 59
AUTISTIC PRONOUNS AND DEIXIS 63
   Self-Differentiation 64
   Non-autistic Pronominal Development 65
   Pronominal "Reversal" and "Avoidance" 70
POST-ECHOIC LANGUAGE 74
   From Sound to Sense 75
   Language Cast in Concrete 77
   Adolescent and Adult Language 80
SUMMARY 84

The previous chapter discussed speaking behavior that is devoid of meaning and communicative intent. Other forms of verbal behavior may appear less automatic and may convey some communicative intent. Although communicative intent alone is not *language*, it is a step in that direction. For behavior to be true language, additional criteria must be met. First, the behavior should refer to something that is ideally displaced in space and time. Second, it should be a product of a series of grammatical and intonational rules capable of defining the relationship between referenced items, speakers, or the environment. With these rules, two or more symbolic acts (words or gestures) can be combined in one situation for one purpose, and the same component parts can be recombined in another situation for another purpose. Such a coding mechanism must far exceed mere efficiency in dealing with single labels or lexical units.

This chapter explores the extent to which speech behaviors of autistic children qualify as language.

ECHOLALIA AND COMMUNICATIVE INTENT

Some autistic children remain forever mute. Others become indefinitely plateaued at a psittacine level of echolalia and self-stimulating vocalizations. Still others progress slowly toward a level of true language even while remaining extensively echolalic. For them the long period of echolalia is more than a static state of unaltered reproductions.

Thus, there are many degrees of echolalia that reflect levels of emergence from an automatic state. Baker et al. (1976) provided subcategories of imitations and echoes for a comparative analysis of autistic and developmental receptive aphasic disorders:

1. Immediate repetitions of self—prompted or appropriate
2. Immediate repetitions of self—imprompted or inappropriate
3. Immediate repetitions of others—prompted or appropriate
4. Immediate repetitions of others—inappropriate
5. Immediate repetitions of others—exact
6. Immediate repetitions of others—reduced
7. Immediate repetitions of others—expanded
8. Immediate repetitions of others—mitigated
9. Delayed echo—communicative
10. Delayed echo—uncommunicative (p. 130)

These classifications define both structural and functional criteria. This section considers immediate, delayed, and mitigated echolalia together with the relative function of each as an expression of communicative intent and of language.

Immediate and Delayed Echolalia

One way in which speakers indicate affirmation is by repeating the interlocutor's utterance ("Wanta go?"/"Wanta go"). Kanner (1946) interpreted some of his patients' exact echoes as "affirmation by repetition" employed in the absence of a "yes concept" for expressing affirmation. Although few exact echoes can be so regarded, children occasionally express communicative intent in this fashion. Thus, a mother about to serve her child asks "Do you want a drink?" to which the reply is an exact repetition of the question. This immediate, communicative echolalia—communicative if he does wish a drink—is at a level of signal behavior and thus seldom reflects linguistic processing beyond the simple interpretation of a label. Is this the highest communicative function we can expect from immediate (exact) echolalia?

Researchers have only recently studied whether immediate echolalia has any redeeming linguistic qualities beyond that of signal behavior and affirmation by repetition. Theoretically, if some common denominator of linguistic achievement could be uncovered from the product and the situation in which it occurs, then we should be better equipped to understand the problem and its potential for remediation.

Buium and Stuecher (1974) analyzed the echolalia of a 5½-year-old boy having a diagnosis of childhood psychosis with autistic features. Sixteen sentences of varying complexities were presented to the boy, and he returned each in immediate echolalia. According to their analysis, the "meaning" of eight of the sentences was retained. Four of these were exact echoes ("Today I play outside"/"Today I play outside"). Three were truncated or reduced echoes ("I might have been playing"/"I playing"). The remaining example was a contraction ("It is very nice"/ "It's very nice"). Interestingly, this contraction was interpreted as a grammatical transformation, but it more logically reflects a simple blending due to nonrecognition of word boundaries. The remaining eight sentences lacked sentential meaningfulness (according to the investigators) because of omission of the subject phrase. The auxiliary *is* and the obligatory *do* were omitted in three sentences. In a highly questionable interpretation of their results, the investigators indicated that the repetitions showed evidence of having been guided by an internal set of linguistic rules, that the subject recognized certain grammatical relations, and that these relations represented part of the subject's knowledge of language. The data indicate the absence of rule guidance, grammatical awareness, and a paucity of linguistic competence. The few deviations from pure echolalia were insufficient to impute linguistic competence for even the specific utterances involved.

Echolalia rarely occurs in conjunction with message comprehension (Fay, 1967, 1969; Fay and Butler, 1968). Although understanding of individual components of the triggering stimulus may be demonstrated, the message has failed to register if the echo is forthcoming. Therefore, an echoer's capabilities to process language may be more likely revealed by the stimuli he does *not* echo. This is illustrated in the speech of an autistic 5-year-old (Fay, 1969). An analysis of the child's tape recordings showed consistent echo/error scores of 4/4 for stimuli having the carrier phrase of "Show me the _____." In marked contrast, he neither echoed nor failed the succeeding stimulus of the protocol, "Pick up the man." Thus the presumably easier item of "Show me the man" was echoed and not acted upon, whereas the man was then picked up on request without an accompanying echo. The critical variable was obviously not the noun *man*. To explore this further additional testing was done upon completion of the investigation. "Show me the _____," "Where is the _____?" and "Point to the _____" were used in multiple permutation of phrases, objects, and pictures of objects. With almost perfect consistency, echo plus error were registered for "Show me the _____" and "Where is the _____?"; yet for the carrier phrase "Point to the _____" the responses were consistently correct without echolalia. One might explain this phenomenon on the basis of a more abstract "Show me" and Wh-question. Conversely, the finger pointing and picking up (in the earlier instance) involved concrete action on the part of the boy: a direct motoric involvement. What is not clear is how the phrase per se seemed to derail the utterance either into an echo/error or into a silent identification. But it was apparently sufficient to tally an incorrect response for identification of a noun-object which the child clearly could make under the right pre-noun conditions. Although this is only one case, it may have generalizable implications to both psychometric testing and intervention for echo-stifling comprehension.

Why some stimuli should be "gated through" for processing whereas others are rejected is perhaps the most critical issue in understanding immediate echolalia. It was earlier postulated that the Wh-question is itself a key variable (Fay, 1975). However, a careful analysis of the linguistic competence of an echolalic boy (age 4½) by Panagos (1975) suggested otherwise. Deficits of comprehension in this case were traced to an inadequately developed system of adverbials rather than to Wh transformations. Panagos concluded that delayed development of semantic rules—as in the case of time distinctions—were possibly blocking acquisition of those syntactic rules dependent upon them. Thus, the comprehension difficulties leading to an echo-reaction may encompass problems involving many levels of cognitive and linguistic interaction.

We are clearly in need of more definitive answers before we can even begin to understand the variables underlying verbal comprehension and its relationship to echolalia. Numerous individual differences no doubt exist together with some as yet unappreciated correlates that could be generalized across children. But, thus far, the notion that immediate and persistent echolalia continues unabated after linguistic competence has been demonstrated lacks empirical support.

Delayed echolalia is the repetition of stored, usually echoic, utterances in new and usually inappropriate contexts. Griffith and Ritvo (1967) reported a dialogue with a 9-year-old in which most of her apparently spontaneous comments were in fact almost verbatim reproductions of remarks she had made days, weeks, or months previously. Such behavior is typical of children with childhood autism, childhood schizophrenia, Tic de Gilles syndrome, and in some blind youngsters. It is rare among other young echoers. Baker et al. (1976) reported delayed echolalia in mean percentages of 5.2 of the total utterances of their autistic children, but only 0.1 for their comparison group diagnosed as receptive aphasic.

Delayed echoing is often viewed as a sign of possessing an internalized, albeit rigid, model. The delay in production from time of registration suggests at least the fidelity of long term verbal storage and retrieval. However, the unusual associations these children make between a word and random aspects of the original context are often reflected in the irrelevant context in which the phrase is later produced. Shapiro, Roberts, and Fish (1970) suggested that the examiner and the child seem to be *attending to different relevancies* as demonstrated by a child who responded to his mother's farewell by saying good-bye 5 minutes after her departure. But by that time a new observer did not recognize the relevance of the child's remark, and the mother had left her "unresponsive" child. The attendant bizarreness can be largely accounted for by the situation at registration, the choice of the particular phrase from storage, the duration of storage, and the time/place/situation of iteration.

The usual proclivity to register and store television commercials for future distribution speaks poorly for the cause of communicative intent. A similar and quite probably related behavior can be observed among reading autistics who repeat seemingly without provocation roadside messages, advertisements from the telephone book's yellow pages, and so on. It is difficult to avoid the conclusion that the desire to repeat in these instances has nothing whatsoever to do with communication. Here would seem to be a legitimate case in which parents, recognizing a degree of verbosity in an otherwise reluctant talker, tend to reinforce (knowingly or otherwise) the recitations.

But delayed echoes can be and are used as a communicative device by some children who associate a phrase and situation instrumentally and then "recreate" the favored situation by repeating the stored verbal signal. Furneaux (1966) wrote of an autistic girl who asked, "Do you want to go in the garden?" as an indication of her immediate desire to do so. No doubt the classic example, however, was Kanner's (1946) subject who said, "Don't throw the dog off the balcony" to check himself from doing something wrong. This was traced back to the time when his mother said the phrase with some irritation because he persisted in throwing his toy dog from the balcony of their hotel room. These communicative efforts together with instances of "metaphorical language" seem to be a product of the children's typically excellent associative memory linking sound pattern to condition or object. As such they demonstrate communicative intent in the apparent absence of linguistic competence. Caution should be exercised, nevertheless, in attributing communication to recycled phrases, unless the behavior can be shown to be applied consistently over time. Even then, it may be necessary to trace the exact origins of the remarks in order to ascertain whether iteration is other than random.

Can delayed echolalia express, in addition to communicative intent, evidence of linguistic competence? The limited evidence available suggests this possibility at a minimal level of competence. Baltaxe and Simmons (1977) analyzed the linguistics reflected by the bedtime soliloquies of an 8-year-old autistic child with marked delayed echolalia. The study revealed that the child may use linguistic strategies only minimally employed by a normal child. The more specific rules governing the syntactic and semantic occurrence of linguistic elements requisite for well formed utterances were found to have been incompletely acquired if acquired at all. Utterances on the level of discourse also reflected limited linguistic competence. The authors hypothesized that the subject might have been progressing toward more functional language by an alternative process of breaking down her stored echolalic patterns.

There is increasing evidence that delayed echolalia is quite a different phenomenon from its immediate counterpart. In fact, the differences are such that one can legitimately challenge the evolutionary implications of the qualifier *delayed* as well as the implied clinical linkage between the two symptoms. Because of its primary association with psychotic illnesses, we may be dealing with a manifestation of the psychotic personality in the case of delayed echolalia, as opposed to the developmental plateauing or stagnation postulated with immediate echo phenomena. The following points may assist in differentiating the two echolalias:

1. An echo-reaction in terms of central nervous system (CNS) function is an immediate reaction. Any temporal extension in terms of

minutes and more is no longer immediate and therefore probably neurophysiologically nonsimilar.

2. Immediate echolalia occurs in the presence of another speaker from whom the utterance is obtained. Delayed echolalia may also have its origins as an immediate echo of an interlocutor and thus share a common genesis. It may, nevertheless, be registered in the absence of an overt echo-reaction.

3. Yet, once registered, committed to long term storage, and iterated one or more times in a variety of circumstances, it acquires as a consequence secondary triggering agents (i.e., new people, objects, situations, surroundings, or even the private meanderings of the mind). Thus, as in the case of more normal imitative processes, at least two variations are apparent: simple and persistent (Baldwin, 1895/1925). As described by Baldwin, "A child imitates automatically a sound he hears—one case; and then remembering it but not hearing it, wills to make it—a second case" (1925, p. 359). In the case of delayed echolalia, the iteration may or may not be willful, but like persistent imitation it emerges, not from audition, but rather from the memory. The trigger of delayed echolalia thus is psychologically as well as physiologically different from the immediate echo.

4. Related to the issue of secondary triggering agents is the influence of reinforcement. Newsom, Carr, and Lovaas (1977) examined the function of extrinsic reinforcers (provided by other people) and intrinsic reinforcers (provided by the organism itself) in the maintenance of private (delayed) echolalia and socially directed speech. Recordings during 90-minute social isolation periods showed that socially directed speech of young psychotic subjects declined, whereas the level of private speech remained constant with no tendency to decrease. From these data, plus those supplied from additional subjects, two types of speaking behavior were postulated. One type, socially directed, was said to be extrinsically motivated and dependent on social reinforcement for its maintenance. The other type, private speech, was posited as independent of social reinforcement. Thus, according to the authors, delayed echolalia is maintained by intrinsic reinforcement whereas immediate echolalia is largely a function of incomprehensibility of verbal stimuli.

One might conclude, therefore, that although immediate and delayed echolalia share a few common characteristics, they differ in several important respects. There is no evidence to show that the delayed variety is an outgrowth or evolution of the immediate variety. In terms of language function, both forms seem to operate on a very low—perhaps common—level of repetition without much or any comprehension.

Undoubtedly they share some (but not all) common neural pathways even though the triggering is extrinsic in immediate echolalia and mainly intrinsic in delayed echolalia. In terms of communicative intent and the ability to signal such intentions, delayed echolalia offers greater potential even though much of it seems totally void of communicative efforts. So where does this leave us in accounting for the delayed echolalia among the autistic?

At least two related yet different explanations come to mind. The first would simply relegate delayed echolalia to the severity of the linguistic handicap. If 1) immediate echolalia represents the only avenue of word accrual, and 2) those word packages continually fail as communication, then 3) the child is probably performing with the only verbal material at his disposal. He repeats heard material resurrected from the mental images of the original auditory experience, perhaps in a conditioned association with circumstances similar to the original pairing of words and event. If not so circumstance associated, then he performs at random or for self-stimulation. But always he is chained to his collected repertoire of sound packages because of his inability to match semantic features to actual words in the lexicon. The alternatives are either silence or phenomena of gibberish, neologisms, or inappropriate use of words. Thus, the particular intensity and duration of his developmental stagnation could account for his retaining, iterating, and reiterating verbal material in the only way he can.

A second tenable explanation relates to certain peculiarities of the autistic personality that transcend verbal functioning. Wolff and Chess (1965) were particularly impressed in their study about the "striking abnormality" of repetitive behavior per se. They noted that the amount of stereotyped repetition seemed to be inversely related to the child's exploratory activities (i.e., deficient initiative, curiosity, and experimentation) and to his accessibility to environmental stimuli. Wing et al. (1977) have made a similar observation in a study of symbolic play of mentally retarded and of autistic children. They found that the majority of children with no symbolic play, or with stereotyped play, proved to have either autistic features or the full autistic syndrome. The authors suggested a connection between autistic repetitive speech (both preverbally and as a development later in childhood) and abnormalities of symbolic play. The exact nature of the connection, according to Wing and her associates, it not yet evident.

Mitigated Echolalia

A variation of echolalia in which language clearly does intervene is mitigated echolalia. The term was introduced by Pick (1924) to describe the slight modifications he noted in the echolalia of some of his aphasic patients. He interpreted mitigation as an indication of the echoer's conflict between the compulsion to imitate and the breaking through of the power of gradually returning voluntary speech. Stengel (1947) noted two characteristic modifications: 1) introducing the first person singular into the repeated utterance, and 2) appending an intelligent response to an echoed question or order.

As a childhood phenomenon, mitigated echolalia, together with the grammatical restructuring and semantic resolution that its two main variations imply, has received surprisingly little attention. Yet the behavior may be observed among the normal and abnormal alike. In this author's daughter's otherwise generally non-echolalic speech, a number of examples occurred between the ages of 29 and 34 months. A sampling is offered below:

Trigger	Mitigated echo
I guess you are.	I guess I'm are.
We'll see if you've got a penny.	We'll see if Betsy got a penny.
Here's the buckle.	There's the buckle.
How are you?	How are me? Oh, pretty good.
Show it to me.	Show it to you.
You think I am.	I think you am?
This is another one.	That is another one.
I'll have another cup after this.	I'll have another cup after that.
Depends on what you're doing.	'Pends on what you're doing. . . .
	'Pends on what my doing.

Note the double confusion due to the presence of two pronouns in several of the triggering utterances. In the following section, "Autistic Pronouns and Deixis," the erroneous strategies exhibited by the echolalia are also evident in the non-echoic expressions of many normally developing children.

In order to demonstrate the existence of non-aphasic mitigated echolalia among children the incidence from the recorded utterances of 40 echolalic children was examined (Fay, 1967a). The echoers were not analyzed according to diagnosis, but included late-abating 3-year-olds as well as older clinical clients. A total of 331 samples were obtained and classified according to three major types: type I, pronominal reciprocation ("Where do you sleep?" / "I sleep"); type II, echoic segment preceded or followed by utterance ("Where does your cat sleep?" / "Cat sleep . . . can't find my cat"); and type III, miscellaneous ("How are you?" / "Am I"; "You have a dog, don't you?" / "Yeah, I have a dog, don't I"; "Where does she put her key?" / "Mom put her key"). A total of 32 speakers contributed 149 samples of type I. The type II samples amounted to 143 from 33 speakers. The type III miscellaneous collection (combined I and II, verb or adverb edit, or noun from pronoun) amounted to 39 samples from 16 speakers.

A few remarks relevant to the above study are appropriate here. The working definition of *mitigation* was obtained from the aphasiologists and used as a tool in search of a childhood analog of the adult echoic phenomena. In so doing, 90% of the samples were categorized according to the two aphasic classifications, types I and II. For type III, only about 10% of the total, a deviation from the aphasia model was made to include miscellaneous grammatical conversions or supplements to the echo which seemed to fit the behavior as defined. Undoubtedly type III could be—and has been—enlarged upon. Older children, for example, might produce more instances. Yet the fact remains that no subsequent research on children or adults has as yet specified additional types and full parameters of mitigation. Nevertheless, it is not uncommon to read broadly interpreted definitions of mitigated echolalia such as "situations in which the autistic child alters some aspect of the utterance he is repeating." Unless the observed alterations are specifically linked to progressive or structural alterations or to functional goals, *they cannot qualify as mitigation.* Moreover, there must be an upper limit imposed on the number and extent of structurally permissible alterations; if not, the utterance may literally upgrade itself out of the classification of echolalia.

It has become widely recognized that forms of imitation can be found imbedded in apparently spontaneous speech (e.g., Clark, 1974; Whitehurst and Vasta, 1975; Moerk, 1977). Where is the line of demarcation between imitation and spontaneity in an utterance containing elements of both? Clark (1974) has described a tactic used persistently by some children to pad an utterance with portions of the previous adult utterance. This device, which she aptly termed *plagiarism*, is thought to be useful for keeping communication going in the absence of full competence. Like mitigation, plagiarism reflects the struggle, but is less automatic and less faithful overall to the triggering utterance. The clinical analog of plagiarism has been referred to as *echo-answer* by Lebrun et al. (1971). At some point mitigated echolalia graduates into plagiarism, echo-answer, or spontaneous speech, and in the process leaves its major echoic component behind.

There is another reason for a cautious interpretation of mitigation: prognosis. In a group study (Fay, 1967b) in which 24 late-abaters were compared with 13 clinical referrals, the ratio of pure to mitigated echolalia was approximately 2:1 for each group (67% and 33% and 73% and 27%, respectively). Later, Fay and Butler (1968) divided the sample of 22 late-abaters into subgroups of predominantly pure echoers ($N = 13$) and predominantly mitigated echoers ($N = 9$). The mean 48-month Stanford-Binet IQ for the mitigated group proved to be significantly higher than that obtained for the pure group: 92.0 versus 77.8. The mitigated group was found also to have clearly outperformed their nonmitigating peers at age 3, on the 36-month subtests of verbal comprehension, verbal expression, and object naming. Nevertheless, neither group did as well on the language subtests as did their controls who were matched individually by age, race, sex, and IQ. The mitigation was interpreted as evidence of the gradual convergence of the audiovocal system with an improving syntactic-semantic system. As such it speaks to a more favorable clinical outcome.

Unfortunately, mitigation and its associated prognostic improvement are not characteristic of autism. Shapiro, Roberts, and Fish (1970) noted the rarity of mitigation, and Baker et al. (1976) reported a mean percentage of 8.5 mitigation of the total utterances analyzed. Amounts observed relate to the level of the children studied as well as to the definition of mitigation applied. For instance, the present authors know of no studies in which type II (echo plus utterance) has been included together with the "grammatical reconstruction" definition, although Baker et al. (1976) did employ an apparent equivalent category, "immediate repetitions of others—expanded."

What the autistic child more often demonstrates by this echolalia is the failure to mitigate. What singles him out is what he has not done to the stimulus (type I) or with the stimulus (type II). These errors of noncommission underscore his restricted linguistic capabilities. By way of contrast, Critchley's (1967) definition of aphasic echolalia specifically included a provision for type I mitigation: *"When the aphasic merely repeats the phrase spoken by the examiner, with or without a change of pronoun, we may use the term echolalia"* (p. 17).

Kanner's (1943) attribution of "pronominal reversal" to echolalia is now generally acknowledged even though he, as well as numerous other authorities, opt for a psychogenic rationale. It is precisely because the echoer is not actively editing that the "reversal" becomes apparent in his echoic utterance (Fay, 1971; Bartak and Rutter, 1974). He is, in effect, *failing to reverse* his received pronouns. He is not editing a speaker-appropriate pronoun to a listener-appropriate pronoun. By failing to intervene, he exposes his nonawareness of the underlying grammatical contrasts. Nevertheless, the problems of pronominal resolution are only partially understood in the context of unmitigated echolalia.

Because it is rare among the autistic, type II mitigation is discussed only briefly below. Here echolalia becomes respectable at last. When an echo is the prologue to an appropriate response, there is good evidence that the echo was in the service of cognition. Such a heuristic function for echolalia is not at all uncommon among normal children and adults. Church (1961) described his impression of the behavior in these words:

"The perception—and comprehension and retention—of difficult material is often a two-stage affair: one first echoes blindly and then attends to the reverberations of one's echoes" (p. 36). This phenomenon was studied as demonstrated by about half of two groups of children who were experimentally administered the Peabody Picture Vocabulary Test (Fay and Butler, 1971; Fay and Anderson, 1977). Confronted with pictures from which to select a response, the child was presented a vocabulary word orally. His tendency to echo the word before manually responding was studied. It was found that there is an increasing tendency to engage in echo as the child grows older (CA 3 to CA 7), and a clear proclivity to engage in more of the behavior as the semantic difficulty level of the stimuli increases. Once again, the close relationship between echoic output and verbal comprehension is evident.

AUTISTIC PRONOUNS AND DEIXIS

Mankind has long been troubled with the label-reference problems embodied in the correct usage of pronouns. In *Sartor Resartus*, Thomas Carlyle asked "Who am *I*; the thing that can say 'I'. . . . Who am I; what is this me?" (p. 57). There are major philosophical and cognitive difficulties in the referential properties, that is, extrapolating one's existence and that of others from the labels. There are also built-in problems with the labels per se.

While developmental confrontation with these difficulties is a challenge for normal and abnormal alike, nowhere are the problems more prevalent than with the autistic child. Language, stress, communicative intent, nonverbal communication, and cognition—all likely areas of autistic weakness—converge in an apparent conspiracy against pronominal resolution. It is not surprising that "reversed pronouns" came to be regarded as "almost pathognomonic" of the syndrome.

How the unedited pronouns of echolalia belie the failure of language development was discussed earlier in the chapter. But simply signaling the deficit does little to explain the nature of it. This section addresses the challenge of personal pronouns by considering not only what went wrong and how it might be mended, but also the possibility that the "pathognomonic symptom" may hold a key to many other linguistic difficulties. To do so it will be necessary to address the challenge from the perspective of both its "labeling" and its "referential" properties. Many years of research on the referential issue have been nullified by a failure of the investigators to consider the labels and their primal relationship to hearing rather than to speaking. The normal child's appreciation of deictic contrasts underlies many more linguistic and communicative operations than simply personal pronouns. By analogy, therefore, nonappreciation of deictic contrasts could account for a number of key difficulties in the autistic child's linguistic development.

Self-Differentiation

Persons who view childhood autism as a form of psychopathology see pronominal difficulties as the result of a confusion of personal identity and its consequential psychic defense mechanisms. "It is not easy to talk constantly in opposites," wrote Bettelheim (1967), "to do quite well in getting across what is wanted, and never make the 'mistake' of using pronouns correctly" (p. 243). Ego-based accounts of the pathological self (differentiation of the self from others and from the rest of existence) formed a natural union with what was obviously a developmental problem in acquiring pronouns. How could one develop skill in the use of symbolic referents to self and others (*I* versus *Not-I*) when one had not yet resolved one's own separate identity?

This ego-based approach has been criticized because of its failure to recognize the language component in general and the echoic etiology of pronominal "reversal" in particular (e.g., Fay, 1971; Bartak and Rutter, 1974). Moreover, the notion as stated by the ego theorists demonstrates an error of logic known as *post hoc . . . ergo propter hoc*, the fallacy of thinking that a happening that follows another must be its result. To infer that self-resolution is an accomplished fact at some point prior to proficiency in the production of pronouns does not warrant the further inference that *because* self-resolution has been accomplished pronouns will develop adequately. This logic was strained even further in accounting for the pronominal problems of the autistic child. Here it is being argued that the inferred requisite event (self-resolution) failed to take place because the resultant evidence of proper spoken pronouns is absent. In effect, this explanation says that what we think occurs (because of what we think to be the normal result of that occurrence) actually did not occur, because our postulated normal result failed to materialize!

The erroneous conclusions of the ego theorists, nevertheless, do not justify total neglect of the self-resolution issue. We must somehow keep in perspective both the "psycho" and the "linguistic" aspects of this psycholinguistic hurdle. Yet one need not invoke Freudian psychology, as Rimland (1964) admonished, in order to understand the "deficient ego" in the autistic child. Rather, we must consider how the development of the self-concept, the ability to perceive one's self as an entity, correlates with the development of personal pronouns. Regretfully, this does little to simplify the task.

Epstein (1973) developed a theory in which the phenomenological views of self-concept are presented within an objective framework.

Without attempting to summarize the theory, Epstein's developmental concept can nevertheless be illustrated with this excerpt:

> Thus, it is evident to the child that he has hands and feet that look more like other people's than like those of the dog or cat who inhabit the same household. . . . Moreover, what cannot be seen can be detected by other senses, or otherwise inferred. . . . In addition to evidence that one has a body like other people's there is also evidence that one's own body is uniquely one's own (p. 413).

Similarly, Erikson (1964) describes the origin of self-identity as the "recognition" that is given to an infant by another face, as if, in the process, seeing and "recognizing" one face "gives face" and therefore identity and a self to another.

The active ingredients of inferential self-differentiation according to these theorists, then, would be sensation (particularly vision), attention, inference, and the presence of people in the immediate environment. From an adult perspective, this seems quite a cognitive challenge for an infant. Yet (as in the case of first-language learning), it must be somehow less demanding than it appears. As Church (1971) cautioned, one cannot infer that just because the baby perceives some of the same things that we do that he perceives them in the same way: "The baby's experience is described as *participative* in that self-world boundaries are very tenuously drawn (which is another way of saying that the body is incompletely schematized and the self is diffusely localized), so that those events that are perceived have an organic impact on the body" (p. 468).

Just how much time is required for the normal differentiation process is, of course, speculation. Undoubtedly some individuals remain in a confused state of incomplete differentiation throughout life. Yet it does seem quite reasonable that at least a beginning to the process of self-differentiation, if not total self-resolution, is requisite to the effective ordering and manipulation of the symbolic referents that designate self and others. There would seem to be no rationale, however, that the differentiation process be completed before the advent of the child's introduction to heard pronouns. In fact, it is not improbable that auditory receipt coupled with visual recognition might be an integral process in the development of the separation of the *I* from the *Not-I*.

Non-autistic Pronominal Development

For many years child psychologists have shown interest in the development of pronouns as an index of attained self-awareness. Boyd (1914) ascribed significance to the incidence of personal pronouns in this manner: "The diminishing *I* and the growing use of other pronouns, especially *we* and *you*, is a significant revelation of the process by which the self-centered child is transformed into a social being" (p. 119). Subsequent developmental studies (e.g., Anderson, 1937; Goodenough, 1938; Young, 1942) followed in this same vein with tallied observations of spoken pronouns being interpreted as indicators of egocentricity and self-awareness. These studies supported the developmental primacy of the so-called ego pronouns. *I* and *me* were treated as a single category, occasionally together with *myself*.

In their efforts to find clues to self-awareness and social awareness from observing the spoken pronouns of children, these early investigators made a number of interpretive errors. They seemingly ignored the listening experiences of the child. Undoubtedly, it was not realized at the time that children generally understand language to some extent before using the language expressively (e.g., McCarthy, 1954; Petretic and Tweney, 1977; Sachs and Truswell, 1978). But even if the child does not understand what he is hearing, his initial exposures are nevertheless just the opposite of the first-person forms (*I, me, myself*), which he subsequently employs for self-expression. In other words, the focus should have been on those pronoun forms that were understood. The immediate problem in dealing with pronouns is an understanding of the referents heard in the speech of others. This is important both as a skill in itself and as an avenue of oral expression. Undoubtedly, unraveling referents is largely a cognitive operation.

But it is only through audition that the raw materials—the sounds that we know as pronous—enter the process. Therefore, the child's eventual expressive use of pronouns is dependent upon the strategies he is able to work out with the auditory material at his disposal. Here the relative state of his egocentric or sociocentric development is irrelevant.

And what is the nature of those heard pronouns? Fickle to say the least! Whoever is the speaker at the moment is the person allowed to use *I* or *me* in self-reference. And that person uses *you* to his addressee. Thus, as a receiver of speech the young child hears himself, presumably the person of his prime interest, referred to as *you*. Furthermore, that *you*-material is worthless as a vehicle for self-designation. For the latter, he needs *I*-material. His dilemma, in part, is how to deal with *shifting reference*. For, as he observes others talking, he may note that the referents *I* and *you* can change with each change of speaker. Changing reference is one of the complications inherent in *deictic* elements of human language. Among Hockett's (1963) list of 10 grammatical universals we read:

> *Every human language has a stock of elements that shift their denotations depending on elementary features of the speech situation.* That is, every language has deictic elements. . . . *Among the deictic elements of every human language is one that denotes the speaker and one that denotes the addressee.* The first and second person pronouns are universal (p. 16).

Deictic terms, deictics, or indexicals are words that "pick out" or "point to" things in relation to the participants in the speech situation. In doing so these terms anchor each reference to the speaker in the here and now (E. Clark, 1977). In the simplest use of *person deixis*, the pronoun *I* picks out the speaker in contrast to the *you*, the addressee. They are at the same time symbols and indices and represent a complex category in which code and message (communication and language) overlap. According to Ingram (1971), person deixis in the form of the person deictic unit is generated at the *most abstract or deep level of grammar*.

As if it were not enough to have to unravel speaker-appropriate *I* from listener-appropriate *you*, at least two further complications of receipt must be dealt with. First, *you* refers to the addressee but also to any number of other addressees in the child's listening environment. Second, *me*, as seen below, is considerably more than merely a synonym of *I*.

Type I mitigation gives us overt evidence that a reciprocal strategy or drill has developed and is being applied to an incoming signal. Similarly, Weir (1962) reported the pronominal drills obtained from recordings of her 28-month-old son's bedtime soliloquies. These drills took the form of an *I* and *you* interchange suggestive of mitigation: "Where are you going?/I am going." Presumably a covert analog of overt mitigation and overt drill is operational in other children. But regardless of degree of overtness, such drills reveal only the application of a reciprocal strategy, not how the strategy developed.

Shipley and Shipley (1969) have suggested a tactic in which pronominal resolution is accomplished through a process termed *relative comprehension*. By this method most children, according to the authors, comprehend pronouns immediately relative to the speaker and the person addressed. The hypothesis holds that the form of pronoun used by the child depends on 1) the child's perception of social relationships and the use of pronouns within those relationships, and 2) the child's perception of himself in such a relationship. The Shipleys' thesis stemmed from a study of the use of *thee* by Quaker children. They noted that if the alternative hypothesis of *absolute comprehension* is correct, one would expect most children's initial use of pronouns to be backward, that is, "reversed pronouns."

Eve Clark (1977) has made allowances for just such an eventuality in her dual-hypothesis approach to the problem: a hypothesis for both shifting and nonshifting reference. Clark offers a number of citations confirming that the first personal pronoun children use is a "first person" form such as *I*, *me*, *my*, or *mine*. It is used only sporadically at first, she notes, usually in alternation with the child's own name or *baby* used in self-reference. Clark notes further that the first use of *I* for self-reference may in some cases be part of a set phrase or formula such as "I can do it" or "Me, too" and gains independent status only after analysis in which the pronoun form is segmented out of the utterance. The same could hold true for idiomatic sound packages such as "/ai/dunno" and "/ai/wandat" in which *I* seems to be functioning as nothing more than the initial phoneme of an undifferentiated chunk that happens to have signal value.

The next pronoun children use, according to Clark, is *you*. In order to decide on the relation of *I* to *you*, she suggests two plausible hypotheses. One, conforming to the general rule of nonshifting reference, is that pronouns are a type of name. Thus, *I* becomes assigned to the adult speaker whereas *you* = child. The second hypothesis, equivalent to *relative comprehension* (Shipley and Shipley, 1969), is that the children work out the contrast between *I* and *you* before beginning to use *you*. This, of course, relates *I* to speaker and *you* to addressee. Most children begin with the correct (second) hypothesis, but many do not. Clark lists evidence from a number of observers in support of the first hypothesis in which *you* is used in self-reference, and in which *I* is used for adults and *you* for children (e.g., "I carry you" = "You carry me"). Clark summarized the sequential development of this "wrong track" hypothesis as follows: They first used the pronoun *I* alone with no contrast; then they used *I* and *you* with a wrong contrast; and finally they came to use *I* and *you* appropriately, with the contrast adults use.

A strong case is made by Clark (and also by Bates, 1976) that this linguistic deixis in which words are used to pick out objects (or speakers) originates out of earlier *gestural deixis* of pointing and showing. Bruner (1975a) advances a similar theory which begins with *indicating*, that is, the gestural, postural, and idiosyncratic procedures for bringing a partner's attention to an object or action or state. Initially what is mastered at this very young age is a procedure for following an adult's line of regard, i.e., homing in on the adult's attentional locus. This develops into a mutual attentional system between caregiver and child under the control of the caregiver and/or the child. Eventually the system becomes managed by joint pickup of relevant directional clues that each provides the other. Bruner (1975a) admits a big step between "behavioral" and "linguistic" deixis since in the latter the context is contained in the message, whereas in the former it lies in the behavioral field of the speakers. Presumably those children who escape problems of person deixis are those who have mastered the contrasts of gestural or behavioral deixis at a much earlier age.

Our concerns, rightly or wrongly, have been less with *I* and more with the *you/me* dichotomy. It is the listener's resolution of the pronouns heard that is more linguistically demanding than the need for self-designation in the role of speaker. There is enough strange activity on the receiving end of *you* to make a moderate case for upgrading its role as culprit, at least among slow language learners. (Not at question, here, is whether *you* = child or *you* = addressee, which would seem to be an issue whether the deictic pair were *I* and *you* or *you* and *me*.)

First, comprehension of *you* when so addressed would have egocentric function on a par with being addressed by one's own name. Second, if as a listener one could manage only the closing cadences of the incoming signal, as is typical of the very young (Leopold, 1949, p. 648), of echoers, and of others with reduced auditory memory, in all likelihood the confronting pronoun would be in the objective case (indirect object or object of the preposition). Thus, the speaker becomes *me* in "Give the rubber ball to me" and the addressee typically *you* as in "Mommy and Daddy love you." Third, inasmuch as the speaker's own speech identifies him as the addressor, the subject pronoun *I* is quite often expendable without detriment to the addressee's comprehension of the message.

Glimpses of the aforementioned activity with *you/me* include the case of 3-year-old Terry (Fay, 1972), who answered questions put to him with either "yeah" or "me." Analysis showed that presence or absence of a pronoun in the question was the potential critical variable. For example, "How old are you?" yielded only "me" in response. In a subsequent tape-recorded interview Terry was bombarded with pronoun-loaded questions (grammatical and otherwise). Of 91 probes containing *you*, 27 solo responses of "me" were tallied together with four "Toto's," his version of his name. The remaining 60 responses were almost all "yeah." The pronouns *he, she* and *we* failed to trigger a pronominal response, but the *I* in 10 questions netted six responses of "you." If the probe contained both a Wh-word and a *you*, the probability of a responsive "me" increased dramatically (26 of the 27 *me*'s came from stimuli with both components). Interrogatives *do, did, can, will*, and *shall* produced a consistent "yeah" regardless of whether accompanied by a pronoun. In Terry's case the uninhibited drill with pronouns was apparently dictated by interrogative ± pronoun.

Another reason for focusing on *you/me* came from an informal study (Fay, 1971) of the response 3-year-olds made to the 34 words of the imitation articulation test of the 36-month examination. Of 652 consecutively tested children, 51 (7.8%) abandoned their faithful imitation of preceding words to produce "me" on #34 instead of repeating the stimulus "you." At no time during this small study nor in the articulation testing of several hundred other 3-year-olds was "I" observed to be triggered by the *you*. The study did, however, uncover one other evidence of deictic contrast on the fourteenth word, *this*. Four of the *you* converters plus one *you* conformist responded with "that" (an example of place deixis).

The question of errors now arises. E. Clark (1977) indicated the children's first use of *I* for self-reference always seems to be correct. Weir (1962) also noted that her son's bedtime pronominal drills were correct in terms of assignment to syntactic slots. An analysis of mitigated pronouns from 32 late-abating echoers (Fay, 1972) also showed good choice of case in the edited echoes. Thus, nominative *I* replaced nominative *you* in the subject position. The one deviation noted, however, was the erroneous assignment of nine *me*'s to the position of sentence subject. This, of course, is not atypical of many children who go through a brief stage of self-designation of *me* in lieu of *I*. They have made the necessary pronominal reciprocation, albeit erroneously. Nevertheless, one cannot avoid speculation that *me* may have once enjoyed lawful nominative status as evident in the diachronic development of Middle English *methinks* and *methought* from Anglo-Saxon *me thyncth*.

Finally, there is the instance in which a small child asked her father what letter was faceup on her alphabet block. To the father's response "U," she replied "me?" All of this suggests that in the earliest stages of development *I* may well be subordinate to *me*. If so, there are a number of implications for clinical intervention in cases of nondevelopment or maldevelopment.

But whether the child's prime concern is on *I* or *me* or on both simultaneously, person deixis militates against an easy road to comprehension. Clark and Sengul (1978) note that, although most children use at least one or two deictic words by age 2½, they do not seem to know some pairs involve a deictic contrast. If this referential/ label challenge is difficult for normal children, what are we to expect from autistic youngsters?

Pronominal "Reversal" and "Avoidance"

Autistic pronouns are not reversed. It is unfortunate that the terminology *pronominal reversal* is now widely accepted to specify the behavior. Rather than deliberately exchanging pronouns as this terminology implies, the children actually do nothing but repeat what they hear. The problem is one of inaction rather than commission and reflects their inability to cope with the shifting reference of person deixis. Although generally an outgrowth of unmitigated echolalia, in cases where echolalia is not a part of the picture the net result remains the same. Listener-appropriate forms are simply "borrowed" for use as speaker-appropriate designations. Lorna Wing (personal communication) described a French autistic child of her acquaintance who reverses pronouns but always calls himself *tu* and never *vous*. He is always addressed by the former and never as the formal *vous*.

The autistic child's difficulties with decoding deixis may be traceable to an undeveloped or underdeveloped gestural behavior. As early as 4 months of age, a mutual system of joint selective attention between infant and caregiver is normally assured (Bruner, 1975a). Such a system depends on sensitivity to and curiosity about the mother's relevant directional cues. Thus it would involve visual cross-checking between mother and child as well as the latter's extension of his hand as an external pointer for noting line of regard. This, in turn, probably eventuates in conventional pointing behavior, which the normal youngster develops by the age of one (E. Clark, 1977). Not only does he use pointing to show to another what he is interested in, but he also responds to pointing by looking at the objects indicated. But the autistic infant is lacking both in the interpersonal and the attentional attributes of such a system. These deficiencies, together with his typical lack of curiosity and of "reaching out" behaviors, could seemingly abort the development of an appreciation of behavioral or gestural deixis long before resolution of person deixis is an issue.

To carry the difficulty one developmental step further, Bruner (1975a) has suggested that the big step from "behavioral" to "linguistic" deixis may be bridged in part through early phonological marking. For example, he noted that vocal "comments" or babbling while manipulating objects were higher pitched than those accompanying exchanges with the mother. The same child used a sharper onset of voicing when reaching toward out-of-reach objects, a possible proximal/nonproximal deictic marker. Again, the autistic child, as noted in Chapter 2, seems to lack such intonational qualities in his babble—if he babbles—and in his later echoing and speaking efforts. Thus, it can be seen that the problem of "reversed" pronouns is only a symptom, perhaps pathognomonic, of more complex difficulties with interpersonal and attentional behaviors of infancy.

Concerns for autistic pronouns are not confined to the problem of so-called reversals. O'Gorman (1970) suggested that the child is not so much confused about personal pronouns as not bothered about them. Bosch (1970) has written extensively on the delayed appearance of *I*, and Bettelheim (1967) focused on what he considers to be the child's avoidance or circumvention of *I*. According to Bettelheim (1967),

> If we are dealing here with no more than echolalia, it should be as simple for them to repeat "I want milk" as to repeat "you want milk." We have tried this with all our autistic children, and always the result is the same. They will readily repeat "you want" such and such, but never before they have begun to say "I" in other contexts do they repeat a statement containing "I" (p. 426).

Bettelheim's observations have been challenged by Cunningham (1968), who found no greater avoidance among his psychotic group than among his equally retarded nonpsychotic group. Bartak and Rutter (1974) exposed spontaneously echolalic autistic children who had never used *I* to a number of short sentences containing several personal pronouns in all positions. There was no tendency to avoid repetition of *I* once sentence position was controlled. Their data indicated that the frequency of echoing pronouns in the final sentence position was higher than for either the initial sentence position or middle position. When considering that 1) final sentence components dominate, and 2) *I* is seldom found among the closing components because of its nominative case, then the pseudo-avoidance can be better understood. Research on short term memory shows that the retention of the end of an input stimulus depends on different memory mechanisms from those used for retention of the beginning of the stimulus (R. Clark, 1977). Typically, final items are reproduced first. According to Clark, retention of the beginning depends on rehearsal, and children will be *unable to rehearse stimuli with which they are not already familiar*. It is noteworthy that short term memory responsible for retention of the terminal input is apparently the same in this respect to what has been termed *echoic memory* (Neisser, 1967), *echo box memory* (Waugh and Norman, 1965), and *PAS* (Precategorical Acoustic Storage) (Crowder and Morton, 1969). Not surprisingly, echolalia demonstrates the same initial preference for the terminal items (Fay, 1966).

Although echoic memory and nonrehearsal would seem sufficient to account for Bettelheim's (1967) postulation of avoidance, an additional comment is warranted. Repeating the sound [ai] in a nongrammatical context should be no more difficult for autistic children than repeating [o]. Therefore, in echolalic speech it should be repeated in a nongrammatical manner *if* it is within the range of echoic memory. It is only when the sound takes on grammatical properties that imitation is likely to be avoided. Studies of *elicited imitation* have shown that children will not repeat beyond their own grammatical competence (e.g., Menyuk, 1969; Menyuk and Looney, 1972). Perhaps the constraint to imitate *I* among older and more competent autistic children can be thus explained.

One could of course argue that a general insensitivity to people begets insensitivity to the symbolic representation of people; therefore, the linguistic handicap is simply a by-product of (or another instance of) the child's absence of social awareness and sensitivity. Such a thesis would be particularly appealing if the problems observed in person deixis were not apparent (or less apparent) in the autistic child's handling of other deictic categories. There is increasing evidence, however, that autistic children have difficulty with the shifting boundaries of place deixis (*here*, *there*, *this*, *that*, *come*, *go*, *bring*, *take*), temporal adverbs (e.g., *today*, *this week*), and articles (*a*, *the*) as well as with the shifting reference of person deixis. Bartak, Rutter, and Cox (1975) observed that the autistic child's biggest problem is with words describing relationships rather than with labels of concrete objects or events. Bartolucci and Albers (1974) have reported a pilot study with autistic children on an aspect of deixis, specifically the inflection *-ed* which locates an event in time by creating a two-way contrast between past and present. Three autistic, three mentally retarded, and three normal children were presented an action in the present tense. They were then asked to transform the verb into the appropriate past tense by the following method: "Ann is drinking the juice. . . . She did the same thing this morning. . . . What did she do?" Imaginary verbs *bing* and *rick* were also used. The normal children proved to be 80% correct, and the mentally retarded were 60% correct. The autistic children gave correct responses 8% of the time. The investigators interpreted these results to mean that a problem for autistic children existed at the level of the relationship between the morphological and the semantic aspects of language in the past tense. No doubt future research will further elucidate the extent of the autistic deictic deficiencies.

This discussion warrants a few additional comments relative to intervention procedures:

1. There are a number of good reasons to postpone the traditional emphasis on spoken *I*. The child does not need *I* to express himself in the initial phases of language learning. Since the self-referent can be identified by the signal source (his voice) it is also unnecessary in dialogue. If a self-designation is needed, begin with the child's proper name to be used by him and those around him.
2. When ready, teach an appreciation of the deictic contrast *you/me*. If resolution of *you* is the initial problem as well as the initial ego concern for normal children, it should be no less a problem for the autistic. If he has been an echoer, look for mitigation of *you* to *me*. These are the forms most likely to be dealt with because of their importance and terminal sentence position.
3. The rule for *you/me* (and later *I/you*) cannot be taught to one person by another. It is therefore important for the child to observe others in conversation. Two adults (clinicians or clinician and mother) can serve this function in dialogue. Philips and Dyer (1977, p. 56) suggest a ball-throwing routine as follows: The question posed is "Who wants the ball?" and the answer either "I want the ball" or (name of child, clinician 1, or clinician 2) wants the ball." The ball is immediately thrown to the named person by whoever had it. Dolls or

hand puppets allow for eventually incorporating the child into the dialogue as the voice of first one puppet, then the other. Heavy reliance upon pointing, gesturing, reaching out, and touching between the speakers is probably the most efficient avenue to label/reference resolution. It may be necessary to establish such interchanges before introducing the first pronoun.

4. As skills develop, possessive pronouns, third person forms, and plural forms may be introduced if there are no problems in decoding gender. To confirm confidence it is sometimes helpful to "derail" deliberately the process by gesturing that the object be given to mother while saying that it be given to *me* or *him*. The more advanced child can later be introduced to utterances containing two personal pronouns and to the nuances of stress as they relate to understanding pronominal co-reference (Maratsos, 1973a).

This section has not defined the role and temporal relationship of the process of self-differentiation to the development of pronouns. This is because of the continuing confusion about how the self develops (Broughton and Riegel, 1977). The problem is somewhat reminiscent of the mind/body controversy that has plagued philosophers for centuries: how does one extrapolate one's knowledge of his or her existence from the symbolism used to denote that existence? The question is perhaps inappropriate to the problem at hand. Considering the grammatical challenge of personal pronouns to all first-language learners, and to the autistic child in particular, it is clear that pronominal learning is a complex and very difficult undertaking even if the self becomes identified as separate. But there is increasing evidence that a much greater problem, ontogenetically more primitive and far more pervasive, underlies the difficulties both with self and with pronouns. This problem seems to be defined by attentional and deictic limitations in the realm of encounter with others. The net result is major difficulties with language, in general, together with a host of behaviors that Hermelin and O'Connor (1970) have aptly termed *social obliviousness*. Our tendency to blame the obliviousness for the language or the language for the obliviousness may have been misdirected. Pronouns are but one intersection of components of his more general problem; the way in which the autistic child communicates exposes many more.

POST-ECHOIC LANGUAGE

The relationship between the noncomprehension of heard speech and the occurrence of echolalia has been repeatedly emphasized in this book. It does not follow, however, that echo abatement necessarily constitutes verbal comprehension. The experience of mentally registering an auditory signal without either comprehending it or echoing it is universal. Yet in the normal progression of language development, echolalia is supplanted by communicative language functioning. In the case of the autistic child who has advanced from an extended mute state through echolalia and beyond, at least a primitive emergence into the world of language receipt and expression can be expected.

The following section considers how this transition from speech to language might occur and in what ways the resultant product deviates from normalcy as the child grows to adolescence and adulthood.

From Sound to Sense

Despite the continuing question of whether imitation can be grammatically progressive (cf. Ervin-Tripp, 1964; R. Clark, 1977; Moerk, 1977), it is doubtful that the echolalia of the autistic child contributes much to his linguistic competence. Therefore, we must look elsewhere for a rationale.

What can be learned from the normal child's progression into competency in receipt and expression of language? Although normal language acquisition remains a mystery, child language studies have provided important insights. The historic trend of these studies is generally from a *structural* and *syntactic* approach to a *functional* and *semantic* description of children's first utterances. In a recent essay on the subject, Feldman (1977) came to the conclusion that the meaning-determining rules of language can be understood only by reference to the function of communication. "From this it would follow that efforts to understand language abstracted from the speaker's use of it are always misleading—more so for language used socially, less so for language used ideationally—and, therefore, that any specific claims made in the context of such efforts are, at best, of limited application" (p. 293).

It is beyond our purpose here to review these new "functional/semantic" products of psycholinguistic research. Such an effort would have to encompass the early syntactic-semantic work including that of Bloom (1970) and of Brown (1973a) as well as the more recent contributions on relational meaning (e.g., Dore, 1974; Bruner, 1975a; Bates, 1976). It would be more productive to examine briefly some of the implications of referential meaning to the language of childhood autism.

Labeling is one of the simplest skills of language development; and if there is one skill that the verbal autistic child seems to master, it is labeling. But does he? Many autistic children have considerable difficulty with individual words (Dalgleish, 1975). Others seem to demonstrate a surface skill of naming what is extremely shallow in meaning. For example, one client showed remarkable skill and great delight in recitations either from memory or by stimulation of stacks of picture cards. In fact, that was often his "reward" for a good session. Yet, when confronted with a poster-size picture of a lion that was so similar to the one in his card deck that it could be taken for an enlargement, he failed to identify it. There are several possible explanations for this failure, explanations that are not mutually exclusive: 1) there is an inability to generalize the visual-perceptual experience from the small to the large, 2) generalization is restricted secondary to a tenacious retention of the original learning situation, and/or 3) the child simply could not construct a general rule for generalization from the picture card to the picture poster. What is necessary here is not specifically linguistic, not just the capacity to learn names as they are specifically taught. Yet that appears to be exactly the nature of his limitations. He cannot analyze regularities in the language as they relate to the world.

Bronowski and Bellugi (1970), using the concept *chair*, provided a particularly illuminating example of how the child relates human thought to the environment. They suggest that the child may first learn the word for chair with one particular chair, as in the above example of the lion pictures. The normal child may then go on to extend the word *chair* initially to all pieces of furniture. Then, through his analysis of sentences about chairs in his parents' speech and his experiences with these sentences, the child may gradually narrow his use to the range of objects that we might also describe as chairs . . . a quality of "chairness." The authors emphasized that there is no way to give a definition of *chair* in terms of size, dimensions, color, and the like. To recognize another object not seen before as a chair, they suggest, one must ignore many aspects of the differences between chairs and attend to criteria that might include a moveable seat that accommodates one person, a back, and four legs. In other words, a *specific function or action* is implicit in the definition. Thus, even this seemingly simple concrete labeling excercise calls upon a "deeper human capacity for analyzing and manipulating the environment in the mind by subdividing it into units that persist when they are moved from one mental context into another" (p. 673). Bronowski and Bellugi stressed that we cannot separate the naming of concepts (objects, actions, and properties) from the rules governing their permissible arrangements.

Assuming some lexical success, what is the challenge of combined words? Leonard (1976) used the term *semantic notions* (relational meanings such as agent, action, object, instrument, and location) to identify permissible arrangements that express semantic relations beyond referential meaning by assuming responsibility for meanings expressed by relations between words. He offered the example of "Mommy wash," the meaning of which is not totally contained in the single words *Mommy* and *wash*, since no means would be available to distinguish "Mommy wash" from "wash Mommy." Focusing upon such semantic relations as a method of analyzing language acquisition, Leonard and his colleagues (Leonard, Bolders, and Miller, 1976) obtained language samples from 40 children, some of whom were language disordered. Normal–disordered comparisons were interpreted as supporting the notion that the disordered language use reflected semantic relations consistent with an earlier level of development.

A critical union of linguistics with cognition is dealt with whether considering individual words, semantic notions or, sentence comprehension. Again, quoting Bronowski and Bellugi (1970):

> The match between a sentence and the reality it maps strikes us now, when we know the language, as made by putting the sentence together; but it begins in the first place, in the beginning of language, by taking reality apart (p. 673).

The decomposition of reality is not a linguistic operation but rather a cognitive one (see Chapter 5).

One of the most puzzling theoretical questions of language development and remediation is: how do children come to *improve* on their language once development is well underway? How do they come to move steadily in the direction of the adult model? Why do they learn to say more if what they already convey works reasonably well? Brown (1973b) has provided an excellent discussion of the notions behind improvement in the normally functioning child. He notes that most people assume that improvement is a response to selective social pressures of various kinds; ill formed or incomplete utterances must be less effective than well formed and complete utterances in accomplishing the child's intent; parents probably approve of well formed utterances and disapprove or correct the ill formed. Although Brown acknowledges that such ideas sound sensible and may be correct, the still-scant research on the subject does not support them. He concludes, "We presently do not have evidence that there are selective social pressures of any kind operating on children to impel them to bring their speech into line with adult models" (p. 105).

Language Cast in Concrete

When policymakers in our society are having difficulty convincing a discordant minority of their group to accept the wording of a statement, they often resort to the disarming tactic of suggesting that "It isn't to be engraved in stone or cast in concrete . . . it can always be changed." If there is one pervasive theme in the study of the language of childhood autism it is *the permanence of the initial learning situation*. How can speech be brought into line with adult models if the *only associations are first associations* that are tenaciously stored and recycled as if they were indeed cast in concrete?

This semantic binding is the pathognomonic feature of post-echoic autistic language. Kanner (1949) noted it first when he observed that the meaning of a word apparently cannot be used with any but the original connotation. Scheerer, Rothmann, and Goldstein (1945) remarked that the autistic child and the idiot savant cannot detach the words from their experienced "belongingness" in the actual situation, and Rimland (1964) emphasized the inability to relate present sensation to past experience. The case of the young client who could not generalize from the picture card to the picture poster was discussed above. This, as well as almost all language and language-associated symptoms (repetitions, stereotypes, preservation of sameness, unedited pronouns, delayed echolalia, literalness, abnormalities of symbolic play, and so on) point to initial associative learning and its corollary, the failure to generalize meanings. One need not go far into the literature to find numerous examples of undetached words, but perhaps the best example is the case of 3-year-old Alex (N. Simon, 1975, p. 1442). When riding home at dusk with his mother one day, he was told by her that they would have "sea scallops to eat" for supper. Just as she said this, the car ahead (Mercury Comet, 1960 vintage), which had peculiar slanting tail lights, stopped and the tail lights lit up. For 3 or 4 years afterward, Alex would recite "sea scallops to eat" whenever he saw this type of tail light. When told of this at age 12, Alex related that he had thought that kind of light was called *scallops-to-eat* (although he then knew what sea scallops were), and thought his mother had said, "see, scallops-to-eat." There is no doubt that the preservation of the original symbol-object association is a major, if not *the* major, contributor to post-echoic language stagnation as well as to a host of future developmental difficulties in communicative and cognitive functioning (see Chapters 4 and 5).

Just what the basis is for the "initial-fixation" approach to language remains to be seen. Yet, as in the case of immediate echolalia, the difficulty appears to reflect a developmental absence of certain links in the hierarchical chain necessary for ascendancy to the next higher phase of learning (Hebb, 1949). And, as in echolalia, the coding operations appear to function independent of the presence of a higher level of mental function.

Quite obviously any tendency to fixate on the original learning situation has tremendous implications to any program of intervention. The choice of what is to be taught initially takes on a far greater importance for these children than for any other clinical population. But beyond the issue of initial learning choices is the far more pervasive problem of failure to generalize to new learning situations. *One should be extremely cautious, therefore, in attributing failures of generalization to innocent parties: the child, his family, the tutor, and the methodologies employed.*

The tardy appearance of the *yes* concept, as in the case of the non-use of "I," is further evidence of linguistic confounding. And, as in the case of *I*, it is rarely found in the echoic territory of terminal triggering words (Philips and Dyer, 1977). It denotes once again a developmental failure in verbal comprehension or in relating experiences. To reply "yes" to a probe usually requires decoding the question, mentally responding to the message, and choosing the appropriate response. For a child who tends to be concrete-centered this is indeed an abstract task. Often the term of assent can be considered a statement about a statement. Not uncommonly the probe refers to objects or events removed in place or time, making the level of abstraction even greater. Add to this the "moral obligation" of truth value, and yet another dimension of nonconcreteness enters the scene. A key ingredient in the normal child's acquisition of "yes" is the intonational clue (upward inflection) of the terminal word of the probe (Fay, 1975). Operating on this clue—once again a weak area for autistic children—children learn to respond often without reference to the message, the adequacy of the reply, or truth value. When 120 normal 3-year-olds were offered the declarative stimulus *El Camino Réal*, 24% responded affirmatively, 5% negatively, 37% silently, and the remainder opted for such responses as "Oh, good," "I don't know," "I can't say dat," "Two," "Four," "Just Jerry," "Because anyhow Mom said," and "What is dat?" When the pitch-inflected "question" *El Camino Réal?* was asked the same children, the affirmative account rose to 62%!

In addition to noncomprehension, high abstraction, nonappreciation of pitch inflection, and the morality of truth, there is in the *yes* concept, as well as in all question responses, a listener obligation to the prober. This communicative deficit in autistic youngsters is evident from the early absence of gestural communication.

The child can be taught to say "yes," but the concept is not acquired via speech. When one of the author's young subjects first arrived, he had learned "yes" by operant techniques in his nursery school. For many weeks he responded to probes with "Say yes." (Johnston, 1968, p. 190, also reports this problem.) It did not prove difficult to extinguish the prefix "say," but this only resulted in a more normal sounding response. The real problem arose in getting an appropriate *yes/no* dichotomy. This he could eventually manage, but for some time he was inclined to answer affirmatively to nonsense questions such as "Do you wear socks on your ears?"

Additional anomalies of language form and use have been summarized in the literature. Abnormalities of grammatical construction such as dropped prepositions, conjunctions, and pronouns from phrases ("go walk shops") or incorrect usages ("you sit for chair in table") were evident in the expressions of just over half of a group of 20 autistic children studied by Wing (1969). Also observed were temporal sequencing problems involving phonemes as well as words ("put salt it on"). Words of similar sound or related meaning were muddled ("teapotmental" for "departmental"; "on" for "off"; "sock" for "shoe"; "Mommy" for "Daddy"). The Wing study also uncovered numerous instances of invented words (neologisms) as well as instances in which objects were described by their use (e.g., broom: "sweep-the-floor"). Ricks and Wing (1975) noted a marked tendency for the contraction of sentences, phrases, and words into minimal packages. They gave as an example "Home after bread" which meant "Can we go home after we buy the bread?" In addition to faults of voice, articulation, and rhythm, Goldfarb et al. (1972) listed abnormal features of preteen autistics, which included misnaming, miswording, perseveration, irrelevancies, repetitions of thought, excessive questioning, distortion of ideas, agrammatisms, limited use of language, literalness, and problems with pronouns.

Adolescent and Adult Language

As the near-normal autistic child grows older, his concerns become less those of language usage and more those of interpersonal communication. In the follow-up study by DeMyer et al. (1973) the top 20 children (those rated "normal" on at least one measure: social, speech, or work/school) were generally higher functioning at subsequent reevaluation and had fewer signs of neurological dysfunction than the remaining 126. Fourteen percent, according to DeMyer's data, emerge into adolescence and adulthood having somehow circumvented an array of obstacles that could almost constitute a conspiracy against language learning. Yet even these "favored few" are not without continuing problems in the receipt and expression of the mother tongue.

The characteristics of the language of this group have only recently been subjected to systematic observations. Simmons and Baltaxe (1975) used Goldfarb's observations of preteens as a checklist for the types of faults detectable in a group of seven autistic adolescents. Four of the seven demonstrated pathological linguistic features, while three did not. The abnormal features included voice and phonation, rhythm, voice quality, and articulation. The most prevalent feature of articulation was overprecision attributed to equal stress across syllables. The most frequent and general anomaly was a disfluency affecting normal speech flow and temporal sequencing. Violations of linguistic rules and constraints (semantic, syntactic, and situational) characterized the language-based difficulties. Semantic constraints were violated most often in

the samples analyzed. Syntactic constraint violations involved prepositions, tense agreement, subject/verb agreement, deletions, and
constraints on negative constructions. In contrast with the categories of
semantic and syntactic constraints, situational constraints—in particular
the inability to switch codes depending on listener, social situation, and
topic—proved to be most vulnerable to constant violation. The subjects
practically always used a formal style and were judged to be incapable of
switching to an informal one.

The difficulty with prepositions mentioned in the Simmons and
Baltaxe report has been particularly well illustrated in an anecdotal
account by Creak (1972). A 20-year-old was to be included in an
informal picture-taking session with his parents beside a particularly
admired plant.

> He persistently stood too far off to come into the picture until finally I said,
> "Stand in here between mother and father." He seemed puzzled and
> annoyed and walked away so that we had to do without that one. This
> ordinary incident prompted me to think: I came to the conclusion that his
> irritation resulted from my incomprehensible request. I had, after all, asked
> him to "stand in," to "stand here," and to "stand between." How could he
> possibly do all three? (p. 4)

In addition to these problems, a confusion with gender is noted in a
follow-up interview with a 19-year-old first studied at age 7. Gender is of
importance in English only in the selection of third person pronouns *he*,
she, and *it* (Berit-Hallahmi et al., 1974). The interviewer talked about his
father's employment while deliberately referring to his father as "she"
and "her." In replying, Jim would typically pick up the erroneous
pronoun in framing his reply. Similarly, his mother, designated as *he*, did
his work at home. When queried about what was wrong, he finally said,
"You don't talk right." In a related manner, Jim would answer the question "Where do you put your keys?" with "In the pocket." His tendency
to use the definite article in lieu of the more "natural" possesive pronoun
my contributed to a formal, computer-like tone to his delivery.

A panel composed of parents and professionals from the British and
the American national societies for autistic children generated through
correspondence a comparison of approximately 50 predominantly male
older children and young adults (Dewey and Everard, 1974). Their language findings were summarized under the headings of nonreciprocal
speech, literalness, and irrelevant speech. As might be expected, the
nonreciprocal category included mostly problems of communication such
as giving the listener more than he wanted to hear. Parents often
reported that their children were poor listeners, in part because they
needed more time to process heard remarks. The difficulties of verbal
comprehension, together with perseveration of first impressions and

meanings, characterized the difficulties in the section on literalness. An example was given of a young adult who called his parents to find out what would be suitable to clean the keys of his piano. His mother suggested a moist rag with plain Ivory soap. Some time later, he called back to say that he had searched in vain for this special *ivory* soap. Another example of literalness was the response to the question "Do you have a hobby?" To this the respondent answered "Yes . . ." and nothing more. Irrelevant speech was viewed as harmless yet symptomatic of inattention and inability to recognize the flow of ideas. An example here was a dinner-table conversation which included mention of a familiar name to the adolescent. He then interjected comments about that person's ultimate voice switch from high soprano before the eighth grade to tenor thereafter.

Formal language analyses, surveys, and clinical anecdotes help us appreciate some of the challenges encountered by these mildly autistic young people. Yet probably the most valuable resource for the outsider's appreciation of how it was (or is) to be so handicapped is to be obtained from the autistic people themselves. They certainly have a message for us. And it is through the dedication and study of parents such as Margaret Dewey that that message is being communicated. One of her four children has struggled with the autistic handicap all of his life, and, now 29, is self-supporting as a piano tuner, living in his own home. Trying to understand Jack's problem, she has taken graduate courses and read extensively on the subject of the older and post-autistic person. Still not satisfied, she went to the source material and, over a period of 8 years, has researched and published the results of her studies and interviews with parents and their offspring. Although much of her work relates to recreational, social, and vocational problems, language difficulties have not been neglected.

At a conference of the British National Society for Autistic Children, Dewey (1976) summarized some "bad experiences" shared by autistic individuals up to and including adulthood. Major difficulties were encountered because of 1) misunderstanding directions, 2) following advice too literally, 3) listening to the wrong "authority," 4) failing to recognize that some "advice" is a joke or trick, and 5) failing to adapt advice to changed situations. These language/communication problems were listed together with related difficulties of resistance to change and difficulty, if not impossibility, in focusing on more than one thing at a time. One of the high functioning adults who participated in a panel chaired by Mrs. Dewey at the San Diego conference of the National Society for Autistic Children (Dewey and Everard, 1975) illustrated a number of these points:

> I do not know what subjects to talk about with different people. I have
> commented that certain girls are sexy, because I have heard guys say this

about girls. Once I told a bank teller to her face that she was sexy, and that was probably not the right thing to say. But I heard guys talking dirty to each other and I told them this was not right, and they got angry with me. I have learned that it is normal for guys to talk this way to each other, but I still do not think it is normal to do it around girls. Yet, sometimes I do hear guys say fresh things to girls and the girls don't get mad at them. But they do with me.

Mrs. Dewey gave a better appreciation of the autistic's experience with language and communication. Professor and Mrs. Dewey's assistance helped get a recorded interview from Jack Dewey. Jack answered questions too extensive in number to include here. However, the main points concerning language function are summarized below:

> He has poor recollection and no particular feelings about muteness, echolalia, and pronominal reversals. He has been and is still aware of using stock phrases repeatedly. He often rehearses speaking performances prior to encounter. Such rehearsals, he maintains, "prevent trouble" and provide an opportunity for editing. Jack recalls pronoun-gender difficulties in early elementary grades: "Mrs. Jones is a nice teacher, isn't he?" He also recalls concern by the school authorities about his repeated failures to understand his teachers. This resulted in numerous special hearing tests in which his acute responsiveness and perfect pitch were further recognized. As a child he always missed the story line of children's TV and has continued to have this problem with movies and TV. For several years he watched with his parents the "Mary Tyler Moore Show" as therapy for his difficulty. Yet he seldom understood more than 50 percent of the action, even with their commentary to help. Jack also expressed concerns about his tendency to overanswer questions by providing more information than "what people want to hear." Although he has healthy awareness of his personal talents and verbal accomplishments, Jack realizes that he has problems in self-expression and, to an even greater extent, comprehension. He seemed almost to plead for an appreciation on the part of teachers and others that message-receipt difficulties be not interpreted as hearing, listening, or attentional failures. Such accusations, he recalled, "were more humiliating than anything else, because I was trying to understand. . . . It was not willful . . . I was anxious to please, but not pleasing."

Could anyone have said it better? There is nothing more to add, unless it is this concern for the communication of feelings expressed by Jack in his role as one of the participants in the 1975 San Diego conference (Dewey and Everard, 1975):

> It is very important that an autistic person be able to talk to somebody when he is troubled, someone who doesn't immediately assume that all the trouble is in his head. We get pretty upset when we can't figure out what went wrong, when somebody misunderstood us and we don't know how to set it straight. That is a real problem whether we were misunderstood by a policeman or a friend. If the trouble is in our imagination, we have to be helped with that too.

SUMMARY

As children grow older they tackle, with varying degrees of success, the challenge of acquiring their native language. For many autistic children the lyrics of a popular song a few years ago seem to capture their despair: "Everybody's talking at me; I can't hear a word they're sayin'—Only the echoes of my mind." The inadequacies of immediate echolalia and its distant cousin, delayed echolalia, for interpersonal communication are apparent to others, if not to the child. But just how any child makes progress toward adult forms of language once the process is underway remains largely a mystery. It is possible that the echoes of adult utterances form a storehouse of information from which the more capable gradually induce the rules of language. Evidence of such an inductive operation, nevertheless, is meager. Mitigated echolalia tells us that the child is doing something structurally *to* the received signal or functionally *with* the received signal. It is a positive prognostic sign too rarely observed among autistic echoers.

On the other hand, object naming in the form of acquiring nouns is the most readily acquired language skill of autistic youngsters. But even these efforts are confounded. One major pitfall is evident in the permanence of the initial learning situation together with its corollary: the failure to formulate general principles or inferences. These coding operations apparently function oblivious to higher mental processes which are, themselves, engaged in a struggle of mapping reality. If reality is effectively taken apart, the result is likely to be the assignment of concrete labels rather than rule-linked conceptual units. Their memorized words denote but fail to connote.

Further evidence of the invariant approach to analyzing and coding experience is illustrated in those linguistic confrontations in which flexibility is not merely desirable but essential to understanding: personal pronouns and other deictic forms. The autistic child's reputation for pronominal errors and avoidances may reflect some difficulties in self–other resolution, but more immediately they indicate a failure to appreciate the shifting nature of the referents according to the demands of the speaking situation at the moment. This failure to appreciate deictic contrasts could be an outgrowth of early infancy when the mother's pointing gestures escaped recognition, visual tracking, or meaning. Although traditionally the pronominal difficulties have focused on the expressive use of *I*, research in short term memory and echoic behavior indicates that the focus has been misplaced. As a listener, the child must initially cope with resolution of *you*, the fickle pronoun that 1) designates himself (and others) as addressee, and 2) is most likely retained in short term storage because of its position in the closing cadences of the stimulus. The problem then becomes one of contrasting listener-appropriate *you* to speaker-appropriate *me*. Because nonresolution of deictic contrasts is not limited to personal pronouns in the case of the autistic child, the basic handicap is regarded as being one more of the language of self in respect to others than of ego development.

By adolescence or young adulthood the high functioning autistic person may well have gained functional linguistic competence despite continuing difficulties in comprehension and communication. Isolated structural skills sometimes become the bridge to communication. Other autistic people continue restrained by their earlier linguistic difficulties together with ever-emerging new hurdles such as prepositions, adverbials, gender confusion, and so on—society's callous reward for having acquired some of the basics of language. Their crippled language cripples their communication. But perhaps even more detrimental are the ways inadequate language distorts their view of the world. Young people learn to view the world as adults do, both by communicating with themselves about what happens and by hearing adults communicate with each other. Thus to the extent that he remains handicapped both in speaking and listening, the maturing autistic person is likely to get a distorted view of the world and his place in it.

chapter 4

Aspects of
Communication

Adriana Luce Schuler

Department of Special Education
San Francisco State University
San Francisco, California

contents

FEATURES OF COMMUNICATION 89
LEARNING TO COMMUNICATE 93
COMMUNICATION IN AUTISM 99
    Functions of Speech 99
    Communicative Competence 105
SUMMARY 110

The previous chapters discussed various ways autistic children use speech, from speech as a nonrepresentational sensorimotor behavior to speech as a vehicle for language. But spoken language is not the only tool that serves human interaction. Intentions and feelings can be expressed through gestures, facial expressions, eye contact, and body posture. While the study of language over the last decade has focused predominately on the study of language structure, the language acquisition process cannot be divorced from its early communication context. This chapter deals with communication behaviors in their broadest sense, incorporating verbal as well as nonverbal means of expression. This discusson will help clarify how autistic children differ from other children in interacting with their environment.

The first part of the chapter discusses the relationship between language and communication and the formal characteristics of communication systems. Particular emphasis is placed upon the role of verbal versus nonverbal expression. The second part of this chapter examines: 1) how children normally learn to communicate before they acquire their first words, 2) how one can differentiate among the various functions that children express thereby emphasizing functional, rather than structural, aspects of language and 3) the extent to which autistic children exhibit deficiencies of communicative behavior rather than deficiencies of language in a more restricted sense. These issues concern nonverbal children as well as children with varying levels of echolalic behavior. The ways that nonverbal behaviors are used for communication either in support of, or as a substitute for, verbalizations are discussed in relation to the various levels of verbal functioning in autism.

The extent to which childhood autism can be interpreted as a communicative—rather than as a strictly linguistic—problem is examined on the basis of the evaluation of communicative competence in autism. This is an attempt to clarify the interrelationships among an array of seemingly disjointed behavioral characteristics commonly associated with autism.

FEATURES OF COMMUNICATION

The mere production of speech sounds does not necessarily result in communication. Speech sounds may be produced with complete disregard for social context. The rate of production may not vary as a function of the availability of social reinforcement. Lovaas et al. (1977), in their study of delayed echolalia in autistic subjects, demonstrated the limited effects of social consequences by showing that the rate of such speech production was not affected by social isolation. The repetitiveness of such speech is another demonstration of the limited communicative value of such utterances. Speech is not remodeled in the absence of anticipated listeners' responses. This implies a lack of concern for listener attitudes or possible changes of listener behavior.

Judgments about communication deficits in autism depend largely on the way communication is defined. Definitions depend upon the discipline and philosophical orientation of the scholars involved. Some scholars maintain that any signal produced by one organism that influences the behavior of another is a communicative act (Frings and Frings, 1964). More limited definitions include those of MacKay (1966, 1972), who views behaviors as communicative only when communicative intent is clearly demonstrated. This distinction is helpful when describing speech behavior in childhood autism. According to MacKay, there is a difference between an animal acting in a way that brings about an event and one acting in a certain way *in order* to bring about an event. In the former case, the behavioral outcome is merely an accidental consequence, whereas in the latter, goal directness is demonstrated. The classification of behavior according to communicative intent or automaticity may seem to be methodological mayhem because functions of behavior can only be inferred. While behavioral topography can be described with painstaking accuracy, purpose or function of a behavior cannot be observed. But communication in autism cannot be understood merely on the basis of behaviors observed. For instance, a detailed phonetic analysis of echolalic phrases is interesting, but largely irrelevant, in terms of why that behavior occurs.

Conclusions about the automaticity of a behavior should be based upon inferences about a series of observations rather than upon a single observation. Judgments about automaticity and intent may be inferred from the study of behavior in relationship to its context, and through the experimental manipulation of that context. Since this chapter does not attempt to disentangle philosophical controversies about the primacy of structuralism versus functionalism, its scope is limited to observations of communicative behavior in autism.

First, goal directedness of a behavior may be inferred when alternative courses of action are taken to correct a mismatch between anticipated and actual behavioral outcome. Infants demonstrate such a capacity for corrective action (sometimes referred to as *repair*) at a very early age, when intensity or frequency of vocalizations are altered once anticipated consequences are not met. Much remains to be learned about how children direct their actions through actual or anticipated behavioral consequences to become steadily and increasingly able to depart from reflexive and automatic action.

Second, automaticity of behavior may be inferred from the degree to which a behavior is determined by preceding stimuli. The automaticity of an echolalic phrase is a function of how well it can be predicted from preceding stimuli. For instance, a phrase such as "Don't do that" uttered when a child reaches out for a particular toy (no matter the outcome) is probably automatic rather than intentional. In more general terms, the more a behavior can be divorced from its triggering stimuli, the greater the evidence of intentionality. These differences between intentional and automatic behaviors are seen in the different effects that laboratory-simulated or reproduced alarm calls have on birds compared to chimpanzees. While birds respond to such calls in a predictable manner, chimpanzees do not. Chimpanzees seem to incorporate contextual information that contradicts the alarm calls. They are less easily *tricked* into set responses (Menzel and Johnson, 1976; Orne, 1973). Field observations of chimpanzees support the notion that they are able to respond selectively to one of several simultaneous cues and are able to discard others. This may indicate judgment and incorporation of contextual information rather than automatic action (Langer, 1942; Menzel, 1977). Behavioral heterogeneity or lack of stereotyping may thus reflect goal directedness rather than automaticity.

Communicative intent can be coded in many different ways. Examples of the systematic coding of intentions and meanings through channels other than speech are found in sign language, traffic signs, and plastic (abstract symbol) language systems that have been taught to chimpanzees as well as to people with language problems. (For a discussion of such alternative systems of communication, see Chapter 6.) But other less formalized behaviors, such as gestures, eye movements, and facial expressions, may also have communicative value. The signals that invariably accompany and support verbal exchanges are sometimes referred to as *paralinguistic* as opposed to *linguistic* (Lyons, 1972). In fact, so-called nonverbal means of communication form an integral part of everyday dialogues and may be crucial to early communicative development. The use of nonverbal means of communication was studied in detail by Argyle (1969, 1972), who regarded body orientation, posture and proximity, facial appearance, head movements, and gaze as the main nonverbal signals used by man.

Differences do exist between these various forms of nonverbal communication, both in terms of deliberateness of expression and in terms of coding potential. Much of the so-called body language may not qualify as an intentional form of communication. For instance, facial reddening may have informative value, but be nondeliberate. While nonverbal forms of communication may convey information about the signaler and thereby influence the behavior of the recipient of these signals, they are used with varying degrees of deliberateness. Gesture, posture, and eye movements, for instance, can be used intentionally with remarkable eloquence, as illustrated within the context of an argument or fight (see Morris, 1977). But demarcation lines between intentional and nonintentional forms of communication are not easily drawn. Therefore, it may be useful to refer to degrees of intentionality and to view communicative behavior along a continuum ranging from reflex-like action to deliberate voluntary action.

Further differences between various forms of communicative behavior can be found in terms of coding potential. Formalized coding systems that incorporate smaller units of behavior into larger ones allow for the coding of a greater amount of information. Formalized language systems that rely on separate signs or separate speech sounds that can be combined in many different ways increase the number of response options available to both speaker and listener.[1] At any given time, a speaker may express one of an entire array of possible messages within a particular context. Large numbers of response alternatives may be the most striking features of systems of communication that are most intentional and least automatic. It is at this point that function and structure of communicative behavior interact because the number of response alternatives is determined by the structural complexity of the code.

Linguistic behavior is a subclass of communicative behavior that allows for maximal coding efficiency and for reflective rather than automatic actions. As pointed out by DeLaguna (1927), language frees speech from the conditions under which it was heard or uttered. This enables us to affect each other's immediate behavior and each other's future behaviors. But verbal as well as nonverbal behavior may express communicative intentions of a speaker or a group of speakers and thereby facilitate interaction. To quote Menzel and Johnson (1976):

> They are the mechanisms whereby humans or non-humans solve the basic problems of coordinating and regulating their societies; discriminating each other's specieshood, sex, age, social background, group membership, emotional motivational states, and state of other objects and events in the environment; transmitting the capacity for similar accomplishments to subsequent generations, and thus ultimately securing all of the requisites for the survival and reproduction of the phenotype (p. 131).

The study of communication deals with the multitude of means by which different species affect the behavior of other members of that species. Humans use interacting verbal and nonverbal modes of communication, and are capable of simultaneously conveying intent through various channels. Coding potential is thus enlarged because formalized verbal expressions are combined with deliberate gestures and body movements, as well as with more automatic forms of body language. While tone of voice, intonation, facial expression, and so on, accompany spoken or signed words, discrepancies may be found between body language and

---

[1] Because of the systematic use of a verbal code, the term *verbal* in contrast to *vocal* may apply to nonspeaking but signing children, as well as to speaking children.

verbal messages. Deliberate forms of communication may be used both to conceal and to reveal information. The high degree of intentionality of human communicative behavior may serve purposes of prevarication, which requires an ability to anticipate and incorporate the view of the other.

However, much remains unclear about how children acquire verbal and nonverbal communication skills. It is not clear how children learn to use various channels of communication in a congruent manner, how they eventually learn to blend separately learned systems so gestures and intonation support speech, or how primitive and limited systems of communication provide the emergence of elaborate and sophisticated systems to increase behavioral alternatives for both speaker and listener.

While fussing, screaming, or throwing a tantrum may not seem similar to the use of an indirect polite request ("It feels warm in here," meaning "Would you please open the window?"), their functions may be the same: they each may get someone else to act in a desirable way. The latter form of requesting is much more sophisticated than the former in terms of communicative intent, and it could be argued the earlier forms should not be characterized as communicative.

Children become more and more sophisticated in terms of their ability to engage in, and to code, complex interaction involving others. But much remains to be learned about how children normally acquire linguistic abilities and how they learn to communicate. Careful studies of why some children fail to learn to communicate and use language may shed some light on the ontogenesis and, possibly, the phylogenesis of human communicative ability.

LEARNING TO COMMUNICATE

During the last decade much has been published about how and when children use their first words and how they put those words together to form meaningful sentences. While this work provides information about the acquisition of language structure, it provides much less information about the ways children communicate and to what extent communicative abilities may be a prerequisite for the acquisition of grammar.

During the past few years, much work has concerned the *pragmatic* aspects of language, that is, how language is used for various purposes (see Rees, 1978). Much of the recent shift in emphasis away from purely structural toward more functional issue has been propagated by the work of Austin (1962) and Searle (1969), who laid the basis of a "speech act" approach to language. According to their views, sentences are not context-free propositions but are acts or events in themselves. As part of this approach, distinctions are commonly made between the locutionary and illocutionary aspects of language, the former having to do with a sentence as a grammatical construct and the latter being concerned with someone using that construct to make a statement, request additional information, or pose a question. The terms *proposition* and *performative* make similar distinctions.

Revived interest in the pragmatic aspects of language acquisition has resulted in different approaches to the study of child language. Emphasis is now placed on how children learn to put language to work rather than on descriptions of the course of grammatical development. The acquisition of language skills cannot be divorced from the ways in which children learn to interact with others. However, knowledge of language structure does not necessarily imply communicative competence. Similarly, many language functions can be accomplished through nonverbal means. For instance, a child who cannot speak may be able to move his eyes or his hands to get others to do certain things. Such nonverbal forms of communication are interspersed with verbal behavior and are important in studies of communicative behavior.

For children to become effective communicators, they must learn about words and word combinations and about the context in which words are used and the ways words interact with nonverbal communication. In addition to learning these skills conjointly, they also learn the rules of human interaction, the rules of address, and the logistics for making conversation. Contextual cues may facilitate the acquisition of linguistic skills. Because of the redundancy in conversational exchanges, contextual cues attribute meaning to sounds and sound combinations. Understanding the context in which people talk together and share intentions may help a child crack the linguistic code.

Concern for pragmatic issues has shifted the emphasis from children's early syntactic constructs to earlier periods of development in which language function may be expressed through single words, or word approximations, or even nonverbal cues. The latter involves the acquisition of means-end behavior in general, independent of the particular modality through which it is perceived or expressed. Close observation of infants suggest that they readily learn to affect their environment through crying and smiling. But it is not always easy to determine whether those behaviors are intentional and, if so, what their functions are. From a study of preverbal development of three Italian children, Bates, Camaioni, and Volterra (1975) concluded that the children could communicate long before they started to produce words and that functions normally served by speech could be accomplished in alternative ways. With regard to the function of preverbal communication, a distinction was made between so-called *protoimperatives* and *protodeclaratives*. The former was used in reference to the ways children make requests through vocalizations or body movements. The term *protodeclaratives* was used in reference to the children showing objects to adults as if they were making statements about them. The use of gestures as means to an end was observed at approximately the same time that Piaget's fifth stage of sensorimotor development was attained.

Prelanguage communication skills were studied by Sugarman (1973), who developed a descriptive framework to analyze children's "speech acts" during the first year of life in terms of their function. Sugarman developed a system to reflect the child's actual behavior rather than a system based on presumed analogies with adult behavior. She looked for a difference between children's learning to orient themselves toward persons as opposed to external objects. She observed that actions would start out as being either object oriented or person oriented and that children at age 1 learned to coordinate object and person orientations. While infants initially reached out for desired objects, they did not try to direct the adult's attention to the object desired. They learned to do this at a later stage. Sugarman viewed this development as the basis of social growth. This view may be of particular relevance to the common observation that many autistic children seem to relate more readily to objects than to people. Objects are often handled in remarkably coordinated ways, e.g., the skillful ways in which objects are spun. This raises the question whether, and to what extent, the acquisition of object-oriented means-end behavior may diverge from means-end behavior geared toward people.

While little is known about the relative contribution of different sensory channels and modes of processing to cognitive, linguistic, and social growth, some interesting comparative work has been reported. Chevalier-Skolnikoff (1976) developed a framework for comparative analysis of communicative skills in humans and nonhuman primates in an attempt to study the ontogeny of primate intelligence and communicative potential. She reported that macaques do not complete any of the stages of sensorimotor development as far as the gestural and auditory modes are concerned, but do attain some of the first stages within the visuo-facial and vocal modes. In contrast, apes complete the whole sequence of sensorimotor development within the gestural, but not within the vocal, modality. This enables them to use nonstereotyped forms of motor behavior voluntarily for gesturing and signing. Since this study required the careful comparison of early learning as a function of the input and output modalities involved, the design may prove useful for in-depth studies ranging from self-stimulatory to more intentional behaviors in autistic children.

Both prelinguistic behaviors and first words have been analyzed in terms of their functions. It is not always easy to decide whether or not a child's vocalizations should be classified as words. The mere occurrence of words or word approximations does not suffice. Words must be used in a systematic and purposeful manner and be uttered with apparent communicative intent. Ryan (1977) discussed methodological problems she encountered during her analysis of the communicative context of early language development. She noticed that children's early vocalizations often bear little resemblance to adult speech. Even if "words" are recognizable, there is no guarantee that adult words have the same meaning when spoken by a child. There is a tendency to read meaning into sounds, even when there is little evidence that those sounds are anything but self-stimulatory or contextually conditioned vocalizations. Ryan recommended careful descriptive studies of means-end behaviors, preverbal "dialogues," and other reciprocal exchanges between adults and children. Maybe some experimentation should be superimposed upon purely descriptive studies. One could set up situations where a child would solve problems. For example, what happens if the object a child reaches for is moved away from him rather than toward him? Would the child reach out again, or would he try to obtain that object by changing body position or seeking assistance from an adult? True communicative intent would probably trigger such corrective action if first attempts were to fail.

Despite methodological problems, attempts have been made to classify children's early utterances. Dore (1975) described two-word utterances as "primitive speech acts," consisting of rudimentary referring expressions as well as a "primitive force" (e.g., an intonation pattern), functioning as an indicative device. He identified the following functions: labeling, repeating, answering, requesting (action), requesting (answer), calling, greeting, protesting, and practicing. But such a classification system is based on adult categories and on the presumption that the functions of early vocalizations parallel those of adult speech.

Halliday (1975) developed a classification system by analyzing the speech of his son. Distinctions were made among *instrumental, regulatory, interactional, personal, heuristic, imaginative,* and *informative* functions. Instrumentals were observed at the age of 10.5 months and were used to express demands corresponding most closely to the "I want" functions of adult speech. Instrumentals were followed by regulatories, which serve to regulate the action of others as intermediaries to meet certain goals. Interactionals were observed next, functioning as a means of forming a bond between the child and the others, expressing a "you and me" relationship. Personals were observed at the age of 16.5 months, allowing for the child's self-expression. As noted by Halliday, these first four functions could also be performed by nonverbal means, particularly within the context of stereotyped interactions. The same did not apply to the three language-bound functions that appeared subsequently. Heuristics were used in the explanations behind actions, statements, and events, requiring that one's own actions be separated from the actions of others, and giving rise to questions keyed by *what* and *why*. Utterances having to do with "let's pretend" and "make believe" functions were characterized as imaginatives. Informatives, the last functions to appear, convey information not apparent to the listener on the basis of his own direct experiences. This point (around 18 months, in the case of his son) is a major transition because it is marked by the emergence of word combinations as well as by the ability to engage in dialogue. In addition, it is marked by an ability to represent objects distant in time and space, together with an ability to code the relationship between separate elements of meaning. These last three language-bound functions were called "mathetic" by Halliday, in contrast with the earlier functions called "pragmatic" or extrinsic to language. The mathetic functions are ideational, and the pragmatic functions are interpersonal. This distinction, according to Halliday, is marked by differential pitch inflections. Rising inflections were observed when speech was used for purposes of doing, and falling intonation for purposes of knowing and learning. According to Halliday, such pitch distinctions provide the basis for the later distinctions between the interactive and informative aspects of speech.

While Halliday's work is of a rather impressionistic and intuitive nature, leaving criteria for classification rather unspecified, it reports an interesting developmental progression across the various speech functions. Furthermore, it is helpful for our analyses of communicative development in autistic children.

The growing interest in pragmatic issues has resulted in studies of the different functions of verbal and nonverbal behavior, and has created an interest in how children learn to communicate in the context where early social interactions take place. The more basic question is: how do children's behaviors become more and more intentional? How do behaviors evolve from the reflexive and automatic and become increasingly susceptible to voluntary control? While such questions remain largely unanswered, some answers are related to the establishment of communicative intent. Bruner (1975a; 1975b) emphasized the importance of social games and interactive routines that have an element of reciprocity and joint action. Routines such as feeding and bathing are crucial in the establishment of communicative intent because children learn about turn taking and role shifts before learning to speak. These interactions may serve to synchronize gaze and attention of child and adult. Such preverbal topicalization might provide the basis for later topicalization in the context of speech. To summarize, the repetitive interactional routines of early childhood aid in the acquisition of communicative intent along with the ability to anticipate and influence the course of future events.

The growth of communicative skills in young children is sometimes attributed to the use of "motherese" (Newport, 1976). This term refers to baby-talk by mothers as a means of simplifying the linguistic code. But opinions on this matter differ considerably (Bates, 1976; Newport, 1976). While the speech addressed to children in terms of vocal characteristics and structure differs from the speech addressed to adults, it is not clear whether these differences facilitate the acquisition of linguistic rules. Nelson (1973) says that these simplified interaction patterns may serve to maintain functional communication between mother and infant.

That the communicative social context of early speech acts may indeed affect the acquisition of communication skills is supported by the extent to which individual differences can be observed in the course of development. Nelson (1973) described such differences in detail along with their relevance to developmental issues. In an earlier study she made a distinction between "referentially" and "expressively" inclined children. The former capitalized primarily on what Halliday called the mathetic function of language and not so much on the pragmatic functions. The term *expressive* is used to refer to children who put language into immediate action and rely less on syntactic structures or vocabulary than do children who are more preoccupied with the language code. Such differences may reflect the context in which communication skills are acquired, that is, the context and style of social interaction. Nelson (1973) suggested that the style of mother-child interaction may determine the communicative style the child develops. She showed that children may proceed through different courses of development, depending on which speech functions are most prominent in their environment. Whether children become more "referential" or more "expressive" is influenced by whether their mothers tend to talk about objects and events in an informative style, thus setting the stage for referential speech, or whether they are more action oriented with more prominent use of pragmatic or expressive speech functions. Although the extent to which such differentiation can be made, and the implications for further development of communicative competence remain unclear, communicative styles do have an impact on the course and nature of communicative development, and they are also apt to affect the development of linguistic and cognitive styles and skills.

Given all these uncertainties, one can only speculate on the possible effects of communicative context and styles on the genesis of communicative deficiences. Styles of interaction may play a role both in whether or not communicative deficits develop and on the way they evolve. A child with a specific linguistic coding problem may survive quite well in an environment that is so direct and action oriented that that child must rely on nonverbal means of expression. On the other hand, that same environment will not improve linguistic skills.

An increased awareness of pragmatic issues may at least help establish more refined criteria for differential diagnostics to determine which speech functions are most problematic for which children. Furthermore, it is important to know whether a child is able to express himself nonverbally with apparent communicative intent. New developments in the area of pragmatics will help us deal more effectively with the needs of children who fail to learn communication skills.

COMMUNICATION IN AUTISM

Severe language impairment is a characteristic of early childhood autism. Language impairment may be the basis for other symptoms of autism (Rutter, Bartak, and Simmons, 1971; Churchill, 1972; Rutter, 1974), but the nature of the language deficit has not been clearly defined. The meaning of the term *language deficit* is rarely specified. There is a difference between children having problems with grammatical aspects of language and children who fail to communicate verbally or nonverbally. While the former children may have problems with the linguistic code per se, they may still be talkative or have learned to get their messages across with gestures, intonation patterns, or eye movements. Children with a paucity of linguistic coding should be differentiated from children with broader deficits. Some children may not learn prelinguistic transactions in their environment and may be unable to influence the actions of others through speech or other modes of expression. Because communicative intent is lacking, vocalizations will be limited to sound play or rote reproduction of previously stored utterances and will be intertwined with other self-stimulatory behaviors. The next section of this chapter discusses the communicative abilities of autistic children in terms of the functions of their speech and their style of interacting.

Functions of Speech

Chapters 2 and 3 discussed echolalic behavior along a dimension of intentionality. The notion of communicative intent was used to differentiate forms of echolalia that may indicate emerging language skills from those that are merely rote and automatic and do not serve any purpose beyond the sensory stimulation inherent in the behavior itself. Consequently, it should be determined whether a child engages in vocal behavior as a means to an end or as an end in itself. Such a judgment requires a knowledge of the types of vocalizations, their variations, and their sensitivity to contextual variables. If changes are observed as a function of the presence of people or the degree to which communication goals are met, more is involved than merely reflex action. We are often inclined to give vocalizations meaning according to our own values and ideas. Such anthropomorphic tendencies interfere with the study of animal communication systems as well. As pointed out by Lancaster (1968), primate vocalizations do not necessarily serve to serve to convey meaning. They may merely be signaling devices, serving to emphasize or enhance the effect of visual and tactile signals. Danger calls of birds, for instance, generally will not specify the nature of the dangers, but only signal the existence of the danger.

In judging the relevance of vocalizations we should guard against such overinterpretations. These become even more tempting when observed speech behaviors resemble our own speech. Distinctions must be made between a child who incessantly says, "Shut the fan, Dan," in a random fashion without reference to fans or climatic considerations, and a child who says, "Shut the fan, Dan" because he feels cold. Since a child does not usually volunteer information about his intentions, it is not easy to determine which functions various vocalizations may serve. Even when single words or complete utterances are produced within an appropriate context, it does not necessarily follow that they are intentional. For instance, the authors observed a girl who would always say things like "Be quiet now, everything is all right . . . stop crying," whenever she was spoken to loudly or when she was apparently upset. The phrases uttered in that context were always identical in structure and produced with a rigidly invariable, but appropriate, intonation pattern. One would hesitate to view such speech as propositional or intentional because it merely consisted of the rote and stereotyped reproduction of phrases stored within that particular context. Such context-dependent speech recall resembles the almost ritualized ways routines are carried out. Kanner (1943) referred to this as "desire to maintain sameness." More examples of such situational and ritualized speech recall are easily observed among children with extensive delayed echolalic repertoires. One boy was noted to say, "The damned potatoes are burning" in the context of food and kitchens. Later he would say the same thing when he wanted food. At that time the utterance seemed to acquire a requesting function; that is, it became a means of obtaining food. While it is difficult to determine at what point the utterance started to take on such an instrumental function, it seemed to be a result of its repeated occurrence with the actual consumption of food. The sight of food had become a discriminative stimulus for "The damned potatoes are burning," reinforced by actual food consumption. Food-linked phrases being used within a communicative context can get to be rather elaborate and ritualized, for example, "Do you want juice? . . . Say, I want some juice, please. . . . Good girl," followed by reaching for the juice bottle.

Communicative use of stored phrases is not necessarily limited to food items. Children have been observed producing apparently echolalic phrases such as, "Do you want to be tickled?" and "Say, tickle, please," while placing their bodies in anticipatory and approaching positions. Thus, echolalic speech may be used for communicative purposes, but little is known about how this is accomplished and about the different functions that echolalic speech may serve. Some of the current research relating to speech functions and pragmatic issues may clarify these matters. Prizant and Duchan (1978) reported preliminary findings of detailed functional analyses of echolalic behavior. They made a distinction between the following functions: self-regulation, affirmation, checking, and rehearsal. In terms of echolalia in social interaction, they differentiated between indiscriminate nonfocused echolalia and echolalia used in a turn taking or a declarative manner.

It is possible to express speech functions through other than verbal means. The first four speech functions identified by Halliday (1973, 1975) could be expressed through other than verbal means. Nonverbal communication has hardly been studied in childhood autism. From the few studies available, it seems that autistic children do not excel in nonverbal communication. Various forms of self-stimulatory finger movements and hand postures may sometimes be interpreted as communicative, but close observations of those behaviors within their contexts do not support such conclusions. Self-stimulatory behaviors are not triggered or shaped by external events, but tend to occur completely independent of other persons and other social events. Autistic self-stimulatory vocalizations differ from the usual babbling that occurs as a stage of normal language development. Interactional functions can be expressed through normal babbling because children seem to learn about the interactional dimensions of discourse before they learn to speak. Normal children's babbling eventually honors the rules of discourse as they learn to wait for their turn. Child-caregiver interactions show an element of reciprocity as children seem to practice the give and take of normal interactions while they are still babbling.

Nonverbal communicative behaviors in autistic children consist of instrumental and regulatory functions. From an analysis of sensorimotor and communicative behaviors of 12 mute autistic children, Curcio (1978) concluded that protodeclarative acts were absent among autistic children. If pointing did occur at all, it always served a requesting function and never indicated the location or properties of an object. Protoimperatives were expressed in various manners. While 5 of the 12 children simply guided their teacher's hand to get a container opened, 6 others used eye contact and another child simply banged the container.

Protoimperatives tend to be expressed through screaming and temper tantrums. Stereotyped self-stimulatory behaviors, such as pacing and hand flapping, may even be used as a means to obtain physical contact or other reinforcement. It is also common to see chidren manipulate the hands of other persons, guiding the hands to get food or drink or to be tickled or scratched. The authors frequently observed children holding out their hands to get goodies upon completion of responses that were previously reinforced. While such behaviors may be purposeful or communicative, the behaviors are primitive in the sense that they are strictly tied to one context and are not representational (see Chapter 5). In general, autistic children differ from children with other language disorders because their nonverbal expressions are more limited and relatively few speech functions are served.

The comments here about communicative behaviors pertain to children who are either mute or completely echolalic. Children whose speech behavior is limited to rote and stereotyped reproduction memorize phrases without signs of mitigated echolalia or grammatical productivity. Some children diagnosed as autistic will eventually move beyond that point and master the roots of language. Little is known about the functions of first grammatical constructs. Such developments deserve to be studied to determine whether there are analogies with a more normal course of development and to develop curriculum designs to avoid teaching meaningless and nonfunctional phrases.

Schuler, Fletcher, and Davis-Welsh (1977) analyzed how speech was used by a 9-year-old boy who was diagnosed as autistic and who had remained mute during the first 5 years of his life. Self-stimulatory vocalizations had been shaped into speech approximations and eventually into some first words through the use of operant conditioning. The first words to become functional and spontaneous were related to food. The first productive strategies consisted of a combination of *want* with various members of a class of desired objects and activities. This "want plus X" construction functioned similarly to the pivot-open constructions described by Braine (1963) in the grammar of 1 1/2-year-olds. A second productive strategy served a similar function by combining *no* with undesirable things and events. During the study the boy's repertoire of appropriate speech expanded. In order for the researchers to determine which speech functions were operating within the boy's verbal repertoire, an experimental setup in a television studio with a separate remote control room was used. A playback picture on the television screen was controlled by verbal instructions given to a person in the control room. From this control room, two types of instructions were given. One type requested the boy to carry out instructions such as "Raise your arms" versus "Raise Cheryl's arms." The other type required him to give verbal instructions to his teacher, "Tell Cheryl to. . . ." In addition, toys and picture books were supplied to trigger other speech forms. An analysis of the videotaped speech samples showed that the most productive speech forms consisted of instrumentals and regulatories. A relatively small number included interactionals, of which the phrase, "I love you too, Cheryl," was an example. It was produced when instructions were given in a foreign language. While these would have been echoed at an earlier time, they now resulted in a puzzled face and an attempt to restore contact. The phrase "I love you, too," which was apparently of a delayed echolalic nature, was produced when he bent over to give his teacher a hug. As far as dialogues about pictures and future and past events were concerned, some pseudo-heuristics and informatives were produced. They were predominately of a delayed echolalic nature. Interestingly, the rote and echolalic phrases differed from the grammatically productive and functional ones in terms of articulatory characeristics and vocal delivery. Delayed phrases were produced with a quaint singsong intonation and in a muttered and barely intelligible manner.

While instrumentals and interactionals were most prominent and expressed most distinctly, they were unsophisticated. The boy generally failed to establish eye contact or call his teacher's name in an attempt to secure her attention. Attempts to correct failed communicative efforts were limited to additions of either "I," his own name, or "please" to *I want* structures. If all of these failed, he was observed to increase the volume of his speech, use upward pitch inflection, whine, or throw a tantrum. Raising pitch inflections seemed to be consistently used to mark instrumental and regulatory speech functions such as requests. This observation is of interest because this corresponds with Halliday's (1973, 1975) observations on requests being linked with rising pitch patterns. While these repair endeavors indicated communicative intent, at the same time they revealed rather limited strategies for social interaction.

In conclusion, this 9-year-old boy used frequent requests and seldom used descriptive statements spontaneously. This usage is in accord with the authors' clinical observations, as well as with reports in the literature (Ricks and Wing, 1975; Baltaxe and Simmons, 1975; Curcio, 1978). Most functional speech occurs when speech acts are of direct relevance to the immediate needs of the autistic person. Thus, most speech serves instrumental and regulatory functions, or, in Skinner's (1957) terms, should be viewed as *mands*, which differ from *tacts* because they are controlled by following rather than preceding events. The consequences have to be concrete and immediately relevant. The requests have to do with food consumption, physical contact, favorite activities, or changes in environment. Typical examples of the latter are requests to leave, to go home, or for other persons to leave the room. Such immediate requests are often expressed with remarkable clarity when compared to the rest of the children's speech, the function of which is not easily described. While some may maintain social rapport, or ask for or comment about events to come, these functions, described by Halliday (1973, 1975) as *mathetic* (having to do with language for language's sake), are rare. Much speech that could be taken for dialogue may be self-stimulatory vocalizations that have become somewhat diversified through the incorporation of related fragments of stored discourse. Speech may serve other than strictly communicative functions. Piaget (1926) extensively discussed what he called *egocentric speech*, which is not directed toward others but rather to the child himself. Similar types of speech were described by Vygotsky (1962) and by many investigators of child development. It has also been referred to as *private speech*. Some, such as Vygotsky, suggest that such private speech is merely a precursor of inner language, serving as a means for representational and imaginative gains. Others have attributed different functions to such forms of speech. Weir (1962), for instance, described some of this type of speech as bedtime monologues and inferred that these might function as grammar acquisition devices. She based this idea on the observation that her son would repeat and systematically alter the structure of *recycled* utterances to which he had been exposed at earlier times of the day. Similar observations (Baltaxe, 1977) with respect to autism appear in the literature (see Chapter 2). It may be too early to draw conclusions, but the function of nondirected speech may vary across children of various levels of development and with varying degrees of autism. If echolalia aids in the acquisition of grammar, this should be evidenced by structural changes. In order to make such judgments, the researcher must show that a series of varied utterances occurred within the same context.

Whatever the functions of self-directed, egocentric, or private speech may be, not all speech is maintained through primary or social reinforcement. Humans will talk for the sake of talking. Experiments with and observations of "non-extinguishability of the speech of both autistic and non-autistic children" (Lovaas et al., 1977) suggest that some type of sensory reinforcement is inherent in speech production. If such reinforcement does operate, it would account for the large amount of nonfunctional echolalic speech that is marked by preoccupation with sound effects and repetition of particular structures.

The occurrence of nonfunctional, stereotyped, and repetitive speech may be part of an overall lack of means-end behavior. Self-stimulatory behaviors and stereotyped, repetitive play are characterized by their limited impact on the immediate environment. Both seem to serve no other purpose than sensory stimulation. They are stereotyped without evidence of the adaptive alterations and refinements that are so characteristic of purpose-oriented, means-end behaviors. If objects are involved, they are handled in a nonpurposeful, repetitive, or formalized manner. Similarly, ritualistic behaviors are concerned with serial reconstruction of memorized actions, rather than with the achievement of a goal. Behavioral anomalies in autism are thus a reflection of limitations in goal-directed, means-end behavior. But further research is needed to clarify whether the ability to handle objects purposefully may be better developed. Serifica (1971) found that object permanence was well developed in autistic children when highly motivating objects were used. Similar findings were reported by Curcio (1978). The children in his study, who were largely noncommunicative, showed object permanence but were less able to use objects, for instance, a rake, to reach out for other objects. Performance on tasks requiring an understanding of causality was even poorer. The tasks described all required a notion of an adult as the cause of action. Further research should clarify whether the greatest deficits are exhibited on tasks that require an understanding of causality tied to human action.

Communicative Competence

Ricks and Wing (1975) have commented on the peculiarities of autistic language even when grammatical abilities are relatively well developed. Such peculiarities cannot be explained on the basis of word choice or sentence construction. This is evident in clinical descriptions that pertain to how speech is produced. Kanner (1943) referred to monotone speaking manners as well as "bizarre voice characteristics" when he described autistic speech as "flat in affect." Similar comments were made by Despert (1951), who noted a "failure to express personality" and a "poor emotional tone." A lack of feeling was also postulated by Bettelheim (1967), who went so far as to infer an expression of anger "being seduced into speaking." Attempts to describe autistic speech peculiarities use terms such as *wooden, robot-like*, and *mechanistic*.

Because the peculiarities of speech may be considered to reflect the ways speech is produced, as well as used, these two aspects are discussed below separately.

Peculiarities of speech production are associated with mechanisms of articulation, voice production, and intonation (Goldfarb, 1961; Goldfarb, et al., 1972). As pointed out in Chapter 2, autistic speech is often unintelligible because of deficiencies in articulation and voice production, and because pitch and volume are not patterned appropriately across time.

The problems encountered cannot be blamed solely on defective speech production mechanisms, since both verbal and nonverbal forms of communication are involved. Ricks and Wing (1975) pointed out that autistic children seem limited in the use of nonverbal, as well as verbal means of communication. Neither gestures and facial expressions nor head nods, "uh-hums," smiles, and so on—all of which are the normal concomitants of conversational exchanges—are used to support a conversational exchange. Whereas other children with speech problems often excel in making body parts speak, autistic children typically fail to do so, as if they have not learned word meanings within the context of social interaction.

Communicative ability is determined by the content of messages, by the proficiency with which messages are coded, and by the ways messages are conveyed to the listener. The latter is determined by the dynamics of speaker-listener interactions. Speaker and listener roles have to be continuously shifted if proper "floor appointments" (Argyle, 1972) are to be kept and the conversation is to flow smoothly. Autistic persons generally are not adept in such role shifts. Troubles with speaker-listener relationships were described by Baltaxe (1977) as one of the characteristics of speech of autistic adolescents. Problems with the flow of conversations are easily illustrated. Autistic children may ask the same question over and over after the answer has been supplied on repeated occasions. Similarly, they may not ensure their listener's attention as they might through, for example, eye contact, using proper names, or making exclamations such as "Hey you."

Problems with the give-and-take of speaker-listener relationships may be further illustrated by a general failure of autistic children to maintain social rapport when speaking. As listeners, autistic children seldom reinforce the speaker through smiles, head nods, or other signs of approval. Similarly, they fail to guide their own speech with cues that express approval, amazement, disbelief, or boredom. It is not uncommon for autistic children to carry on about topics that have no interest to the listener or that may even irritate or annoy the listener. Ricks and Wing (1975) found that autistic children tend to talk *ad nauseum* about something that is of interest only to them. Such talk is extremely repetitive, with no room for questions or changes of opinion. Such pseudo-dialogues are similar to the rote echolalic recall of a song or a television commercial because they are not to be interrupted by requests for explanation or elaboration. An interruption almost invariably results in a reinitiation of the complete routine. Even when there is supposed to be turn taking, there tends to be little adherence to social conventions. For instance, a particular answer may be expected to a stereotyped question asked over and over with no allowance for different replies.

A normal flow of conversation is further thwarted because autistic persons do not properly introduce the topic of conversation with phrases such as "By the way," "Remember that . . .," or "Talking about . . ." and also fail to use *this, that, here,* and *there* appropriately. Consequently, there is room for misinterpretation, and the immediate purpose of a statement will often remain unclear. Baltaxe (1977) referred to these unclarities as *foregrounding* and *backgrounding* failures. She concluded that autistic adolescents were not able to distinguish old from new information. Such a problem might at least partially account for the commonly encountered intonational peculiarity. Odd intonation patterns may reveal an inability to highlight pieces of information that should be most relevant to the listener.

Conversational clumsiness may also be attributed to a poorly developed awareness of discourse rules and of rules of conduct in general. Speakers and listeners must adhere to a code of conduct superimposed upon a common linguistic code (Keenan, 1974). Bates (1976) referred to such rules of conduct as "conversational postulates." These rules concern address, politeness, and the appropriateness of an utterance in its social context. The speech of autistic children conflicts with such rules of conduct. Ricks and Wing (1975) reported that autistic children speak too loudly in public places and are unable to make situational judgments. Baltaxe and Simmons (1977) found that German autistic adolescents were generally unable to differentiate between polite and casual forms of address. In her analyses of the speech of autistic adolescents, Baltaxe (1977) found that politeness principles were frequently violated. But such violations may be by-products of echolalia rather than deliberate code violations.

Poor conversational skills may reflect an inability to place oneself in the position of the listener. Keenan and Schieffelin (1976) stated that speaker and listener must be able to adopt each other's perspectives as interactional partners. In order to conduct a meaningful conversation, one needs to have an idea about what a listener knows, is supposed to know, or may want to know. Communication failures may result because of a lack of awareness of and an inability to make presuppositions about the listener (Krauss and Glucksberg, 1969; Glucksberg and Danks, 1975; Bates, 1976). Without such an awareness it would be impossible for the *other* to be the focus of communicative intentions, and the rules of *you* versus *me* would be irrelevant. The *other* person would not be a means to accomplish an end, for instance, to obtain a desired object. While some autistic children may manage to word some simple requests, they rarely modify their requests when they turn out to be ineffective. Corrective action would require an ability to make judgments about the other person to whom the request is addressed. Based on such judgments, the request would be reworded or additional information supplied. Autistic children do not often make judgments that require them to take the perspective of the other into account.

While it is evident that autistic children do poorly in terms of the dyadic aspects of communication, we can only speculate about why their interactional skills are so poorly developed. Little is known about how children normally learn the rules of interaction. According to Bruner (1975a; 1975b), children develop a notion of reciprocal action before they learn to speak. He postulated that such action takes place through early interactive routines (see discussion in previous section) which lead to joint attention and joint action. Case reports on the early development of autistic children frequently note that such children often stiffen up when touched or handled, suggesting an early interference in the development of interactive routines.

Much remains to be discovered about how normal children learn to distinguish their points of view from those of the listener. But it has been hypothesized that children progress from an egocentric[2] stage into a role-taking stage of development (Flavell et al., 1968). Role-taking activities have been reported as early as 2 1/2 to 3 years of age (DeVries, 1970; Maratsos, 1973b; Bates et al., 1976), but much remains to be learned about how such learning takes place.

The difficulties autistic children demonstrate in learning the rules of human interaction may be compounded by the stimuli that normally guide human interaction. Learning about the *other's* perspective is facilitated by subtle and largely nonverbal cues that are inherent in the production of speech. Not only are autistic children unable to coordinate their own speech with such nonverbal forms of expression, but they are also unable to interpret cues used by others. They do not use facial expressions as deliberate means of communication, nor do they seem unable to "read" faces. As pointed out by Ricks and Wing (1975), it is not unusual to see an autistic child actually holding an adult's face while gazing intently, "as if searching for a meaning that eludes him."

Some communication failures of autistic children may be due to their inability to be cued by subtle social stimuli. Similarly, behavioral problems may be linked to an inability to anticipate the behavior of others and to interpret subtle social cues. Appropriate behavior requires

---

[2] The term *egocentric* may be misleading in this respect because it suggests a strongly developed notion of self. It is, however, questionable to what extent a concept of *self* can develop separately from a concept of *others*. It may be more realistic to assume that children gradually learn to differentiate self from others.

that discriminations be made between prohibitive and nonprohibitive contexts. In order to sustain any type of social dialogue, one needs to monitor one's own behavior through the behavior of the others so that corrective action can be taken to correct communication breakdown. Socially appropriate behavior requires an ability to engage in and redirect intentional behavior, and an ability to hide or cover up intentions and to role play in accordance with the contextual demands of the moment. Lack of such abilities in autistic children is amply demonstrated by the pervasive disorders of social behavior that are so typical of childhood autism. Autistic children typically behave in ways that are socially inappropriate. They tend to flip their fingers, rock, engage in excessive nonsense talk, and so on, despite clear-cut signs of social disapproval. Similarly, they seem unable to reword a request more politely or to ensure the listener's attention when demands are not immediately satisfied. Normally, children learn that talking loudly, laughing, giggling, or masturbation are tolerated in certain contexts but not in others. Self-stimulatory behaviors are not unique to autistic persons; we merely discriminate between those conditions in which they are appropriate and those in which they are not. People learn to engage in those side activities that are socially tolerable. Twiddling or rotating body parts, chewing gum, and watching television are permissible under certain conditions but not under others. In more behavioral terms, we learn to differentiate between those stimuli that signal reinforcement (S^Ds) and those that do not (S^Δs). Such stimulus control is not easily acquired by autistic children. Many of their behavioral, as well as communicative, deficits could be interpreted as a failure to learn to direct their behavior by subtle social cues.

Stating that autistic children cannot monitor their behavior on the basis of subtle social cues does not explain why they do so poorly. While we can only speculate about the origin of such social monitoring problems, it may be useful to point out that social cues are transient. They fade over time. This requires an attentional flexibility as well as an ability to attend both to various simultaneous cues that accompany speech and to the context in which they occur. Autistic children usually do poorly when required to track moving objects visually or to direct and shift their gaze. Nor are autistic children equipped to attend simultaneously to more than one thing (see Chapter 5). In addition, they reportedly do better when presented with nontransient stimuli that have been coded in space rather than in time (see Chapter 5). Children normally learn to attend to and interpret social stimuli (for example, tone of voice, smiles) within the context of early social interaction. Autistic children may be ill equipped to learn within the context of joint attention and action. Their body movement may even be dissynchronous with the body action and vocalization of adults (Condon, 1975). As yet, we can only speculate about the relevance of attention to human stimuli and social interaction to further linguistic and cognitive growth.

Speech and language problems in autism are part of a more general problem with the basics of communication. Speech is often not used for communicative purposes, and the range of speech functions served often remains limited to the expression of concrete demands. Limitations in the deliberate use of speech as a vehicle to accomplish interactional goals may be related to a more general limitation in goal-oriented behavior, particularly in regard to the use of people rather than objects. Even when some functional speech is acquired, conversational skills may be limited because the autistic child has problems with the give-and-take of a conversation, and an apparent inability to be guided by subtle social cues.

SUMMARY

The intention to communicate is often seen as the most crucial feature of communicative behavior. Communicative intent may be inferred when the behavior of one person affects the behavior of another person in a deliberate manner. This may be evident by corrective action taken when communicative ends fail to be met. Communication should be viewed along a continuum of intent rather than as an all-or-none phenomenon. Increasing degrees of communicative intent may be evidenced by lesser degrees of automaticity, a greater number of response options, and an increasing ability to anticipate and incorporate the perspective of another person within a communicative act. Furthermore, communicative intent may be coded by verbal as well as nonverbal means. Most verbal exchanges are accompanied by nonverbal signals with various degrees of deliberateness ranging from nondeliberate automatic body signals (such as facial reddening and perspiration) to the deliberate use of gestures and facial expression.

In terms of the relationship between language and communication, linguistic behavior merely constitutes a subclass of communicative behavior that optimizes coding potential.

Much emphasis has been placed on how children learn about language structure. More pragmatically oriented issues have also been studied. These concern the use of language as a means to an end. Children learn about the functions of language long before they learn to speak. Children make declarative statements and requests through nonverbal means such as eye movements and body actions. Functions such as requests for objects or people's attention may be expressed through nonverbal as well as verbal means. But much more needs to be learned about which functions are acquired first and how acquisition of nonverbal communication interacts with verbal communication.

In cases of autism, not all speech and vocalizations qualify as communicative; many are of a self-stimulatory nature. Those utterances that are communicative consist largely of concrete requests. Similarly, nonverbal behaviors often fail to serve communication functions, or do so in a limited, stereotyped manner.

Even when autistic children use speech appropriately, their speech is often mechanistic and flat in affect. Such peculiarities are more readily understood as a pragmatic failure than as defective speech production. Poor vocal quality may reflect a failure to monitor vocal qualities on the basis of feedback supplied by the listener. Similarly, poor conversation skills may be attributable to an inability to take the perspective of the listener, and to *read* the listener's responses in terms of facial expression, body movement, and so on. Other behavioral deficiences in autism, such as the prevalence of self-stimulating behaviors in inappropriate settings, may be similar in nature; that is, they may reflect a limited ability to monitor one's behavior on the basis of social cues and therefore reflect communicative problems in a broader sense.

chapter 5

Aspects of
Cognition

Adriana Luce Schuler

Department of Special Education
San Francisco State University
San Francisco, California

contents

COGNITIVE ABILITIES IN AUTISM 115
    Evidence from Testing 116
    Evidence from Other Sources 120
COMPONENTS OF "LANGUAGE-MINDEDNESS" 126
THE INTERACTION OF COGNITIVE, LINGUISTIC,
    AND SOCIAL DEVELOPMENT 131
SUMMARY 135

The previous chapter described how autistic children use speech and other motor behaviors to interact with their environments. Speculation as to whether or not such communicative attempts can be characterized as linguistic was offered. Similarly, this chapter attempts to make inferences about autistic thought processes and discusses the interaction of linguistic, cognitive, and social growth.

The relationships among perception, language, and cognition have intrigued mankind for centuries. This interest is clearly illustrated by the controversies about whether or not thought can take place without words, and whether or not thoughts alter words and vice versa. The current thinking about these matters is influenced by the work of Piaget (1926) and Bruner (1975a, 1975b). Piaget postulates that intelligence is rooted within actions and sensorimotor schemata, and is not critically dependent upon language. Bruner (1975a, 1975b) states that the basis for both linguistic and cognitive development stems from socialization.

However, the interrelationships among perception, language, and cognition offer much room for continuing speculation. What seems clear is that these different aspects of behavior are deeply intertwined. Questions about what may be accomplished by an organism through language raise their immediate reciprocal; that is, what does an organism need to be able to accomplish in order to develop language? Premack (1976a, 1976b) notes that representational ability alone does not suffice. It must be supplemented by skills in cross-modal association, memory, and attention. In other words, input that is perceived must be stored and categorized.

In order to avoid a philosophical morass, what is meant by *cognition* in this chapter should be clarified. Cognition is the process by which perceptual experience is organized and interpreted on the basis of inferred relationships between things and events.

This chapter addresses the cognitive functioning of autistic children. First, to illustrate how opinions regarding the intellectual integrity of autistic children have evolved, earlier beliefs are reviewed. Then, the question of whether a cognitive deficit might reflect specific language problems or a more generalized symbolic disorder is discussed. The final section of the chapter concerns the interrelationships among cognitive, linguistic, and social development of autistic children. It shows how the seemingly disjointed array of behavioral peculiarities of autistic children may, in fact, create a more unified picture of autistic development.

COGNITIVE ABILITIES IN AUTISM

The term *developmental discontinuity* is used to describe the uneven distribution of skills in autistic children, who may operate with remarkable skill on complex tasks while being unable to do much simpler things. For instance, some autistic children may be able to copy elaborate three-dimensional block constructions or describe the size of a room with painstaking accuracy, but be unable to play ball or imitate a simple arm movement. Similarly, they may recall telephone or Social Security numbers of family members, teachers, or other acquaintances, but fail to give appropriate answers to simple questions. While they are often fascinated with music or rhythm, and may be able to sing in perfect pitch, they rarely share such experiences with others. Some may have an amazingly well developed capacity to spell exotic words, but be unable to carry out simple written instructions.

This uneven distribution of skills, along with often unpredictable, if not capricious, behavior on tests, has remained an area of intrigue. Since most autistic children were once considered untestable, much significance has been attached to occasional context-appropriate verbalizations, to signs of manual dexterity, to facial appearance, and to apparent absence of motor impairment. Consequently, "islets of intelligence" (Creak, 1963) or so-called splinter skills were viewed as representative of true potential that could be developed if it were possible to find ways of breaking through the facade of social aloofness and withdrawal. For instance, Kanner (1943) stated, with regard to the mental capacities of the autistic children he studied, that all were unquestionably endowed with good cognitive potential. Failure to perform in a testing situation was not interpreted as a lack of such potential but as a deliberate refusal to cooperate or as a sign of a preoccupation with more interesting things.

Various developments in the research, however, are challenging the older suppositions about the cognitive integrity of the autistic child. Data, gathered through the widespread administration of intelligence and other tests and through observations of how autistic children learn and process information are leading to critical reevaluations of the language and symbolic play of autistic children, and further questions concerning the nature of cognitive skills in autism are being raised.

Evidence from Testing

Detailed reports on how autistic children perform on standardized intelligence tests are available from a number of sources. Alpern (1967) was one of the first to show that autistic children could be tested if tests were administered carefully. A similar point was made by Mittler (1966), who said that the label *untestable* revealed more about the tester than about the child tested. Through careful testing and retesting, Alpern proved that autistic children could perform in a consistent and reliable manner; that is, they would always pass or fail the same test items. Rutter and Lockyer (1967) found that 50% of a group of 63 autistic children functioned at a severely retarded level with IQs below 50. In another study, Lotter (1967) reported that 56% of a group of autistic 8–10-year-olds were functioning at the severely retarded level.

With regard to the prognostic value of intelligence tests, Lockyer and Rutter (1969) found that IQ scores obtained at age 5 for autistic children remained remarkably consistent with subsequent IQs measures taken 10 or 15 years later. These results were noted despite incomplete testing procedures and the administration of only a small number of subtests. A large sample of autistic children provided the basis for intelligence studies by DeMyer et al. (1974). From their studies, they found that 94% of 155 children tested had IQs lower than 67 and that 75% of those children scored lower than 51. With regard to the overall clinical picture, DeMyer et al. found that the higher the IQ, the less severe the social withdrawal symptoms and language impairment. Concerning the prognostic value of intelligence tests, they noted that treated children with IQs above 50 tended to show greater progress than untreated children. Children with IQs below 40 tended to show no change in IQ as a result of treatment. While their mental age might increase, their IQ did not.

On the basis of accumulated data, DeMyer (1976) concluded that the intelligence of autistic children could be measured reliably and that the scores would predict future functioning. Furthermore, they stated that most autistic children tested functioned at a "subnormal" level and would remain subnormal despite intensive educational efforts. Also, autistic children showed more signs of neurological dysfunction than did the mentally retarded children in the control group.

In order to clarify the nature of autistic cognitive malfunctioning, DeMyer (1976) performed a comparative, item-by-item analysis of the performance of autistic and mentally retarded children. Children were divided into three groups—high, medium, or low—according to overall level of functioning. Such a comparison was complicated by the fact that several of the tests relied, to varying degrees, on verbal skills. The fact that some children could have scored correctly on the basis of memorized responses to standard questions could have been another drawback. Nevertheless, DeMyer noted that the perceptual-motor skills of most autistic children were retarded, and that the performance on visual-motor tasks was enhanced when the visual stimuli remained visible at all times. If the children were required to respond to a transient visual cue, their performance dropped. Similar results were recorded when the task was made more demanding from a motor perspective. Retarded children did better than autistic children when asked to imitate body movements or to engage in ball play. The group of low functioning autistic children functioned above an infant level only when asked to use their lower extremities or to match objects. While verbal and abstraction skills were poor, if not untestable, in the lower functioning children, the higher functioning autistic children scored similarly to the retarded group. These results led DeMyer to speculate about the nature of autistic withdrawal behaviors, since such behaviors were not noted among retarded children with comparable IQ scores. DeMyer suggested that the key to autistic withdrawl behaviors may lie within impaired visual-motor, rather than verbal, capacities. But withdrawal and nonfunctional object use also were related to the poor development of symbolic skills.

While the results of these IQ studies suggest that autistic children perform at a retarded level, the implications of the poor performances are not clear. Some questions about the validity of such tests with autistic children are justified. Clarke and Clarke (1965) have discussed the merits and disadvantages of the use of standardized tests with handicapped children in general. One major drawback is that verbal instructions must be given and verbal responses are required. Thus, using verbal tests with children who are mute or echolalic may obscure rather than clarify the ways in which they operate. A more general problem is that IQ tests do not clarify how information is processed. In other words, a description of what someone has learned (or has failed to learn) does not tell how it was learned (or if there is a potential to yet acquire the failed skill). Consequently, IQ scores do not shed light on the nature of cognitive deficiencies in autism. It is even questionable if overall conclusions about the autistic population can ever be valid, given the heterogeneity of the children who, at some point in their lives, are labeled autistic. For example, many children who were once considered *retarded* are now labeled *autistic*.

In an attempt to study conceptual abilities, Schuler and Bormann (1967) developed a nonverbal testing procedure. Using a match-to-sample paradigm, since matching responses are common in the behavioral repertoires of autistic children, they designed a series of matching tasks that required subjects to move from judgments of similarity based on perceptual grounds to selections requiring increasing degrees of conceptual judgment. To avoid the introduction of stimuli that might be irrelevant or distracting, familiar, everyday objects were used. The matching tasks were divided into the following six subtests:

1. *Identical objects:* Subjects were required to match each of six test objects to one of six identical choice objects, e.g., match black plastic comb to black plastic comb and white plastic spoon to white plastic spoon.

2. *Similar objects:* Subjects were required to match six test objects to one of six choice objects on the basis of similarity, e.g., a plastic red toy car to a metal brown toy car.

3. *Broken and whole objects:* Subjects were required to match six broken test items to their corresponding whole choice objects, e.g., a broken clothespin to an unbroken one.

4. *Parts to wholes:* Subjects were required to match six object parts to their complementary counterparts, e.g., the lid of a jar to the jar, the wheels of a car to the car.

5. *Objects and their functional complements:* Subjects were required to match six test action complements to six corresponding choice objects, e.g., a screw to a screwdriver, a comb to a wig.

6. *Objects and their functional equivalents:* Subjects were required to match six test objects with six choice objects that were functionally equivalent, e.g., a comb to a brush, a glass to a baby bottle.

To ensure that the children would not fail because of a lack of understanding of what they were supposed to do, or because of a lack of motivation, all subtests were preceded by a series of differentially reinforced practice trials. In order to proceed with the test trials, subjects had to meet a criterion of 90% correct responses. Both tangible and social forms of nondifferential reinforcement were given on the subsequent test trials to maintain the attention of the subjects.

Preliminary results indicated that all children who could match identical objects (subtest 1) were also able to match broken parts with their whole counterparts (subtest 3). However, they were not always able to match similar but nonidentical objects, such as a red plastic toy car to a brown metal one (subtest 2), a task that would have required a departure from perceptual cues.

Difficulties were encountered on subtests 4, 5, and 6, which required a further departure from purely perceptual judgments. While one group of children was able and eager to match and reassemble disjointed pieces (e.g., wheels to cars), another group had no idea of the relationships between parts and wholes. They responded in a random fashion, perseverated, or followed a single perceptual cue (for example, matching plastic to plastic). All had the most difficulty with the last two subtests, both of which required further abstractions, and on which the performance of most of the children dropped to chance level. To perform correctly on subtest 5, the children needed a notion of tool use, a concept that they were apparently lacking. For instance, although many of the children could use a pencil, they were unable to match a pencil to a piece of paper with pencil scribbles on it. Perhaps the use of tools in context does not presuppose a more objectified notion of tools as instruments to accomplish certain actions. Failure to perform correctly on the last subtest may reflect similar inabilities, such as an inability to perceive the functional similarity of objects despite perceptual differences. Correct performance, on the other hand, does not necessarily guarantee that such functional similarity is indeed perceived; correct matching of combs and brushes, for example, may be explained because those two objects are often seen together.

While the testing procedures described need refinement and larger-scale application, preliminary findings support the notion of a conceptual deficiency. Most of the autistic children tested were able to use perceptual cues, but were unable to make abstractions about conceptual relationships.

Evidence from Other Sources

Further evidence of cognitive deficits in childhood autism was found by Hermelin and O'Connor (1970), Hermelin (1971, 1976), and Frith (1971). Rather than focusing on the achievements of children diagnosed as autistic, they chose to examine how autistic children process information in comparison to deaf, blind, or retarded children. Comparisons with the first two groups were made because of the behavioral similarities between autistic children and children with sensory impairment. (For a discussion of the apparent sensory deficits of these children, see Rimland, 1964, and Wing, 1974.) These researchers found that it would be an oversimplification to assume that the basic disorder in autism lies within perceptual processes or within an abnormal hierarchical structure of the sensory channels. Hermelin and O'Connor found that their autistic subjects used visual information when it was presented in a codable form, for instance, in spatial configurations. One of their well known experiments examined how autistic children code positions in space when they are presented with a choice between an absolute visuo-spatial and a kinesthetic framework, that is, one linked to the position of their fingers in space. In responding to spatial location rather than to finger cues, autistic children behaved more like normal or retarded children than like blind or blindfolded children.

Other experiments dealt with how autistic children respond to temporally structured information. More specifically, Hermelin and O'Connor examined whether or not autistic subjects are able to detect patterns. Experiments employed both auditory and visual sequences. Hermelin (1971) reported that autistic children could recall random series of words as well as series of words that were thematically related, e.g., words referring to kitchen utensils. Similarly, they were equally able to recall ungrammatical, anomalous, and meaningful grammatical sentences.

While normal and retarded children were always able to do better in the recall of meaningful information, autistic children did equally well in the recall of sense as compared to nonsense. This applied to the recall of auditory material, as well as visual information. When children were asked to reconstruct a series of cardboard squares of decreasing size, they did not do any better than when they were required to construct random sequences. To minimize the perceptual-motor complexity of the tasks, the children were also presented with random versus patterned combinations of two elements, such as numbers and dots. The autistic children were not able to profit from the systematic and rule-governed (rather than random) presentation of stimulus material. Hermelin (1976) concluded that autistic children suffer from a central deficiency in the processing of incoming and outgoing information. She postulated that coding and categorization are deficient in autistic children and that they employ an echo-box memory store, a finding relevant to their often noted echolalia (see discussion in Chapter 2).

Other experiments (Hermelin, 1976) examined how autistic children recall digits when both temporal and spatial cues are available. When a series of three digits could be recalled, either as a function of the order in which they were visually displayed or according to their spatial configuration, the autistic children in Hermelin's study invariably guided their recall by spatial cues, performing in a manner similar to deaf children. From these experiments Hermelin concluded that temporal ordering depends on hearing or listening and may relate to the adequate use of language as a storage code. Hermelin suggested that this uncoded processing may account for the problems that autistic children exhibit in language and social interaction, both of which require an ability to extract flexible rules. According to her views, the language deficiencies constitute only one aspect of a more general inability to use signs or symbols, which in turn relates to other coding deficits. Thus, autism is viewed as a central disorder of cognition, characterized by an inability to reduce information through rules and redundancies.

Ricks and Wing (1975) and Wing et al. (1977) expressed a similar view of autism as a generalized cognitive deficiency. Their studies of language and play behavior revealed stereotyped play and noncommunicative use of speech that were void of symbolic capacity. Analogies between the particularities of language and play behavior were also noted by Frith (1971). She suggested that the language of autistic children is impaired for the same reasons that their play is impaired: both activities require that rules be learned and then applied.

The extent to which autistic children engage in symbolic play was the focus of a study carried out by Wing and co-workers (1977), who studied 108 children diagnosed as having autism, severe retardation, and

Down's syndrome. Based on observations of children playing with toys, they grouped children according to levels of symbolic activities. A distinction was made between symbolic and stereotyped play; for the former, children were expected to be able to produce appropriate noises while pushing a toy car or to play with dolls as if they were real babies. Higher symbolic skills were assumed when children were able to take part in pretend games or draw pictures on imaginative themes. For play behavior to be considered symbolic, the children had to exhibit a variety of such behaviors, as well as diversified, i.e., nonstereotyped play.

Play activities were described as stereotyped when there was evidence of limited symbolic play with an apparent inability to modify play activities on the basis of a contextual or social demand. Along with stereotyped behavior (such as self-stimulatory behavior) and level of social responsiveness, the mobility patterns exhibited by the children were a further point of concern. Children without symbolic or stereotyped play were further categorized as functioning below or above a mental age of 20 months. Most children diagnosed as autistic were functioning above a 20-month level of development, but were lacking in symbolic or even stereotyped symbolic play. These children had extremely limited comprehension skills and could understand only single words or instructions presented within a familiar context. Four children out of the 24 who exhibited stereotyped play showed the complete autistic syndrome. Lack of social behaviors and language abnormalities were noted in seven other children.

Repetitive, stereotyped speech was found in 11 of the 19 children who also demonstrated stereotyped play. While most of these children functioned above the 20-month level, three children functioned below that level. Children who exhibited stereotyped play were able to imitate simple symbolic behaviors but were unable to initiate those behaviors on their own. Differences between children with Down's syndrome and autistic children were noteworthy in this respect. Symbolic play activities occurred frequently within the former group. Interestingly, children who exhibited symbolic play were more likely to exhibit stubbornness and rebellion.

From their studies, Wing et al. concluded that varied and flexible forms of symbolic play do not occur below a mental age of approximately 20 months and that stereotyped play should be viewed as a precursor of symbolic play. Even though the presence of symbolic play seems to be linked to language comprehension skills, the nature of such a relationship and the implications for proposed etiologies of autism remain to be clarified. But the authors concluded that the central problem in childhood autism may be "a severe impairment in the normal human ability to abstract concepts from experience, to give abstractions symbolic labels, to store the concepts in symbolic form, and to draw on them for relevant association when thinking of the past, relating to the present and planning for the future."

Although the studies by Wing and Hermelin and their associates could be criticized for their methods of subject selection and group assignment, as well as for their experimental procedures, they are impressive in their commonality of findings across a large group of subjects and experiments. Their findings redefine the nature of autistic impairment as a disorder of symbolic thought. While this concept is helpful because it unifies an otherwise disjointed set of behavioral characteristics, it does not explain why such a deficit occurs. It does not identify which anomalies of early development or intrinsic neurological deficits may lead to an inability to use symbols.

More basic processing deficiencies have been identified through a series of experiments dealing wih so-called stimulus overselectivity and on the basis of identified learning strategies. The phenomenon of stimulus overselectivity was initially described by Lovaas et al. (1971). They taught autistic and normal children to press a lever when simultaneously presented with auditory, visual, and tactile stimuli. Subsequently, the three single components of the stimulus complex were presented separately in an attempt to determine which stimulus components had controlled the children's responses. It was found that the responses of the autistic children were under the control of one stimulus element only. Autistic children tended to be overselective in their responding. In contrast, normal children continued to respond in the presence of all three stimulus components. They were able to attend to more than one stimulus at the same time. This finding has been repeated in several additional experiments. Lovaas and his co-workers (1971) showed that overselectivity also occurred when only auditory and visual stimuli were presented, and Koegel and Wilhelm (1973) found that autistic children were overselective when presented with a visual stimulus complex, for example, two visual cues on one single card. Other evidence of overselectivity within the visual modality was presented by Schreibman and Lovaas (1973). They taught autistic children to discriminate between clothed girl and boy dolls. After the discrimination was acquired, the heads of the dolls were systematically interchanged in an attempt to determine which stimulus component had guided the children's responses. Again it was found that a single stimulus feature, such as the doll's jacket, had controlled the children's responses, whereas normal children's responses were determined by the doll's head, together with other body parts. Reynolds, Newsom, and Lovaas (1974) showed that autistic children also exhibit overselectivity when presented with multiple auditory stimuli.

These studies are consistent in their picture of autistic idiosyncrasies in attention and learning. However, it is difficult to determine whether they are inherent to developmental stagnation and therefore transitory. It is not clear whether they should be viewed as a cause or a result of impaired language development. Recent studies have indicated that overselectivity is not an irreversible phenomenon. Koegel and Schreibman (1977) showed that autistic children who first responded in an overselective manner could be taught to respond to multiple cues. In another study, Schreibman, Koegel, and Craig (1977) found that autistic children would cease to respond in an overselective manner when separate stimuli were presented in various combinations along with the original stimulus complex. This finding was replicated by Leland et al. (1977). Overselectivity may be a normal phenomenon, characteristic of children of a low developmental level. Schuler and Bormann (1978) found many children who did well when asked to match objects on the basis of perceptual identity (see discussion in previous section). In order to perform correctly, they needed only to attend to more than one cue at a time (for example, they could respond to shape, color, or transparency of the objects displayed). Further studies should determine whether lack of conceptual development in autism is related to overselectivity.

Eimas (1969) and Hale and Morgan (1973) have suggested that stimulus overselectivity is a function of developmental level. Ross (1976) has stated that autistic children who demonstrated overselectivity may be functioning similar to normal children below the age of 2. Strong evidence to this effect was presented by Schover and Newsom (1976). How stimulus overselectivity may interfere seriously with learning was discussed extensively by Ross. He pointed out that learning in a natural environment (such as incidental or observational learning) would be thwarted by stimulus overselectiveness.

Autistic children often demonstrate serious learning problems once their behavioral problems are alleviated and teaching begins. DeMyer (1976) found that many children demonstrate insurmountable blocks to learning. Many autistic children do poorly on discrimination learning tasks because they fail to respond to the relevant stimulus dimension (Donnellan-Walsh et al., 1976). Hermelin and O'Connor (1970) and Hermelin (1976) reported that their retarded autistic subjects were unable to discriminate between two boxes marked with different shapes. The children's responses were found to be a function of the position of the boxes in space (left-right positions) rather than of the shapes portrayed. The same subjects performed considerably better when the discriminations referred to positions in space. As pointed out by Donnellan-Walsh et al. (1976), many autistic children fail to respond to relevant stimulus dimensions and rely instead on the presence of inadvertent cues (such as those supplied by the position of the teacher's hand in space or by the position in space of the stimulus object presented). From the analysis of incorrect responses on the conceptual test described earlier, similar response patterns became apparent (Schuler and Bormann, 1978). Many children selected objects by their position, probably on the basis of previous reinforcement. Other children matched objects on the basis of shape or color characteristics. These tendencies suggest that the children tested (i.e., those who could be trained to perform on a matching task) operated in a systematic and rule-governed manner. Similar findings were reported by Frith (1971), who studied how autistic children perform on guessing games and tasks that require them to make patterns. She noted that some of her autistic subjects would perseverate, while others operated in an alternating manner. (The latter pattern supposedly suggests a higher level of development, Schusterman, 1964; Jeffrey and Cohen, 1965). Frith interpreted this as indicative of an ability to apply rules, and as counterevidence of the claim that autistic children operate in a random fashion. However, knowledge of rules is not quite the same as acting in a rule-governed manner. Implications in terms of cognitive functioning remain unclear.

Failures of autistic children to generalize newly learned behaviors were reported by Rincover and Koegel (1975) and Koegel and Rincover (1977). This lack of generalization may be due to overselectivity or to inadvertent or irrelevant cues. While motivational variables play a major role, cognitive variables can play an additional role. If a behavior is exhibited only within the particular context in which it was originally taught, it could be explained on the basis of an ability to derive a more general rule from a specific context-tied instance of that same rule. Given that autistic children have difficulties with extracting rules, with notions of similarity, and with the separation of relevant and irrelevant stimuli, failure to generalize can be explained on grounds of poor conceptual development. A tendency to process in a wholistic, rather than analytic, manner and to insist on sameness might further complicate the picture. Such processing would interfere with the extraction of single stimulus dimensions.

The fact that autistic children tend to respond overselectively and often fail to generalize newly learned skills could be viewed as a further indication of cognitive impairment in autistic children, possibly of a particular type distinct from more generalized forms of retardation because many retarded children generalize in spite of a slow learning rate. The autistic tendency to learn narrow situation-specific rules and to adhere to them in a strict manner (Frith, 1971) is suggestive of a more specific form of retardation or cognitive deficit.

Paucity of symbolic functioning may be attributed to an overall cognitive disorder as well as to language disability. As pointed out by Premack (1976a, 1976b), language is so deeply enmeshed in intelligence that a discussion of the psychological prerequisites for language is also a discussion of the mechanisms of intelligence. In order to clarify how the autistic profile of skills may relate to language development or lack of it, the discussion below turns to some of the basic cognitive operations that are crucial to the development of language.

COMPONENTS OF "LANGUAGE-MINDEDNESS"

Many autistic children function at low developmental levels despite some precocious skills that require memory or visuo-spatial abilities. Although many autistic children do poorly on tasks that require visuo-spatial integrity, some deal very well with visual stimuli that are coded in space rather than in time (DeMyer, 1976; Hermelin, 1976). Because language components of cognitive functions are not easily separated from nonlanguage components, it is not known how such discrepancies arise. In addition, visuo-spatial ability in autistic children has not been fully explored. Investigators have focused on assessing weaknesses rather than strengths. Consequently, we can only speculate about the dimensions of cognitive abilities in autism.

With regard to the dichotomy between spatial and temporal skills, Hermelin (1976) has suggested that spatial coding may depend less on the extraction of rules and the use of redundancy than does the coding of temporally ordered sequences. Furthermore, she has suggested that spatial information may require more precise memory functions and less processing. In her studies, she also has noted that space may be directly perceived but time is inferred. Little is known about how normal children develop concepts of the structure of space as opposed to the structure of time. Interestingly, wholistic processing of visuo-spatial stimuli is attributed to the right hemisphere of the brain, in contrast to analytic and temporal ways of processing which are attributed to the left hemisphere (Levy-Agresti and Sperry, 1968; Bogen, 1969; Sperry, Gazzaniga, and Bogen, 1969). In this light, it is of interest that many autistic children are most accurately described as left- or mixed-handed (Colby and Parkinson, 1977). Much remains to be learned about the interaction of normal development, lateralization of functions, and hemispheric specialization. It is not known if hemispheric imbalance is at all relevant to autism. Even if it were, it would be difficult to determine whether such an imbalance is primary or secondary to the developmental problems of autism.

Given our limited understanding of normal development, the uneven distribution of skills in autistic children is not easily explained. Claims that autism is primarily a disorder of symbolic thinking are premature. It is not clear how symbolic deficiencies relate to the various aspects of autistic processing and behavioral idiosyncrasies. Consequently, opinion is divided on whether autism should be viewed primarily as a cognitive, a linguistic, or an interactional disorder. In order to clarify some of these issues, the following discussion examines the relationship between cognitive and linguistic skills and how those skills may relate to the behavioral and attentional characteristics of autistic children.

First, in order for language to develop, there must be an awareness of persons and things in the environment, and how persons and things interact; without such an awareness, there is no basis for the linguistic coding of nonlinguistic knowledge. However, little is known about how autistic persons perceive or experience their environments. Given the commonly noted "desire to maintain sameness" (Kanner, 1943; see discussion in Chapter 1), it is apparent that many autistic children are not oblivious to their environment and are able to note differences. Insistence on sameness may be indicative of an inability to perceive regularity and conceptual relatedness despite perceptual differences. But some degree of nonverbal understanding may be inferred from the ways children learn to turn keys, climb fences, or make wheels spin. Such behavior may be based on a inexplicit experiential knowledge derived from previous experience rather than on a concept of causality.

The results of the nonverbal conceptual tests (Schuler and Bormann, 1978) discussed earlier in this chapter indicate a very restricted understanding, not only of conceptual relationships but also of how things work. The inference that autistic persons may have some understanding of sequences of events can be gathered from the experiments carried out by Hermelin and O'Connor (1970), who found that many autistic subjects were able to order temporally related pictures, such as those portraying the gradual burning down of a candle. However, more evidence would be required to support the hypothesis that the coding of relationships rather than the relationships themselves functions as the stumbling blocks for autistic children. Future investigations of the extent to which autistic children are able to judge causality may answer some of these basic questions. So far, it appears that the nonverbal understanding of objects and actions is limited in autistic individuals.

In order for language to develop, conceptual understanding alone is insufficient. There must also be a need to communicate this understanding or to bring about changes. In other words, communicative intent and means-end behavior in general (for a more detailed discussion of these issues, see Chapter 4) are additional prerequisites for language. The latter requires one to understand the impact of one's actions. Connections must be made between actions and consequences. The commonly reported attentional idiosyncrasies of autistic children (for example, their tendency to be overselective) could interfere with the formation of such connections. Limitations in means-end behavior in general suggest that the problems of autistic children are not limited to verbal stimuli. The limited understanding of the effects of human action indicates that the problems encountered are of a cognitive and/or interactional nature rather than a linguistic one.

Attentional idiosyncrasies may not account for the problems described. Insistence on sameness suggests that the order of action sequences is perceived, but it is not clear whether separate components of such sequences can take on representational value. Representational capacity may be inferred from the ways in which some autistic children manipulate parts of other persons' bodies to meet certain ends. Typical examples of such enactive representation (Bruner, 1964) may be found in their efforts to move someone else's hand to get a drink, to be tickled, or to push an adult away. While this suggests communicative intent, such behavior may also be taken as an indication of limited representational capacity. If such signaling behaviors are representational, they should be viewed merely as the roots of representational activity embedded within action sequences. In order for truly symbolic representation to emerge, greater degrees of abstraction are needed. As pointed out by Bates et al. (1979), conventionalized communication becomes symbolic when we can infer that a child has objectified the vehicle-referent relationship. A child must learn that vehicle and referent (the symbol and what is symbolized) can be interchanged for certain purposes. According to Bates and her co-workers, symbolic capacity develops gradually, as evidenced by a child's increasing ability to separate vehicle and referent. The process of gradual "decontextualization" takes place between the ages of 9 and 13 months.

The ability to attend to a series of events does not suffice for the acquisition of labels with symbolic rather than enactive representational value. Symbolic labeling comes with the ability to give simultaneous attention to label and referent and to make continuous comparisons. If labels are used in a truly symbolic manner, they must stand for isolated features and attributes of referents as well as for referents as a whole. The latter requires that features be abstracted from a stimulus complex so they can be categorized accordingly. Color and size attributes, for instance, must be divorced from their physical occurrence and made abstract if concepts of color and size are to develop.

Our understanding of the ways in which children normally acquire symbols remains rudimentary. Nevertheless, inferences concerning the degree to which autistic children develop representational capacities can be drawn from attentional characteristics and limitations of their language and symbolic play.

As far as attentional characteristics are concerned, stimulus overselectivity interferes with the acquisition of representational capacity.

Inability to make associations between smiles, vocalizations, and their context obviously thwarts the acquisition of meaning. However, stimulus overselectivity may be a result, rather than a cause, of poor representational capacity. Whatever its nature, it will interfere with the expansion of linguistic or cognitive abilities. Paucities of symbolic play, whatever their origin, are a further indication of poor representational skills.

If autistic children develop any functional speech it often seems to serve as a signal rather than a symbol. A vocalization or even a complete phrase may be meaningful because it functions as a signal for an action to come, but still not be symbolic in a true sense. An extreme literalness of meaning has been attributed to the speech of autistic persons since the publication of the first case reports. Whenever words are used meaningfully, they tend to refer to concrete referents. Consequently, most autistic children do better when concrete objects are labeled than they do when labels are used to refer to persons and their actions. Not only are the latter transient in nature, the labels used refer to relationships between elements of meaning. This makes the referent-label relationship more opaque and less perceptually salient. Furthermore, language functions that rely on imaginary activity, such as pretend and make-believe games, are poorly developed in autistic individuals. Thus, teachers generally face insurmountable problems when concepts pertaining to sameness and difference are to be taught. In spite of an ability to match objects that are the same, many autistic students are unable to use verbal labels. Similarly, they are often unable to respond appropriately to yes/no questions because such answers require a verbal label for referring to abstract relationships, such as the relationship between a perceived state of affairs and a verbal label referring to it. Interestingly, Premack (1976b) has suggested that yes/no questions code the relationships between someone's knowledge of an item and a representation of that knowledge. According to him, yes/no questions require that representations of one's self be recognized as such. His studies show that chimpanzees can be interrogated in such a manner, which apparently separates them from many other species.

While observations of language and behavior in general support the notion of autism as a symbolic disorder, little experimental data have been gathered in support of that notion. Hermelin (1971) has suggested that autistic children respond to acoustic stimuli as a whole rather than separate features. For instance, she noted that while retarded children separate words from nonspeech sounds, autistic children respond to intensity cues. In a recent study, Bormann and Schuler (1978) investigated the extent to which autistic adolescents are able to discriminate between words on the basis of isolated features; for example, subjects were trained to respond to one- versus four-syllable words. Preliminary analysis of the results seems to indicate that autistic children are unable to generalize from one set of words to the next. This suggests that autistic children learn isolated discriminations rather than underlying rules. These findings support the view that autistic children do not perceive regularities, patterns, and structure (Ricks and Wing, 1975; Hermelin, 1976) since they reveal an inability to classify and categorize, which interferes with conceptual development. Nevertheless preliminary data suggest that autistic children demonstrate such skills when only visuo-spatial stimuli are involved (Schuler, 1979b).

Further experimental evidence of poor representational capacities was found in another study by Schuler and Bormann (1978), which focused on the representational ability of severely retarded autistic children when modalities other than the auditory were involved. Most children described as nonverbal (unable to consistently use labels) were unable to match tactually presented objects with their visual representations despite extensive practice trials. In addition, the same subjects were unable to perform on a modified object-matching task in which they were required to move a marker instead of the object itself. Comparisons with non-autistic children should clarify whether we are dealing with a deficiency specific to autism.

Without further data it is difficult to determine whether representational inabilities are language specific or are indicative of a more generalized deficit. In order to resolve this question, it should be determined to what extent autistic children are able to process static rather than time-varying visual information. Many of these children are adept at finding their way around, but it is not known whether they are guided by some internal representation (cognitive map) or by stored sequences of motor behavior.

Besides the ability to discriminate, associate, and represent, additional skills are needed to develop language abilities. The effective use of language demands syntactic as well as semantic skills in order to perceive and express grammatical relationships between separate words; it is imperative that the temporal relationships between single elements of meaning be perceived. The experiments reported by Hermelin (1976) indicate that autistic children are unable to detect the internal structure of temporally ordered stimulus material. Whether this is a result or a cause of their language impairment remains unresolved, but it is of interest that autistic children behave in ways similar to the deaf. Both tend to code visual sequences in spatial rather than temporal terms.

No definite conclusions can be drawn about the interaction of linguistic and cognitive deficits in autism. However, autistic children tend to do poorly, not ony on language tasks, but also on language-related tasks that do not depend on verbal instruction or expression. For example, they have difficulty matching conceptually related objects and detecting patterns. Given the increasing evidence of the interrelationships among social, linguistic, and cognitive growth in normal children, the question of whether autistic deficits are primarily linguistic or cognitive must be approached within a broader framework of attentional and interactional processes.

THE INTERACTION OF COGNITIVE, LINGUISTIC, AND SOCIAL DEVELOPMENT

Separate discussions of speech, language, communication, and cognition in autistic children have been offered. The following summation reassembles these interconnected aspects of development and allows us to review the controversial issue of whether autism should be viewed as an emotional, a language, or a cognitive problem.

Autistic children may or may not produce speech, but if they do it is rarely used as a means to communicate. This indicates that speech skills can be divorced from linguistic, communicative, and cognitive skills. If speech is conventionalized in intent and meaning, its meaning tends to be literal and narrowly defined by the context in which it was acquired. Other problems of speech/language production in autistic children are demonstrated through pervasive comprehension deficits, a poor ability to use grammatical rules in novel ways, and the persistence of echolalic and stereotyped speech. Problems at the level of communicative behavior are illustrated by the limited use of gestures, facial expression, and intonation for purposes of social interaction. Similarly, conversational skills are generally poor. Autistic children do not incorporate the perspective of their discourse partners; it is as if they have not arrived at the rules of *you* versus *me*. Consequently, they do not easily learn in the context of social interaction.

Cognitive deficiencies are indicated by developmental delays, learning problems, limitations in representational capacity, and problems with cognitive operations that require notions of analogy and similarity or an ability to isolate features of stimulus complexes (e.g, distinguishing parts from the whole).

While the interactions among cognitive, linguistic, and communicative behaviors are evident, the nature of these relationships remains elusive. In addition, considerable variation in level and profile of functioning can be found among groups of children as heterogeneous as autistic children. For instance, some children's communicative efforts may be limited to temper tantrums and screaming, while others may use functional speech. Nevertheless, the unsophisticated ways in which communicative intent is expressed may eventually illuminate the interrelationships between communication and cognition. Autistic communicative behavior often seems largely nonsymbolic and rooted within rote memorized sequences of concrete actions. This behavior is illustrated in the case of an autistic boy who brought his mother her coat, her shopping bag, and her car keys in an apparent attempt to arrange a visit to the market.

It is difficult to find support for theories of the nature of autism that focus on one aspect of development. Interpretations of autism as a severe language disorder (Churchill, 1972), as a severe form of receptive aphasia (Rutter, Bartak, and Newman, 1971), or as a language-related cognitive handicap (Rutter et al., 1971; Hermelin, 1976) deserve cautious consideration. First, comparisons with childhood aphasia are by nature elusive, since the term *aphasia* comes from poorly documented and nondescriptive inferences about brain damage. Second, children described as aphasic do not exhibit the severe behavioral problems that are common among autistic children. In addition, other signs of developmental delay are also common in autism. In a retrospective developmental study of 78 autistic children, Ornitz, Guthrie, and Farley (1977) found that motor delays are often apparent before signs of language delay are noted and that both forms of delay are correlated. They argued that cognitive or linguistic impairment does not offer a sufficient explanation for the development of childhood autism. These more general delays were interpreted as evidence for a neurophysiological basis of childhood autism, suggesting a problem at the level of sensorimotor integration. Other evidence of early developmental problems has been reported by Massie (1977, 1978) on the basis of his interactional and cognitive analyses of filmed samples of early "pre-psychotic" development. However, interpretations of autism as emotional, cognitive, linguistic, or sensorimotor in nature are premature in the absence of more data pertaining to these various aspects of behavior. In addition, more descriptive definitions are needed in order to understand what constitutes a language disorder. Since language development is intertwined with prelinguistic sensorimotor development, language disorders cannot be studied from an isolated structural perspective. Attempts to illuminate patterns of autistic development must include descriptions of behavioral characteristics that are consistently found in specified groups of children. Commonalities within various subsets of autistic behavior might indicate how autistic development diverges from non-autistic development. The specific profile of autistic developmental breakdown must be identified if autism is to be separated from retardation and other developmental disorders, particularly those disorders that pertain to the development of language.

In order to clarify how course and rate of autistic development may diverge from normal development, a better understanding of the interaction of social, linguistic,and cognitive development in normal children would be helpful. While much remains to be learned about autistic as well as normal development, some findings about early development of normal children may be of particular relevance to the pathogenesis of the autistic syndrome. According to Bates and her co-workers (Bates, 1976; Bates et al., 1979), a distinction should be made between the development of static and dynamic aspects of cognition. The former are concerned with knowledge of objects, even if momentarily invisible (object permanence), and with the construction of objects in space. These static elements of cognition seem to develop independent of imitation, symbolization, and the use of tools. Bates and her co-workers made careful comparisons between measures of development obtained in a longitudinal study of a group of children. They found limited correlations between static and dynamic components of development, a finding supported by the work of Snyder (1975) and Corrigan (1976). The development of dynamic capacities was attributed to an ability to coordinate people and object-oriented action sequences, which reportedy develop separately during the first 9 months of life (Sugarman, 1973).

These distinctions are of interest because impairments in imitation, communication, and symbolization may reflect idiosyncrasies in the development of dynamic skills in autistic children. Relatively better developed skills in the use of objects imply that the static dimensions of cognition are well developed. The supposition that the dynamic aspects of communication are acquired in the context of early social interactions is compatible with the fact that autistic infants appear socially unresponsive. Their obliviousness to social stimuli may thwart the development of interrelated dynamic skills that are normally developed in early social interaction. This would explain why most autistic children are more adept with objects and visuo-spatial tasks than with other persons. (For a further discussion of these issues, see Schuler, 1979b.)

However, it is as yet difficult to draw conclusions about autistic children's style of thinking and about the extent to which they are able to move beyond purely perceptual strategies. It is not clear to what extent representational and abstraction abilities are based on early socialization. According to Bates, the notion of substitution is acquired as a function of social interaction. This is congruent with the views of Bruner (1975a, 1975b), who attributes crucial value to joint attention and action in early interaction rituals because these action rituals teach the child the rules of *you* versus *me* as agents or recipients of action. In Bruner's (1975b) words: "The joint enterprise sets the deictic limits that govern joint reference, determines the need for a referential taxonomy, establishes the need for signaling intent, and provides the context for the development of explicit predication." The often noted problems with personal pronouns and other deictic manners thus may be a problem of social rather than linguistic development, analogous with the inability to express communicative intent through other than linguistic channels. It is as if autistic children have been unable to learn from interaction with and imitation of the other, creating a developmental stagnation of a complexity that cannot be attributed to one single aspect of development. While the biological basis of such an inability is still not understood, the early social achievements of non-autistic children are remarkable. For instance, Scaife and Bruner (1975) reported that infants at the age of 5 months are able to follow the line of regard of adults, while Condon and Sander (1974) noted that newborn infants synchronize their body movements with the vocalizations of adults. In contrast, it seems as if autistic children are ill equipped to participate in social interaction.

Interpretations of autism as either an emotional or a linguistic disorder may have been polarized because of a preoccupation with language structure isolated from its interaction with cognitive and communicative development. It would be of interest to reexamine the psychoanalytic notion of *ego-development* in relation to what has been learned recently about early social development. Analogies can be drawn between failures of self-differentiation and poor ego-development and an inability to participate in and learn from social interaction.

The interaction among social, linguistic, and cognitive development may, furthermore, serve to clarify how the various behavioral characteristics of the autistic syndrome are interrelated. Paucities of intentional communication and play reflect deficiencies in means-end behavior in general. High frequencies of self-stimulatory and stereotyped behavior are a further indication of limitations in goal oriented behavior. Idiosyncrasies in language use, poor conceptual and abstraction skills, and prevalence of stereotyped rather than symbolic play are all indicative of poor representational abilities. Such deficiencies could easily lead to behavioral excesses, e.g., temper tantrums, when visual discrimination skills are relatively well developed. For instance, if slight changes in environment, e.g., a chair out of place, are noticed but not understood as the result of human action, one has to deal continuously with novelty. Temper tantrums may thus be associated with a poorly developed concept of sameness, confounded by limitations in purposeful behavior, i.e., a failure to bring about environmental changes.

Future studies that capitalize on the interaction of cognitive, linguistic, and communicative development may ultimately clarify how autistic development diverges from non-autistic development. Use of labels such as *autistic*, *aphasic*, and the like, should be avoided to clarify matters of differential diagnostics. A careful profile of social, linguistic, and cognitive development might be more helpful to identify the problem at hand and to design proper intervention procedures. Too many forms of developmental delay are grouped under the common demoninator *language disorder*. More careful differentiations should be made. For instance, some children may have problems with the structural aspects of language that is, with syntax, phonology, and morphology. Others may lack communicative intentions because they fail to understand the benefits of language use. Still others may have trouble expressing communicative intent in a socially appropriate form and according to the rules of discourse.

An interesting example of how the interactions among social, linguistic, and cognitive development could be studied has been given by Snyder (1975). She studied the early pragmatic development of language-disordered children in respect to their abilities to use single words as compared to sensorimotor (i.e., nonverbal) forms of expression. She found that the language-disordered children were less able to mark novel information with verbal means than with nonverbal means. She interpreted this finding as evidence for a specific representational deficit that affects the dynamic aspects of symbolization. Snyder based the specific symbolic deficit on the fact that the children were able to code the same information nonverbally. This was viewed as counterevidence for attentional or intentional deficits. In autism, the latter could easily be compounded with symbolic deficiencies.

Studies of the interaction of social, linguistic, and cognitive growth might clarify to what extent and at which point autistic development diverges from normal development. Such studies might provide information about the integrity of neurophysiological mechanisms, if developmental stagnation could be correlated with the neurophysiological organization of behavior.

SUMMARY

In the first section of this chapter, the state of knowledge on the cognitive functioning of autistic children was reviewed. It was pointed out that increasing evidence has been gathered indicating serious intellectual impairment, which apparently contradicts earlier held presumptions about the cognitive integrity of the autistic child. The following sources were reviewed: 1) results of large scale administration of IQ tests and other forms of assessment, 2) systematic experiments pertaining to the ways autistic children perceive and store stimulus input, 3) studies of the ability to engage in symbolic play, 4) literature suggestive of so-called stimulus overselectivity, and 5) accumulated data indicating idiosyncrasies in learning and a failure to generalize newly acquired skills.

Some questions were raised about the interpretation of the studies reviewed. Much of the experimental data gathered are not free of methodological flaws, and serious questions can be raised about the validity of the testing results. In addition, most tests and assessments focus on weaknesses rather than on strengths. Although autistic children seem to do better when presented with nontransient, as opposed to transient, stimuli, the extent to which they respond to transient stimuli remains to be investigated. It is unclear whether we are dealing with a stimulus-specific deficit or with a more generalized cognitive deficiency. For instance, we do not know what abilities may be inferred from a surprisingly adept performance on tasks that require assembly skills or discrimination of visuo-spatial stimuli. The abilities to derive and to apply rules and to develop concepts within visuo-spatial dimensions need to be studied if conclusions are to be drawn about the cognitive functions of autistic children.

Studies of autism should avoid a narrow focus on a single aspect of development; emphasis should be placed instead on the interaction of social linguistic, and cognitive development. Such an orientation should help to 1) separate patterns of autistic from normal or otherwise aberrant development, 2) identify criteria for differential diagnosis, and 3) clarify the nature of the autistic syndrome.

Pragmatically oriented studies of child development that focus on different aspects of development might help clarify the nature of the autistic syndrome. An example was given of how a better understanding of normal development might clarify the pathogenesis of autistic disturbances. A discussion was presented to a series of longitudinal studies of child development which delineated two separate lines of development, i.e., a static and a dynamic line. Behavioral disturbances might be explained on the basis of interferences of the dynamic, people-oriented line of development with the object-oriented, static line of development being preserved. Because the dynamic aspects of development are apparently acquired within the context of early social interaction, controversies about the linguistic or social-emotional basis of childhood autism may have been needlessly polarized.

chapter

6

A Review of
Intervention
Techniques

Adriana Luce Schuler

Department of Special Education
San Francisco State University
San Francisco, California

contents

BEHAVIORAL APPROACHES 139
    Description and Review 140
    Discussion 145
ALTERNATIVE SYSTEMS OF COMMUNICATION 148
    Teaching Language to Chimpanzees 149
    Teaching Non-oral Systems of Communication to Autistic
      Children 153
DISCUSSION 158
IMPLICATIONS 162

Treatment procedures have undergone major changes during the last decade as have views on childhood autism (see Chapter 1). Emphasis in treatment was once directed toward the normalization of emotional and psychodynamic variables rather than toward language behaviors per se. These latter behaviors have now become the focus of remedial efforts. Traditional approaches were based on the assumption that language disorders were secondary to emotional disorders and that language functioning would normalize as soon as the child learned to relate to people and to feel safe and secure. Therapy was permissive and supportive, giving the leading role in the therapeutic interaction to the child, with play and music as the main modes of treatment.

Language impairments have now come to be viewed as the most striking characteristic of autistic children and have become the prime focus of teaching efforts. This shift in thinking came with the introduction of new intervention approaches, among which the use of behavior modification and signing are probably the most publicized. The availability of new intervention options has inspired teachers and parents with new hopes and perspectives, despite the fact that the various intervention techniques may present a somewhat disjointed and confusing picture.

In this chapter both behavioral procedures and signing are examined in order to identify variables that are consistently associated with progress. Although the behavioral procedures outlined in the following section are explained largely in relation to speech training, the reader should realize that the techniques discussed do also apply to non-oral forms of language teaching, including signing.

BEHAVIORAL APPROACHES

The behavioral approach focuses directly on observable behavior rather than on presumed underlying causes. Efforts are made to change (i.e., increase or decrease) behavior based on what is known about learning and the experimental analysis of behavior. A variety of treatment approaches claim to be behavioral, but the approach that has been predominantly used with autistic or autistic-like children is commonly referred to as behavior modification or operant conditioning. In this discussion simply the term *behavioral* is used to cover approaches based upon reinforcement theory. Such approaches view behavior in terms of its consequences. Behaviors that are followed by reinforcing events are apt to reoccur, whereas those followed by punishing events are not (Thorndike, 1931).

Behavioral procedures are designed to consequate carefully defined target behaviors in order to decrease or increase their occurrence. This means that eye contact, appropriate sitting, imitation, social behaviors, and so on, are reinforced, while tantrums, screaming, and self-injurious and self-stimulatory behaviors are punished or ignored. Stringent control procedures typically constitute a major component of behavioral programs, particularly during the early phases of training. In order for the clinician to work with a child's off-task behaviors (such as throwing tantrums, screaming, and engaging in self-stimulatory behavior) emphasis is placed upon the teaching of appropriate sitting skills and eye contact. While a behavioral approach does not deny that maturational factors may influence behavior, they are not a primary concern in treatment. The main ideas are that behavior is primarily controlled by its consequences and that the autistic child's environment can be arranged to encourage appropriate and discourage inappropriate behavior.

Description and Review

One of the earliest detailed reports on the application of behavioral principles was the case study by Hewett (1965) on speech training with a 4½-year-old mute autistic boy. In order to control the interference of disruptive behavior, the experimenters used a specially designed experimental booth consisting of two sections separated by a shutter. The child was located on one side of the shutter and the clinician on the other. As the child engaged in off-task behavior, such as screaming, the shutter was closed and the child was deprived of light, rewards, and the presence of the clinician. Once the child had quieted down, the shutter was again raised. The initial emphasis was placed upon the reduction of disruptive behavior rather than on the teaching of speech and language skills. Actual speech training was implemented as soon as the boy had learned to stay in his seat and remain quiet. The boy reportedly developed a repertoire of 32 single-word labels by the end of a 6-month verbal imitation treatment program. The rationale behind speech training was that improvement in the verbal ability of the autistic child would provide him with naturally occurring social reinforcement opportunities, and thereby reduce his social isolation.

Programs for speech behavior focus on the ability to imitate speech and are commonly referred to as *verbal imitation skills*. Once speech imitation skills are taught, attempts are made to connect meaning to the speech behaviors taught and to teach the functional uses of words and phrases. The implicit assumption is that children learn to speak by attending to and repeating the speech of others, and by being rewarded for closer and closer approximations to adult speech. Examples of the use of behavioral techniques have been given by Lovaas (1977; Lovaas et al., 1966), Wolf, Risley, and Mees (1964), Risley and Wolf (1968), and Kozloff (1974). The procedures are similar, but there are differences in the sequence in which teaching steps are presented, as well as in terms of specific teaching procedures (e.g., use of reinforcement versus use of punishment).

In teaching speech imitation skills, distinctions should be made between children who exhibit echolalia and children who are mute. In dealing with muteness, an attempt is usually made to establish speech from occasional vocalizations. All vocalizations are reinforced if the overall rate of vocalization is low. Frequency of vocalizations is thereby increased. Once the rate of vocalization is sufficiently high, criteria for reinforcements are changed. For instance, children may be reinforced for the production of a greater variety of sounds in an attempt to diversify their repertoire. In order to establish and stabilize imitation behavior, vocalizations are reinforced when they follow vocalizations produced by the clinician within a predetermined time lapse, for example, 10 seconds. While the time criterion is gradually tightened, an additional similarity criterion is introduced. Vocalizations are reinforced when they sound more and more like the carefully selected speech sounds or words uttered by the clinician.

Once an initial speech sound is produced consistently (in response to the model presented by the clinician), the imitation of a second speech sound begins and discrimination training is initiated. Additional vocalizations are taught until a generalized imitative ability is demonstrated. Past research suggests that speech imitation training is a time-consuming procedure, particularly when it comes to discriminating between speech sounds. Lovaas (1977) reported that it took 30 days of almost continuous training (7 hours a day) to establish vocal imitation skills in two previously mute children.

Attempts to teach verbal imitation skills to echolalic children have been considerably less time consuming. Children with echolalic behavior usually fail to produce speech upon command and in an appropriate context. Consequently, teaching speech imitation skills does not depend upon establishing novel behavior, but rather on a shift in stimulus control. Poor stimulus control is apparent when commands are repeated rather than carried out or when words or phrases cannot be deliberately imitated even though they are high frequency items within a most likely delayed echolalic repertoire. Teaching appropriate speech to echolalic children may be viewed as the teaching of increasingly refined discriminations between appropriate and inappropriate speech imitation.

Teaching imitation and stimulus control can be conceptualized as prompting and prompt fading. The latter is used to teach discriminations between those conditions in which it is appropriate to repeat and those conditions in which it is not. One of the most frequently used techniques is volume prompting. The discriminative stimulus (e.g., a question, such as "What is this?") is presented almost inaudibly while the verbal prompt (i.e., the answer, such as "This is a ball") is presented loudly, such that only the prompt is imitated. The volume of the discriminative stimulus is gradually increased while the prompt is decreased in volume. In addition, manual prompts (e.g., the clinician holding the child's mouth shut), as well as pausing prompts, have been used. Use of these techniques has been reported as effective in teaching echolalic children to imitate when asked to do so, for example, in response to "say, . . . X." Case studies by Lovaas (1977), Lovaas et al. (1966), and Risley and Wolf (1967) illustrate how these techniques can be used effectively in conjunction with extinction, time-out, and verbal instructions such as "Don't echo" to further inhibit inappropriate echoic responding.

Complete elimination of echoing behavior is, however, never the objective of behavioral procedures. Attempts are made to use echoing behaviors to establish more appropriate speech. But while many children learn not to echo questions addressed to them, appropriate verbal responses to such questions usually need to be separately taught (Carr, Schreibman, and Lovaas, 1975; Lovaas, 1977; Palyo et al., 1979). Consequently, teaching efforts focus upon the ability to imitate speech upon command, and upon the attachment of meaning to, and the functional use of, imitated speech. Much emphasis has commonly been placed upon the teaching of appropriate rather than echoing responses. In addition, children may learn to say their names in response to the question "What's your name?" This requires that discriminations be made between speech that should (i.e., the verbal prompt), and speech that should not (i.e., the question asked), be repeated.

Such discriminations are not easily taught when verbal instructions and prompts are presented by the same person. It is a common practice for clinicians to present instructions such as "What are you doing?" along with verbal prompts such as "I am sitting." While this is based on practical rather than theoretical concerns, it does not clarify the dynamics of a normal dialogue when the speaker-listener relationships are thus confounded. But alternative teaching methods may facilitate discriminations of this kind. Tramontana and Shivers (1971) used cue cards with written words in their work with a child who demonstrated excellent written word discrimination skills, an ability that is not uncommon in autistic and other language-impaired children. Another means of differentiation between verbal instruction and prompt was reported by Palyo et al. (1979), who use audiotaped recordings of verbal prompts. In this case, the children learned to repeat tape-recorded phrases rather than the clinician's speech. This strategy may have circumvented the need to rely on irrelevant cues such as volume shifts or manual prompts.

A slightly modified prompting technique was reported by Ausman and Gaddy (1974) and by Freeman, Ritvo, and Miller (1975). They presented the verbal prompt before questions or instructions were worded. For example, the clinician would say, "Sitting—what is the girl doing?" and reinforce as soon as the child repeated the word *sitting* without the child's having a chance to repeat the question. A similar technique was reported by Ratusnik and Ratusnik (1974), illustrating that these techniques lend themselves easily to informal application in the context of everyday conversations with parents, teachers, and peers. The detailed case study presented by Ratusnik and Ratusnik also shows how this can be applied with higher functioning children who still demonstrate echolalic tendencies. In order to facilitate a non-echoic response the child's response alternatives would be presented along with the question asked, such as:

"Here is the food we have for lunch: Pot roast, potatoes, milk, chocolate pudding . . . what do you want?"

In using verbal prompts with echolalic children, it should be realized that some of the problems that are commonly encountered may be due to the excessively lengthy and complicated verbal instructions and prompts. For example, fewer problems might be anticipated when instructions are presented nonverbally. Rather than asking the child "What is this?" objects could be held up or placed on a response pedestal, then gradually verbal instructions could be faded in. Use of excessive verbalizations may be harmful rather than beneficial in the initial stages of speech training.

Behavioral approaches have not only been applied to the teaching of speech imitation skills or to the teaching of a series of stereotyped answers to common questions. Imitation skills can help establish and expand a functional repertoire of verbal behavior. Attempts to connect meaning to imitative vocalizations have focused on teaching a simple labeling response (Lovaas et al., 1966; Schell, Stark, and Giddon, 1967; Johnston, 1968; Sulzbacher and Costello, 1970; Kozloff, 1974; Lovaas, 1977). Children learn to repeat names of objects and actions when presented with the appropriate stimulus materials (usually series of pictures) and questions such as, "What is this?," "What is the girl doing?," and so on. Verbal prompts are faded gradually until the child is able to name objects and actions through the use of single words and phrases such as, "This is a _____," or "The girl is _____." Teaching such expressive skills is preceded by receptive labeling tasks requiring the child to pick up objects or to point to objects when presented with a verbal label. Simple requests and rudimentary conversational skills are also developed through such teaching efforts.

Whether or not the teaching methods reported are effective depends on how the particular teaching objectives were defined. Task mastery is assumed when a child is able, for example, to label any of a set of 10 pictures presented in random order, performing at a level of 90% correct responses. The child need not be able to generalize use of the labels, that is, apply the labels taught to a different group of objects or pictures that all carry the same name. In other words, it is not always apparent that once a child has learned to say "shoe" when presented with his shoe, that he will also apply that same label to other shoes. Similarly, mastery is usually not defined as the ability to apply these newly acquired skills at home or at school with different persons. Involving parents and teachers is one way to maximize this generalization. Speech behaviors taught should always be relevant to the child's interaction with his daily living environment.

The most detailed account of a behavior modification techniques in teaching speech to autistic children is given by Lovaas (1977). He describes how shaping and chaining and prompting were used to teach vocal imitation skills, and how meaning was attached to the speech behaviors taught through the use of systematic discrimination training and reinforcement. Procedures used to teach abstract terms that define simple relationships in time and space, as well as relationships among people, objects, and events, are discussed in detail. Examples are given of how personal pronouns and notions such as *first* versus *last*, *more* and *less*, *same* and *different*, and so on, are taught. In teaching children to use speech in social interactions, Lovaas reports a variety of techniques ranging from conversation training to the systematic recall and description of past events.

While behavioral principles have been used extensively in the development of language-training programs for the retarded, comprehensive language programs specifically designed for autistic children are still scarce. Nevertheless, some attempts have been made to include autistic children in communication programs with other children. Marshall and Hegrenes (1970) presented a "programmed communication therapy" to be used primarily with mentally retarded, but also with autistic children. Their goal was to prepare children, through a series of teaching steps, to learn from an environment conducive to more natural language acquisition processes. They suggested that the following skills be taught:

1. Object identification, requiring a child to label objects
2. Object description, requiring a child to imitate action phrases such as "The girl is walking"

A more active role followed these passive stages. The child was required to describe his own observations ("I see a horse"), to label his own action ("I eat with a spoon"), and to interact with others through language ("I want a cookie"). The authors hypothesized that this would provide a basis for further language acquisition in a natural environment. The rationale for their approach as well as for the program steps selected is not clear. Gray and Ryan (1974) presented a *Language Program for the Non-Language Child* to be used with a variety of children with language problems. The nonlanguage child is defined as someone who does not perform with the linguistic code who may or may not have some non-verbal language. Autistic children are included. The program consists of structured teaching steps designed to teach specific grammatical structures through imitative prompting and fading. The report concerns a group of autistic children divided into four groups on the basis of their speech behavior. Progress data are not easily interpreted. First, only a weak tendency toward an increased use of structurally more complex utterances was noted. Second, the dependent measures were based on the amount of verbalizations during a 10-minute sampling period. No provisions were made for the elimination of inappropriate echolalic or perseverative speech routines. Apparently autistic children could end up with high scores for meaningless speech.

It is not clear whether the same type of programs should be used with noncommunicative as well as communicative children. While verbal imitation drills (as used by Gray and Ryan) may be useful for children with specific linguistic coding problems, children who already exhibit adequate speech production skills but miss the underlying concepts may not benefit from this type of verbal imitation training.

A more semantically based language-training program by Guess, Sailor, and Baer (1976) is used with severely handicapped children, including those labeled as autistic or psychotic. One of the main assets of the program is its functionality and flexibility. The program was designed so children would rapidly experience speech as an effective means to control their environment.

The dimensions of control employed were *reference* (learning that words represent objects or events in our environment), *control* (the controlling function of language), *self-extended control* (how to request more complete, specific information), *integration* (how to put together reference, control, and self-extended control skills), and *reception* (concepts are taught at the receptive level). The program includes a 60-step training sequence divided into six content areas: persons and things, actions with persons and things, possession, color, size, and relation/location.

Discussion

Behavioral techniques are widely used to teach self-help skills and to manage behavioral problems. The various case studies reported suggest that such techniques also can be applied to teach speech imitation skills. But it is not clear to what extent imitative speech leads to the development of functional communication skills or language abilities in their broadest sense. Johnston (1968) commented on the speech peculiarities in an echolalic boy to whom speech had been taught. She described his

newly learned responses as automatic and marked by rhythmic peculiarities and rigid intonation patterns. Intonational irregularities have
frequently been reported (see discussion, Chapter 2) irrespective of treatment variables. According to the case reports by Lovaas (1977), most
children who received speech training were unable to generalize and
failed to use speech in a spontaneous and context-appropriate manner.
Further evidence of lack of generalization comes from follow-up studies
by Lovaas, Simmons, Koegel, and Stevens-Long (1973). These studies
suggest that many children may not generalize beyond a limited
repertoire of context-tied speech.

It is not easily determined whether language rather than speech
skills can be taught through a systematic application of a behavioral
paradigm. (See Hollis and Carrier, 1978, for further discussion of
this issue.) Limited teaching successes may reflect limitations in the user
rather than in the paradigm itself. Much depends upon how language
skills are defined and how the behavioral paradigm is applied. It is
apparent from the studies reported in previous pages that behavioral
techniques allow for a range of language instruction designs. Lovaas
(1977), for instance, referred to the teaching of speech as a "set of
responses and stimulus functions" to be taught through discrimination
training techniques and differential reinforcement. The critical question
is whether or not separate component skills can be assembled into a
repertoire of functional communicative skills. Language is an extremely
complex composite of an array of skills. Difficulties are encountered
when those composite skills are taught on the basis of component skills.
Intervention efforts may focus on a limited aspect of language, for
example, on the teaching of a set of labels or on the teaching of certain
grammatical rules. But language behaviors are characterized by communicative intent, as well as by operations of reference and grammar.
Consequently, it becomes more of a challenge to design an effective
teaching program. Failure to teach composite verbal skills may reflect
an inadequate teaching program rather than inadequate teaching
procedures. For instance, decisions about the order in which particular
speech functions should be taught have often been based on the complexity of the speech response itself rather than on the complexity of
underlying notions and assumptions. For example, yes/no responses are
often taught before conceptually simpler, but structurally more complex,
responses. Also, conversational skills, for example, should comprise
more than an ability to reproduce a set of specifically trained verbal
responses to high frequency questions.

The selection of specific teaching objectives is often based on questionable, if not arbitrary, grounds. For instance, labeling behaviors focusing on structures such as "That's a . . . (noun)" may be the initial target

of training. Such phrases may not be the most appropriate place to begin. Objections could be raised from both motivational and structural points of view. Because the function of such descriptive statements is tied to the maintenance of social rapport, they may not be relevant to autistic children. The latter are not likely reinforced by smiles, head nods, or other signs of social approval. Spontaneous use and generalization demand a greater sensitivity to those forms of social reinforcement. From a structural perspective, objections could also be raised against teaching structures such as "This is a . . . (noun)." They are semantically empty in the sense that the first three words are not easily associated with a referent.

A crucial question in assessing the merits of a behavioral approach for teaching language concerns whether or not such a paradigm allows that rules are taught rather than isolated behaviors. This is particularly relevant to language programming because it is impossible to teach appropriate responses to all possible stimulus conditions (Guess, Keogh, and Sailor, 1978; Wetherby and Striefel, 1978).

Attempts to teach grammatical rules to children with various language problems have been reported. Guess et al. (1968) taught a pluralization rule, while Baer and Guess (1971) taught the morphological marking of comparative and superlative concepts (small/smaller/smallest). Schumaker and Sherman (1970) showed that imitation and reinforcement techniques could be used to teach tense markers, a finding also reported by Lovaas (1977) in his work with autistic children. Lutzker and Sherman (1974) found that retarded children could be taught to construct sentences of a particular type by using a syntactic rule.

This work demonstrates that the teaching of one particular behavior (rule) affects the probability of occurrence of other related behaviors. This finding implies that something more than a single response is learned. A similar notion may underlie "response acceleration" (Lovaas, 1977), a term that refers to the fact that it is easier to teach additional labels once the first labels are taught. This may be explained by the postulation of an underlying notion of reference, i.e., an understanding of the fact that things have names. But alternative explanations could be offered, such as the formation of a learning set (Lovaas, 1977). Without additional research, it is difficult to define the extent to which operant procedures allow for the teaching of language-related behavior. It is difficult to assess the limitations of the behavioral paradigm in terms of teaching language structure, and even more difficult to draw conclusions about its potential for teaching language functions. Neglect of functional issues may be partially responsible for lack of generalization. However, such difficulties beset any program of explicit training. Issues of generalization, both internal to the program and external to the training setting, are due to receive intensive research for years to come.

ALTERNATIVE SYSTEMS OF COMMUNICATION

Language programs have come to include alternative means of communication such as signs, abstract-shaped plastic symbols, written words, communication boards, and even computer consoles. Signing has probably been used most commonly as an alternative system of communication. The signs used are, in essence, analogous to the signs that constitute American Sign Language (Ameslan or ASL), the visual language used by the deaf. Signs correspond to words, but they are produced by systematic hand movements that acquire their meaning on the basis of their configuration and direction of movement as well as on their proximity to the rest of the body. Linguistic analyses of sign language have shown that a systematic rule-based grammar underlies the use of signs. Signing is linguistic in nature and not merely a context bound signaling system (Stokoe, 1972; Klima, 1975). The grammar that underlies Ameslan is different from English grammar. In order to approximate spoken English more closely, modifications are made, particularly when the two systems are presented simultaneously as in "total communication." The increased use of alternative systems of communication with handicapped populations reflects the extensive efforts directed toward the teaching of alternative modes of communication to nonhuman primates (Gardner and Gardner, 1969; Premack, 1971, 1976a, 1976b). Their uses also reflect a growing awareness that language is not exclusively a vocal-auditory phenomenon, that speech behavior does not necessarily imply language skills, and that language can be expressed through means other than speech (see Schiefelbusch and Hollis, 1979; Schiefelbusch, 1980).

Speech is not crucial to language. In his writings on the relationships between language and thought, Vygotsky (1962) viewed speech as a coding artifact. The fact that apes do not produce speech could be due to highly specialized mechanisms of auditory and vocal coding rather than an inability to use a language system. In attempts to circumvent speech processing, various alternative means of symbols have been taught to chimpanzees and communication-handicapped humans. The systems were designed to bypass the need for functional integrity of the speech-processing mechanisms so that communicative intention and language concepts were expressed by simpler means (Hollis and Schiefelbusch, 1979). Speech requires the ability to plan and execute coordinated movements of vocal chords and supralaryngeal structures. It also requires careful temporal analyses of speech sounds along the dimensions of pitch, intensity, and duration.

The alternative symbol systems used are similar in that they use visual rather than auditory modalities. Signing and speaking share a common element in that they occur along a time dimension. This temporal nature separates them from, for instance, written words and plastic symbols, which are coded along the dimension of space. Signs actually take a somewhat intermediate position since their patterning dimension is spatial as well as temporal. Differences also occur at the level of motor output; signing requires that hand movements be skillfully coordinated, whereas only simple hand movements are required to pick up a plastic chip. Likewise, using plastic chips merely requires a choice between a red piece of plastic of one particular shape and a yellow piece of another shape. This is in contrast to the active coding used in the production of speech and signs, which offers greater coding potential because elements of meaning can be combined in a number of ways. Processing speech may be more demanding than processing signs. Manipulating plastic chips or word cards should be less demanding. Plastic sentences, or sentences composed of written word cards, remain visible over time and allow the listener a second look if the message is not immediately deciphered. While more distinctions could be made between the various coding mechanisms, the main differences are summarized in Table 1.

Reports on success with various alternative systems provide teachers with a range of remedial options, but they also require a rationale to justify the choice of any particular system of communication for any particular child. Unfortunately, this rationale is not easily developed, because it is not always clear how much success is a reflection of a particular teaching technique or of the disorder. Alpert (1980) has developed an experimental procedure for selecting a nonspeech mode for training. Although the method seems promising, it will likely require further clinical application before it can be used widely as a selection procedure.

The following section 1) provides a review of the literature dealing with non-oral systems of communication, and 2) discusses implications for language teaching and communicative systems. The issues involved are introduced by a brief review of the literature dealing with non-oral language in chimpanzees to provide the reader with some general background in the use of alternative systems of communication, with particular reference to the teaching techniques involved.

Teaching Language to Chimpanzees

The question of whether or not speech can be taught to apes has fascinated mankind for centuries. Attempts to teach speech to nonhuman primates have failed. One of the most recent attempts was reported by Hayes and Hayes (1952), who tried to raise a chimpanzee named Vicki in a human environment. Despite extensive teaching efforts, Vicki was not

Table 1. Comparison of communication systems in terms of code characteristics and coding behaviors

Code	Sense modalities involved	Patterning dimension	Response topography
Spoken words	Hearing (and proprioception)	Time	Sequentially coordinated movements of larynx and supralaryngeal structures (oral)
Signed words	Vision (and proprioception)	Space and time	Sequentially coordinated movements of fingers and hands (manual)
Abstract-shaped plastic symbols and written words; pictures and lexigrams	Vision	Space	Single hand movement

able to produce anything but a few vowel-like sounds. Extensive research carried out by Lieberman (1975) using vocal tract modeling and computerized vowel analysis suggests that the vocal tract of nonhuman primates may not be structured to produce the various sounds in human speech. While this does not explain why apes do not speak, it does support efforts to use alternative systems of communication.

One of the most publicized and spectacular efforts to teach language to chimpanzees is the work of the Gardners (Gardner and Gardner, 1969, 1975). They taught signs to Washoe, a chimpanzee who was raised in a human environment. At the age of 4, Washoe had mastered 80 different signs. These signs were used by Washoe in the specific context in which they were taught and also appeared in new situations, which implied that Washoe could do more than just apply context-dependent labels. In using the label *open* in reference to the particular door in which context the label was originally taught, as well as in reference to the water faucet and a soda pop bottle, Washoe demonstrated an understanding of what "opening" was all about. Such conceptual understanding was also demonstrated in the way she made context-appropriate signs when looking through a picture book. The latter suggests even higher levels of linguistic functioning because Washoe's signing went beyond the expression of immediate needs and emotionally colored language use. Washoe made up her own words, for example, the sign WATERBIRD to refer to a duck. She also overextended words (Bronowski and Bellugi, 1970) by using the sign HURT to refer to red stains, as well as to decals on the back of someone's hand.

The Washoe project was a longitudinal effort to study the "natural" acquisition of sign language in a chimpanzee. Different approaches have been taken by other researchers. Premack (1970, 1971, 1976a, 1976b; Premack and Premack, 1972), for example, studied the degree to which a language system, consisting of plastic chips of various shapes and colors, could be taught to a chimpanzee, Sarah. The rationale for the system was based on a functional analysis of language (Premack, 1970). Premack was interested in whether or not Sarah, after having learned a label for similarity, could make independent judgments of similarity when presented with various objects. Sarah demonstrated that such labels did not need to be taught in all new stimulus contexts. Similarly, Premack was interested in whether or not Sarah could answer questions about the relationships between different objects and their labels. Sarah was able to reply with "yes" and "no" markers to questions about object similarity, as well as to questions about the relationships between labels and referents. Sarah could judge whether an object shared features with another object when only presented with that object's label. When, for example, presented with the label for apple, rather than with a real apple, she was able to identify its color and shape. Sarah could also put new word combinations together and go through a question and answer routine independently when left alone with the reading materials. According to Premack, the accomplishments of Sarah demonstrate that she had mastered the cognitive skills that underlie language performance and that a mapping device rather than conceptual skill was taught.

Criticisms in terms of Sarah's accomplishments concern the extremely structured teaching settings and the possible effects of inadvertent cues supplied by the experimenters. It is not the purpose of this chapter to draw conclusions about the nature of Sarah's accomplishments, but Premack's research concerned particular cognitive skills of classification, categorization, and equation rather than natural language acquisition. Sarah developed remarkable cognitive and linguistic skills, but her communicative accomplishments and spontaneous use of the taught structures are not easily evaluated.

The issue of communication, however, was given careful consideration in an experimentally devised keyboard language, to the chimpanzee Lana (Rumbaugh, Gill, and VonGlaserfeld, 1973; Rumbaugh and Gill, 1976; Rumbaugh, 1977). Instead of signs or chips, Lana was taught to use a computer keyboard by touching keys marked with specific lexigrams (Yerkish). This approach circumvented the problems of inadvertent cueing inherent in direct interactions between experimenter and subject. It furthermore eliminated problems caused by extraneous cues provided by the experimenter, provided a continuous 24-hour teaching situation, and allowed for automated continuous recording of all keyboard manipulations by Lana. Lana has developed an extensive vocabulary and has learned to produce novel utterances (Rumbaugh et al., 1979). For example, Lana asked for THE APPLE THAT IS ORANGE when she wanted an orange, a request that indicates an understanding beyond the rote and context-dependent use of taught labels. The most striking example of Lana's accomplishments were her attempts to initiate conversations. She was reported to produce the utterance LANA DRINK THIS OUT OF ROOM, upon watching her trainer drinking a Coke outside her room. In addition, she asked for the name of a box in order to make a request for a box filled with candy. While both these language constructs function as requests, i.e., mands according to Skinner (1957), the latter indicates that Lana was aware of the relationship between labels and their referents.

More research is needed to determine the extent to which nonhuman primates differ from human primates in cognitive and linguistic skills. However, the research reported is of great interest in terms of teaching techniques. Washoe was required to sign in order to have her desires gratified. Food, drinks, tickles, hugs, vertibular stimulation, and so on, were supplied contingent upon Washoe's signing. Sarah's training relied heavily upon food reinforcement. Lana had to push keys in order to get anything varying from food to film and slide privileges. She also received immediate visual feedback because the lexigrams pushed on the keyboard were immediately projected on a screen accompanied by a light flash. In all cases, response forms were selected that were within the chimpanzee's behavioral repertoire and that required someone to make a particular response that could be voluntarily emitted and immediately reinforced. If the response forms selected were only approximations of the eventual behaviors to be taught, criteria for reinforcement were gradually and systematically raised. Lana, for instance, started out having to ask for BOWL in order to get her candy reward. During later phases of training she would get only an empty box until she would request, TIM, GIVE LANA NAME OF THIS. More and more elaborate behaviors were required from Lana in order for her to receive the same reward. Without such systematic training efforts, Lana or Sarah might not have made the remarkable progress they demonstrated in the language system they did not spontaneously develop. That these chimpanzees had to start from zero and proceed on a series of carefully designed teaching steps rather than through mere exposure makes it tempting to draw parallels with the training of language to human beings with severe communicative deficits (Schiefelbusch and Hollis, 1979). Interestingly, more and more efforts have been directed toward the teaching of nonvocal systems of communication to autistic children (Schiefelbusch, 1980).

Teaching Non-oral Systems of Communication to Autistic Children

Among the various attempts to teach alternative systems of communication to autistic children are those directed toward signing. Several reports on the use of signs are available (Miller and Miller, 1973; Webster et al., 1973; Creedon, 1973, 1975, 1976; Schaeffer et al., 1975; Wade, 1976; Fulwiler and Fouts, 1976; Bonvillian and Nelson, 1976).

Creedon's efforts to teach signs to autistic children were based upon work with a large group of children rather than upon single case studies. According to Creedon's rationale, signs are easily "shaped or molded" or, in other words, easily prompted. A topographical similarity was noted between some signs and some hand movements (such as twiddles and posturing) that are commonly part of the children's behavioral repertoire. She also stated that signs provide a child with many opportunities for reinforcement. Signs were taught to children who had no communicative speech, who exhibited limited eye contact, and who did not play appropriately with objects or interact with other peers. Signs were taught in a systematic way by using social praise, hugs, tickles, and the like, during group work. Because the eventual goal was for the children to interact with and learn from each other, peers and parents were included in the training. All children learned the signs related to immediate needs and affective states. Several children learned to sign at more abstract levels and to put signs together in original ways. One child was reported to sign JACKET IS SICK in referring to a broken zipper. Measurable progress was reported for all children on standardized tests, on developmental scales, and in terms of greater socialization and fewer tantrums and self-destructive behaviors.

Creedon made some interesting observations of behaviors during treatment. Several children exhibited echopraxic behavior (i.e., movements relevant as well as irrelevant of the therapist were indiscriminately imitated, for example, the therapist scratching her head). Echopraxia was most prevalent during the initial stages of training but continued to occur when new situations were introduced. Along with overall progress in signing, some children developed spontaneous speech, which gradually was produced more and more clearly. Creedon noted that many children began with rudimentary approximations of single words. These word approximations were followed by imitations of intonation patterns, which in turn were followed by more and more accurate approximations of speech sounds. Furthermore, Creedon noted that the most clearly enunciated speech occurred during rhythmic activities.

Spontaneous (not specifically taught) speech approximations were reported by Fulwiler and Fouts (1976) in their study of the acquisition of signs by a 5-year-old boy with severe behavioral problems. They reported the success of an unstructured teaching procedure that incorporated the boy's momentary needs and interests. Success consisted of the spontaneous production of signs and sign combinations after 20 hours of treatment. According to Fulwiler and Fouts, the boy's progress suggested that autism is a disorder of cross-modal perception rather than symbolic functioning. Caution should be exercised in interpreting these findings because only one subject was involved. The subject was relatively young and the verbalizations at the onset of treatment were not described. It was not clear if the boy used any of his verbalizations or gestures in an intentional manner. The authors may have been dealing with a boy who had already demonstrated communicative intent at the start of treatment and who merely needed a more appropriate expression form. If so, signing was definitely warranted, but its success is not that surprising.

Miller and Miller (1973) reported using functional signs as a part of a "cognitive developmental" teaching approach that also incorporated "body action" and "distance senses." They positioned children on elevated boards on which obstacles were placed so that an immediate need was created for the use of signs.

Sign acquisition in a 9-year-old boy who had failed to respond to various forms of treatment (for example, to the computerized game treatment discussed below) was reported by Bonvillian and Nelson (1976). A systematic approach that incorporated manual prompts and token reinforcement was used. Daily 30-minute drill sessions were conducted over a period of 6 months. At the end of this period, the child was reported to be using 56 signs spontaneously while acquiring new signs at a rate of two per week. Spontaneous sign combinations usually consisted of a verb and an "experimenter" or "agent" semantically analogous to the two-word combinations children normally acquire. Progress was reported in terms of increased scores on the Peabody Picture Vocabulary Test (PPVT), as well as in terms of social development. The boy was able to respond as well to simultaneous communication (sign and spoken word presented simultaneously) as to signs only. But it remains unclear whether he responded to the spoken word alone. In other words, did the signing facilitate auditory comprehension?

The question of whether the simultaneous presentation of signed and spoken words has a facilitating or a thwarting effect was recently investigated by Konstantareas and Leibovitz (1977). They concluded that the simultaneous presentation of both speech and sign was preferable to the presentation of signs only. Whether this would always apply to all children diagnosed as autistic is still questionable, particularly in respect to the phenomenon of stimulus overselectivity (Lovaas, et al., 1971; Koegel and Wilhelm, 1973; Schreibman and Lovaas, 1973). Further counter-evidence may be found in studies by Carr et al., 1978). Carr and his colleagues reported that three out of four autistic children failed to discriminate between spoken words that were presented in conjunction with signs. More carefully conducted comparative studies are needed if any overall conclusions are to be made about autistic or autistic-like children with different behavioral and learning characteristics.

Efforts to teach alternative modes of communication are not limited to signing. Inspired by Sarah's successes with her "plastic symbols," attempts were made to teach a similar language system to humans with severe communication handicaps. Premack and Premack (1974) reported on their work with a mute autistic boy who demonstrated no receptive skills beyond some single word recognition. Use of the coded plastic symbols was taught to this boy, conjointly with efforts to teach this system to two newly arrived chimpanzees, Elizabeth and Peony. Interestingly, both Peony and Elizabeth needed more extensive training to learn their first words than the autistic boy. Elizabeth required 1,699 trials, much more than any human trained on this system. But it should be realized that the acquisition rates for the next series of words were more rapid. As for the autistic boy, an attempt was made to determine whether the plastic symbols could help him acquire language. It was found that a plastic plurality marker did facilitate the acquisition of the English plurality marker.

Extensive studies exploring the usefulness of plastic symbols with a population of mute, severely mentally retardates have been carried out by Carrier and his associates (Carrier, 1974a, 1974b) and discussed by Hollis and Carrier (1975). The main asset of abstract-shaped plastic symbol systems seems to be the simplicity of the required responses. Plastic symbols are objects that do not fade away as do speech and signs. This minimizes the need for intact immediate memory and temporal integration skills. Carrier worked initially with three mentally retarded boys to assess the merits of such a communication system. One of the boys spontaneously began to imitate the speech of the experimenter. Encouraged by these preliminary successes, Carrier decided to work on adapting Premack's work to the practical needs of nonverbal retardates. Color codings were added to aid in the acquisition of grammar rules, and detailed teaching instructions were added. The program thus developed was called the Non-speech Language Initiation Program (Non-SLIP) (Carrier and Peak, 1975) and was tested with 180 retardates. While teaching the first labels, particularly verb labels, was time consuming, additional labels were taught more readily. The program was effective to the extent that 125 subjects completed the program within a 2-year period. This enabled them to begin speech training and to use the symbols for reading, writing, and communication. Interestingly, many of them spontaneously began to initiate speech responses along with their manual responses.

Another application of Premack's work was reported by McLean and McLean (1974), who trained such a language system to three mute autistic boys. The rationale was again based on the lack of success with more traditional approaches and on presumed poor skills in the areas of short term memory and cross-modal association. The researchers used a carefully designed step-by-step training program that incorporated the use of both food and social rewards. Subjects were taught to construct a set of *give* constructions, such as LINDA GIVE BALL or JIM GIVE GLASS. After the children had learned to construct sentences of this type, generalization was tested both in terms of setting and in terms of experimenters. Two of the three children learned to produce a series of six sentences consisting of three elements and were able to generalize their responses across settings and experimenters. The third boy failed to progress because of prevailing perseverative responses. No errors were made between words of different syntactic classes; only within-class errors were observed. However, it is unclear whether this may be attributable to the availability of position cues as a result of the fixed word order or to the existence of conceptual categories. McLean and McLean (1974) concluded that a prosthetic language system could be useful in the initial phases of expressive training and as a device to teach syntax.

Other reports on the use of nonvocal systems of communication include the use of communication boards and lexical systems. An example of the use of a communication board is reported in a detailed case study by Ratusnik and Ratusnik (1974) using written words and blocks. Efforts to teach written words to autistic or autistic-like students often seem met by remarkable success (LaVigna, 1977). Also, precocious reading skills have been noted (Wolf and Chess, 1965), sometimes referred to as "hyperlexia" (Elliott and Needleman, 1975). While it is still unclear to what extent these reading skills may be used effectively, they are of interest because written words are nontransient (as are the plastic, abstract symbol language systems) and, therefore, possibly more accessible to autistic students (Schuler, 1979b). In addition, written words are easily understood by others.

An interesting example of written word training was given by DeVilliers and Naughton (1974), who taught an alternative communication system to two autistic children. Instead of arbitrarily coded chips, they used magnetic particles to each of which a written label was attached. The written labels presented were designed so additional shape and color cues were available to aid the children in acquiring their initial discriminations. The children were then taught to fill in empty slots in chip-play sentences, starting out with labels for food items (such as cracker, mint, nut, pretzel). Initially the children were required to fill in only one single label. Then gradually they were required to discriminate between different food items and between the various persons giving and receiving the various food items (Joe/Jill give cracker Adam/Bobby). The training procedures were then expanded to include various commands. DeVilliers and Naughton suggested that a "small repertoire of meaningful communications might be the basis for constructing a whole system of communication skills," and emphasized the importance of a teaching procedure that requires the child to attend to the behavior of other persons in the teaching situation. Furthermore, use of written words allows for refined program design because the teacher has complete control over the response alternatives. In addition, written words may clarify aspects of language that are normally awkward to teach, such as correct use of personal pronouns and Wh-questions.

Rationale for an errorless discrimination learning technique to teach written word labels was expressed in similar terms by LaVigna (1977). He reported teaching three written words to three mute autistic adolescents. LaVigna was able to apply errorless discrimination learning techniques because the use of written words allowed the systematic presentation of increasingly difficult program steps. As a consequence, the subjects proceeded through the program with only a minimal number of errors (always higher than 90% correct responses). Although reports on use of written words seem encouraging, additional data and comparisons are needed to evaluate the potential of this approach for larger scale application.

Another nonvocal approach to language intervention was taken by Colby (1973), who described a "computer-interaction language program" for nonvocal children. This program used games to engage children in visual, tactile, and auditory language interaction with a computer. The rationale for the intervention was based on the observation that children were fascinated with mechanical equipment. The approach was oriented toward play and discovery. It was not systematic because the children were left by themselves rather than guided through predetermined program steps. No specific reinforcement was supplied except for the reinforcement inherent to manipulating the keyboard and video display. Colby reported the strategy to be effective for 13 out of 17 children. Progress was defined as "linguistic improvement" for purposes of social interaction. While it is not easy to determine how much linguistic progress was actually made and whether or not teaching procedures could be optimized, the use of mechanical devices and machines deserves further exploration. Others have also reported that autistic children are often highly motivated to work with "machines" (Hargrave and Swisher, 1975).

DISCUSSION

The previous review indicates that treatment gains should not be attributed solely to the use of signs. Such claims can also be made by proponents of other nonspeech communication systems. Also, since teaching practices vary widely across the various studies reported, it is difficult to decide whether credit should be given to the particular communication system or the teaching strategies used. Nevertheless, since many ingenious and tenacious efforts to teach speech to mute and to echolalic children have been met with limited success (Lovaas, 1977), the gains may indeed be a matter of mode rather than method. But conclusions about the desirability of a particular system are as yet difficult to draw. Claims made to support alternative systems include: 1) the visual modality is more functional than the auditory modality, 2) the patterning dimension inherent to a nonspeech symbol system is more functional, and 3) the characteristics of the motor responses required are simpler and more readily taught.

Because the various approaches used are visual, intervention successes are easily attributed to that modality (Hollis and Schiefelbusch, 1979). That autistic children may indeed be more inclined to process visual as opposed to auditory information has been suggested by various researchers (Tubbs, 1966; Hermelin and O'Connor, 1970; Condon, 1975). But it is not clear whether problems are related to modality-specific deficits, to defective mechanisms of cross-modal association, or to developmental stagnations. Simon (1975), for instance, postulated the existence of higher order lesions within the auditory system. These would prohibit refined auditory analyses of incoming auditory signals. Specific deficits in the ability to make cross-modal associations between stimulus input arriving through different sensory channels were claimed by Bryson (1972). Initial reports on stimulus overselectivity (Lovaas et al., 1971) support this claim, because austistic children were unable to attend simultaneously to tactile, visual, and auditory stimuli (see discussion in Chapter 5).

However, subsequent investigations of stimulus overselectivity have failed to support the notion of a cross-modal deficiency, suggesting a more generalized deficit (see discussion in Chapter 5). Language-learning problems might therefore be anticipated regardless of the modality used since such a deficit would interfere with any type of association learning. Hermelin (1976) failed to support the notion of a modality-specific cognitive deficit. She found her autistic subjects to be deficient in both auditory and visual modalities when tasks were presented that required the abstraction of underlying rules regarding the temporal organization of the stimuli presented. Such a generalized cognitive deficit suggests that autistic children may face serious problems when they progress beyond imitative signing or the production of a limited set of context-dependent signs. Grammatical combinations of separate signs into larger sentences would require the systematic application of rules of grammar and an ability to use temporal ordering principles. The occurrence of sign echolalia has been reported both as a transient and a persisting phenomenon in the teaching of signs to autistic children (Creedon, 1975). Since temporal order should be less relevant to the use of plastic symbols or written language forms, principles of grammatical ordering might be more readily taught through such systems. However, additional comparative data are needed. Not only should the acquisition of each ordering rule be studied as a function of the patterning dimension (such as time as opposed to space), but whether spatial cues may be used to teach temporal discriminations should also be investigated, the latter being an issue of direct relevance to the selection of an appropriate system of communication.

Proponents of nonspeech modes of communication have furthermore based their rationale on the characteristics of the motor responses taught. Premack and Premack (1974) argued for a language with a simple response mode. The manipulation of plastic symbols was all that was required. Signing has also been promoted on the relative simplicity of the required motor responses, as compared to speech responses. In addition, sign training has been associated with another dimension of the motor response, i.e., with the fact that active motor responses are required from the child. Creedon (1976) speculated that signing might stimulate a growing sense of body awareness or, in other words, would reinforce further sensorimotor development such as more advanced levels of imitation as (e.g., the imitation of nonvisible movements of body parts). But the "magic" of active motor involvement is contradicted by the fact that plastic symbols and written words, which require only a simple motor response, have also resulted in impressive gains.

Further support for the relevance of motor action in learning to sign has been drawn from the observation that spontaneous vocalizations are often produced in conjunction with signs. While learning to sign, many children produce closer and closer approximations to the spoken word. Body movements, particularly hand movements, facilitate speech production otherwise hampered by various types of brain damage (Luria, 1966). Such a facilitative effect may be related to the neural overlap that supposedly exists between oral and manual activities (Kimura and Archibald, 1974). Activities of one neural region might trigger related action in adjoining areas. But such a triggering effect has not been limited to signs. The spontaneous emergence of vocalizations that accompany hand movements was also noted by Carrier (1974a, 1974b). A similar phenomenon was observed by Schuler et al. (1978) in teaching written word labels to a mute autistic child. Such observations of the relationships between gestural and vocal forms of communication allow for speculations about the origins of spoken and gestural language.

Claims about the effectiveness of alternative systems of communication are also attributed to other aspects of the responses involved. Bonvillian and Nelson (1976) suggested that the relationship between a signed label and its referent is less abstract than that between a spoken label and its referent. While such a relationship may apply to some signs, it is not necessarily true for signs in general. As pointed out by Bellugi (1976), signing differs from pantomime in that most signs are arbitrary and formalized. This is demonstrated by the fact that a signed conversation is not easily followed by someone who has not studied sign language. In many cases the first words taught (EAT and DRINK) are to some extent representational of the action expressed. The same applies to signs that use the equivalents of personal pronouns. Interestingly, no incidence of pronoun reversals, which are so typical of speaking autistic children, were observed in the children who learned to sign (Creedon, 1976). As far as the relationships between abstract-shaped plastic symbols or written words and their referents are concerned, it is of interest that it took much more time to teach labels for verbs than for nouns (Carrier, 1974a). Proponents of signing argue that the act of signing may be associated more readily with other action sequences (Creedon, 1975). One might speculate that motor action might allow the formation of a representational framework for other action and thus reinforce the acquisition of meaning. But it is questionable whether autistic children would be able to benefit from strong representational ties between sign and referent. It is doubtful that children normally acquire symbols on the basis of perceived symbolic relationships (Bates et al., 1979.) However, the relationships between labels and their referents as a function of sense modalities and patterning dimensions involved deserves further theoretical as well as applied study.

Signing rationales are also based on other factors, such as the need for proprioceptive stimulation, and the presumption that right hemisphere skills may be relatively well developed in autistic children, allowing them to do better on visuo-spatial tasks. However, such claims are not easily substantiated. All that can be concluded at this time is that the various alternative modes of communication tend to incorporate motor behaviors that already occur or that are easily shaped or prompted. Thus, alternative modes are more likely to be met by success if motivation for both child and teacher continues. Success occurs particularly if words are taught that are functional to the child in his immediate environment and that serve as a means by which to improve the child's capacity to affect his environment and to be instrumental in bringing about changes. Since the consequences are generally relevant to the child (food, hugs, tickles, toys) and administered contingent upon the child's engaging in communicative behavior of some type, the stage is set for the acquisition of communicative behaviors. Once this communicative intent is established, a child may proceed rapidly from rather limited and rudimentary beginnings to more elaborate and sophisticated systems of communication. Alternative modes of communication vary according to their motor and perceptual complexity. Accordingly, decisions to use one particular mode rather than another or to use a combination of modes need continuous reevaluation on the basis of a child's progress (as well as on changes observed in the overall clinical picture). Given that no clearcut criteria can be offered for the choice of one particular mode or training method, data need to be collected so that an evaluation can be made of the effectiveness of various intervention procedures across children, who may differ considerably in spite of a shared autistic label (see Alpert, 1980). In designing a particular program for one child or for a group of children, researchers must make decisions based on a careful weighing of anticipated benefits and costs and based on the behavioral and learning characteristics of individual children. Or, to quote Bonvillian and Nelson (1976), one must "match the characteristics of a communication system with any child's available levels of skill." If this is carefully done along with an assessment of the child's communicative needs, many children may benefit from our increased understanding of the interrelationships of speech, language, and communication.

IMPLICATIONS

Impressive successes have been associated with various forms and modes of intervention; however, conclusions are not easily drawn in regard to the desirability of particular approaches to individual autistic children. It should be realized that the problems exhibited by autistic children as a group may diverge considerably. Consequently, they may respond in different ways to various intervention programs. What works for one may not work well for another child. Lovaas (1977), for example, mentioned that his programs tended to be more effective with echolalic than with mute children. But it remains unclear which behavioral characteristics are correlated with the success or failure of a particular technique. Such enigmas reveal our lack of clear-cut decision-making models in selecting intervention strategies.

Divergent approaches to language intervention have all been able to claim some success. Differences in terminology may hide actual procedural similarities, and apparent procedural differences may be related conceptually. In spite of apparent differences, effective intervention procedures may be procedurally similar. The differences are the products of interpretations made by observers from various disciplines or philosophical orientations. Similarly, it is not always easy to classify particular approachs, because the accumulated clinical or educational experiences of a particular clinician, therapist, or teacher may be reflected rather than a particular theory.

Different approaches to intervention may share more common elements, and be more related, than they first seem. For instance, the various intervention strategies reviewed in this chapter were generally systematic and structured. When language has failed to emerge in a natural context, more structured and intrusive approaches seem most effective. More empirical support has also been gathered in favor of structural orientations. Schopler, Boehm, and Kinsbourne (1971) compared the effect of structured versus unstructured situations (the child decided what activities were engaged in at any time) on five variables: attention, affect, relatedness, vocalization, and psychotic behavior. It was found that developmental level and degree of internal structure interacted—the lower the level of development, the higher the need for structure. Similar findings were reported by Ney, Palvesky, and Markley (1971) in their comparison of the effectiveness of play therapy versus operant conditioning. That structured intrusive approaches do not necessarily preclude a psychodynamic orientation was demonstrated by the work of Clancy and McBride (1969) on mother-child interaction.

Another commonality of the procedures reported is that all used reinforcing consequences. The difference was that some forms of consequation were formally presented while others occurred in more natural contexts. All teaching procedures reviewed relied on some form of reinforcement. Various forms of consequation were used in the various studies on the use of alternative communication systems. For instance, Bonvillian and Nelson (1976), McLean and McLean (1974), Premack and Premack (1974), Carrier (1974a, 1974b), and LaVigna (1977) all used reinforcers, such as food and tokens. Others, including Creedon (1973, 1976), used verbal praise and hugs, while still other researchers, such as Fulwiler and Fouts (1976), used natural consequences, making sure that signs taught were immediately relevant to the gratification of their student's needs. Colby (1973) used immediate visual feedback, contingent upon the subject's pushing of various keys of a console. In summary, some form of clear-cut consequation was always connected with the targeted behaviors.

Such consequation may have been instrumental in the successes obtained. Many autistic children fail to make a connection between their actions and the consequences thereof. Such connections may be facilitated by easy responses that are immediately reinforced. Their strength lies in the clear-cut specification of the relationship between behaviors and their consequences. Even children who normally fail to understand the effect of their actions may do so when immediate clear-cut consequences are presented in the context of operant conditioning.

The teaching of various alternative forms of communication shows another commonality; the forms all incorporate behaviors that already exist within the children's repertoires. Teaching can thus focus on the acquisition of communicative intent rather than on prerequisite motor behavior. In addition, complex grammatical structures are avoided during the first stages of nonspeech training. Generally, only single-word equivalents with clear referents are presented.

In contrast, native users of speech may be more inclined to present nonverbal children with superfluous and irrelevant verbal stimulation. It is conceivable that much of the echolalia exhibited by autistic children is due to complex and perhaps irrelevant speech addressed to them by adults. Speech might be more successfully taught if excessive vocalizations were avoided and if meaning was attached to the vocalizations already existing in a child's repertoire. However, emphasis has generally been placed on the teaching of elaborate grammatical structures. Such preoccupation with the structure rather than with the function of language may contribute to the limited successes of speech-training techniques. Speech-training techniques might be more effective if they are geared closely to the child's current level of development. For instance, failure to generalize simple object-labeling responses can be forseen when a child is apparently unable to match that object with similar objects. As pointed out by Taylor (1976), only meaningless and rote speech can be expected when the conceptual skills that underlie language behavior are missing.

All forms of language teaching may be more effective when objectives are selected that are realistic in terms of a child's current performance. But caution should be applied when developmental information is incorporated. Overly strict, dogmatic adherence to stage-oriented models of intervention can be a misinterpretation of the developmental process.

In addition, formal teaching and natural acquisition of language do not necessarily proceed in an identical manner. For most autistic children, repeated exposure to a speaking environment has not resulted in functional language. Defective mechanisms that have precluded the acquisition of language may necessitate the involvement of compensatory processes in order for language to develop. As pointed out by Premack and Premack (1974), an experimental procedure that is effective in teaching a language system cannot be viewed as a model of language acquisition. Similarly, success of intervention procedures does not prove that language is acquired in this way. The effectiveness of a treatment program is an issue separate from that of the normal course of development. Teaching procedures may be effective despite lack of correspondence with normal development.

Although developmental issues do not provide a basis for the selection of teaching procedures, they do deserve consideration when it comes to the selection of teaching objectives. If skills are taught that incorporate behaviors that already exist within a child's repertoire, teaching may be more effective. Behavioral principles in turn have their greatest relevance in determining how skills should be taught and how progress should be recorded. They allow for the maintenance of attention and for the control of off-task behaviors that might otherwise interfere with teaching efforts.

Continuous reevaluations of intervention procedures should be made on the basis of collected data. Only through the gradual accumulation of case histories and experimental data will we be able to develop a solid rationale for decisions about teaching.

chapter

7

Guidelines for Intervention

Adriana Luce Schuler

Department of Special Education
San Francisco State University
San Francisco, California

contents

ASSESSMENT 167
TEACHING COMMUNICATION SKILLS 174
    Functional Concerns... 175
    Teaching Objectives 177
    Alternative Systems of Communication 177
    Teaching Procedures 180
EXPANDING THE ROOTS OF LANGUAGE 182
    Speech 183
    Language.. 184
    Communication.. 185
    Cognition... 187
CONCLUDING COMMENTS 188

Language and communication disorders associated with autism are of such a magnitude that many children diagnosed as autistic could be characterized as functionally nonverbal, despite ritualized or self-stimulatory vocalizations. There is a lack of data on which to base specific recommendations for teaching language. In addition, it is difficult to decide how much emphasis language should receive as compared to other curriculum components. This latter problem is particularly pressing when dealing with autistic adolescents who perform poorly on language tasks as well as in the areas of self-care and vocational skills. Although language skills are associated with a positive prognostic outlook, the other skills are also essential for a positive intervention outcome. Consequently, the question of whether language teaching deserves the prime attention that it tends to receive must be addressed. Improvements in social interaction skills are not necessarily tied to gains in language skills (Ruttenberg and Wolf, 1967).

Much of an autistic person's capacity to deal constructively with his environment depends on the degree to which the demands of this environment are understood. The extent to which we can expect autistic people to understand us depends on how much we rely on verbal rather than nonverbal modes of communication as well as on the structure and predictability of our environment. Despite their language deficiencies many autistic individuals are capable of learning elaborate routines when guided through the required actions rather than verbally instructed.

To select appropriate teaching objectives the educational needs of the autistic individual need to be taken into careful consideration. Information gathered on the child's history, age, and learning potential, on teaching strategies, and on projections for future development should guide the design of an appropriate intervention program. Decisions in the selection of teaching objectives should be based upon consideration of the following questions: 1) will the objective increase the individual's independence, 2) will it ameliorate behavioral disorders, and 3) will it enhance social interaction and integration? Table 1 provides a more thorough review of this selection process.

Success or failure of teaching efforts depends on what is being taught and how the teaching is implemented. To provide some guidelines the discussion in this chapter covers: 1) assessment issues and practices, 2) the establishment of communicative intent, and 3) the expansion of linguistic abilities.

ASSESSMENT

In order to select objectives that are realistic one must carefully assess a child's level of language functioning as well as the child's language-related behaviors. Assessment is crucial to the selection of suitable teaching objectives. Many problems are commonly encountered in the as-

Table 1.   Checklist for the selection of teaching objectives

1. **Are teaching objectives realistic?**
   1.1   Are objectives congruent with long term prognosis?
   1.2   Are objectives congruent with current skills and level of functioning?
   1.3   Are objectives teachable? Are they defined in operational terms, allowing for the specification of program steps and outcome evaluation?
   1.4   Do the skills to be taught incorporate strengths or weaknesses evidenced by the assessment outcome?
   1.5   Do the skills to be taught rely on other skills that are not within that child's behavioral repertoire?
2. **Do the objectives positively affect prognostic perspectives?**
   2.1   Do objectives allow increased independent living skills?
   2.2   Do objectives pursued positively affect competence/deviance balance in terms of social acceptability?
   2.3   If attained, would the objective decrease autistic behaviors and enhance social integration?
      2.3.1   Could the skills taught help change a child's future living situation?
      2.3.2   Could the skills taught change a child's immediate living situation?
3. **Can the skills be expected to be maintained or generalized?**
   3.1   Do objectives provide a basis for teaching additional related skills?
   3.2   Can the skills be incorporated into other areas of curriculum development?
   3.3   Would the skills provide the child with the motivation to put that skill to use? Can reinforcement be expected in the child's everyday environment?

sessment of students with autistic behaviors. The problems can be summarized as follows:

1. Conventional standardized tests are geared to what a child knows rather than how a child learns (content rather than process orientation).
2. Testing procedures rely heavily on verbal as well as nonverbal interaction skills.
3. Behavioral and attentional problems interfere with testing procedures.
4. Assessment tools that focus on the development of social interaction skills are lacking.

Many assessment tools are designed to provide an overall score that allows for a comparative ranking of the test performances of different children. Although this may be useful in evaluating the magnitude of the problems, the nature of those problems is not clarified. When dealing with autistic or autistic-like children, their developmental discontinuities raise questions about the value of an overall score. A child may perform relatively well in one area and be untestable in another area. In practice it will often be advisable to refrain from the administration of a whole test and rely on selected subtests.

Poor attention and behavioral problems affect any form of social interaction. Assessments are not easily carried out when it is impossible to make even the most rudimentary form of social contact. Consequently, the value of an assessment is largely determined by whether a child can be motivated to interact with or attend to the teacher or clinician. This depends on whether suitable sources of reinforcement have been identified and on the familiarity of the testing environment. In many cases it is desirable that assessments be carried out by those adults who are most familiar with a particular child. Even if social rapport is established, and a child appears to respond in a consistent manner across several tasks, a drop in performance cannot always be attributed to an inability to carry out that particular task. The reinforcers used may have lost their strengths. Also, incompatible behaviors, such as self-stimulation, may preclude proper attention to the task at hand. Because of fluctuations in attention, it is often desirable to initially limit assessment to relatively short periods of time, e.g., 10-minute periods. Similarly, it may be necessary to repeat assessments when doubts arise about the validity of measures obtained. In general, assessment is a step-by-step process; all questions raised cannot be pursued at once.

Additional stumbling blocks should be anticipated when tests rely largely on verbal instructions. It may be necessary to train a child on a series of practice trials that correspond to the task at hand. Even with relatively simple tasks that require imitative skills only, it may be necessary to provide specific training. For instance, if the task requires imitative behaviors, one would reinforce the child for imitative behaviors that are similar but not identical to the behavior being assessed. One must be sure that a child understands what he is supposed to do. Many children will cease to respond if a task is presented that is not completely identical to a previously learned task. For instance, many children will fail to respond if other pictures or objects are used or if the instructions are slightly altered. Similarly, they may not respond at all in an environment that differs from the one to which they are accustomed.

A fourth problem stems from the lack of tools that examine the development of social interaction skills. Assessment of social skills will generally be based on informal observations and descriptive measures. In addition, a child's precocious skills in one particular area may cause someone to neglect more basic skills. For instance, one may fail to assess a child's ability to imitate speech upon command when a child exhibits a large repertoire of context-appropriate delayed echolalic utterances. Context-sensitive recall does not necessarily imply that behavior is intentional or under voluntary control.

Whether assessment will be relevant and helpful in selecting teaching objectives depends on the skills of those who carry out the assessment and on the questions that are asked. In attempting to assess language and language-related behaviors, the most basic question to be resolved is whether the problems exhibited are of a specific linguistic nature or of an overall conceptual or social nature. In other words, the extent to which speech, language, communication, and cognition are involved must be determined. Paucity of speech may indicate that the motor skills needed to produce speech are poorly developed. It may also be indicative of a poorly developed ability to verbally code nonverbal knowledge and intentions. On the other hand, communicative intentions might be lacking altogether. To design an appropriate treatment program it is crucial that such distinctions be made. It would be useless to teach linguistic coding principles (e.g., elaborate syntactic structures) when there is no communicative intent.

To make diagonstic differentiations, questions need to be addressed that pertain to a comparison of social, linguistic, and cognitive development in relation to verbal expression. Table 2 lists a series of questions that may help to pinpoint the crux of the problems. In order to address these questions various aspects of development should be assessed. Table 3 may serve to clarify which issues should be considered.

Both formal and informal forms of assessment should be used to address these questions because they will supplement each other. Formal assessments imply that one looks for responses to a series of tasks designed to sample a child's skills (e.g., performing a motor behavior upon command, labeling objects or pictures, or matching objects and/or pictures that go together). However, it is also important to observe behaviors in a more natural context, that is, when a child is not involved in an assigned task. For instance, it would be important to estimate the amount of time that a child engages in self-stimulatory behaviors versus goal-oriented behaviors. With respect to speech, the child's vocalizations should be described in terms of frequency and diversity as well as in terms of function. It should also be determined whether the vocalizations are automatic and indiscriminate, or selective and discriminate. The latter may be inferred when the frequency of vocalization increases in the presence of people and when the vocalizations are coordinated with gaze and body movements, that is, with nonverbal communicative efforts.

In order to get an idea of the extent to which a child is able to use speech, signs, or other forms of communication functionally, the teacher or clinician needs to observe the child in a variety of situations (e.g., in

Table 2.   Assessment questions to be addressed

1. **Could the problems encountered be due to deficiencies of verbal expression, that is, speech production?**
   1.1   Are the speech sounds or vocalizations produced in a laborious manner?
   1.2   Is there evidence of a problem at the level of motor planning of speech or hand movements?
   1.3   Is there a nasal, harsh, or dull vocal quality to the voice that could dictate poor motor control?
   1.4   Do comprehension skills surpass production skills?
2. **Could the problems encountered be due to modality-specific deficiencies that are inherent to the auditory channel or the the nature of the stimuli?**
   2.1   Is there a discrepancy between verbal and nonverbal means of expression? Are gestures, eye movements, intonation patterns, and body movements used to code intentions?
   2.2   Do nonverbally assessed conceptual skills surpass verbal skills? Is there an ability to match objects that are conceptually related in the absence of labeling skills?
3. **Could the problems encountered be part of a more general problem in symbolic behavior?**
   3.1   Are similar problems exhibited at level of play? Is the manipulation of objects and toys merely repetitive and stereotyped rather than indicative of representational abilities and make-believe play?
   3.2   Are similar problems encountered when attempting to teach pictorial or other nontransient labels for objects or relationships between objects?
4. **Are the problems encountered part of an overall deficiency in areas of intentional behavior?**
   4.1   Is there evidence of means-end behavior involving the use of objects in order to obtain something else?
   4.2   Is there evidence of means-end behavior involving the use of people to get things or using objects to get people's attention?
   4.3   What interaction takes place and in what ways are the child's desires met (temper tantrums, crying, biting, or through guiding an adult's hand to some object)?

play, in stereotyped and self-stimulatory activities, and in social interactions such as at mealtime). Behaviors may be videotaped or audiotaped or a narrative record may be kept to document the degree to which functional communication skills are exhibited.

Not only is it important to evaluate the child's vocal repertoire, but whether or not the child attends to the speech of others should also be determined. Do spoken words serve as a signal to engage in particular behaviors, or is the child oblivious to the speech of others? (For a more detailed discussion of these issues, see Kozloff, 1974, and Lovaas, 1977.) Answers to these questions help to determine whether speech-imitation training should be initiated or whether alternative systems of communication should be considered.

Table 3.   Checklist for assessment: Areas of concern

1. **Knowledge about objects**
   1.1   Is the child able to match identical objects (e.g., a green plastic cup with a green plastic cup)?
   1.2   Is the child able to match objects that are not identical but are similar (e.g., a blue plastic comb with a grey metal comb)?
   1.3   Is the child able to follow objects in space (visual tracking) and locate an object in space when it is not immediately visible or touchable (e.g., find a peanut hidden under a cup)?
2. **Does the child have knowledge about how to do things (means-end behaviors involving the use of people and objects)?**
   2.1   Is the child able to grasp objects in order to get them closer?
   2.2   Does the child cry or fuss when things are beyond reach?
   2.3   Does the child approach others or actively move his body in order to get things?
   2.4   Does the child approach others with eye movements or gestures in order to get things?
   2.5   Does the child use vocalizations to get an adult's attention?
   2.6   Does the child take corrective actions when ends fail to be met?
   2.7   Does the child approach others to show objects in order to get attention?
3. **Representational knowledge (play—nonverbal)**
   3.1   Does the child play with objects in ways that demonstrate a knowledge of how objects are used?
   3.2   Is the child able to show how an object is used when asked to do so or when asked to imitate an adult's actions?
4. **Representational knowledge (labeling—verbal)**
   4.1   Is the child able to use labels for objects (enactive or symbolic)?
   4.2   Is the child able to use labels for people (naming, personal pronouns)?
   4.3   Is the child able to use labels for movement or action (verbs)?
   4.4   Is the child able to label events, noting the interaction between people and things?
   4.5   Is the child able to label spatial relationships?

When children exhibit some speech and are able to produce speech upon command, one can attempt to use those tests that are commonly used to assess the articulation and language comprehension and production skills of children with some type of communicative handicap. However, the use of these tests may present some obstacles. For instance, instructions and picture materials may have to be changed to avoid confusing or distracting the child. Also, tests that are commonly used may be too advanced or irrelevant for many children. For instance, to assess labeling skills it may be helpful to present a child with several common objects in his environment to assess whether he can pick up the appropriate one when presented with the verbal label. Similarly, the child could be asked to name the same objects or to show what actions are to be associated with them (e.g., if the child cannot say "cup," can he nevertheless demonstrate how a cup should be used?). If the child demonstrates an ability to use single labels, more complex instructions may be presented. For instance, does a child understand instructions that require an understanding of the relationships between actions, their agents, and their recipients or complements (e.g., *The blue car hits the jeep*, or *Mary gives the banana to Jimmy*)? To carry out such assessments puppets, toys, and everyday objects are useful. The child can be asked to manipulate these items according to the given instructions. The child can also be asked to describe the actions portrayed by the teacher or clinician or to label actions of adults and peers (e.g., a teacher touching the child's nose versus his or her own nose.)

If a child is not able to label objects and events independently, he may be asked to imitate labels produced by the adult. The proficiency of imitative skills may not always reflect language capacity, but rote speech reproduction skills should be assessed if the overall picture is to be completed. When reproduction skills appear considerably ahead of comprehension and conceptual skills, treatment should not focus upon speech production. Rather, development of communicative intent and conceptual skills, as opposed to articulation skills, should be emphasized.

To determine whether verbal skills are developed congruently with conceptual and perceptual skills it is important to obtain some measure of cognitive development and perceptual abilities. Again, most assessment tools in this area rely on verbal skills, but some nonverbal tests are available. To assess conceptual development everyday objects can be used in matching exercises according to perceptual versus conceptual criteria (see Chapter 5 for a more detailed discussion). This approach provides some measure of language-related cognitive abilities.

To evaluate symbolic and intentional behavior one usually has to rely on informal descriptive measures and developmental scales. However, it should be kept in mind that most scales tend to only ask whether or not a behavior occurs; the function of a particular behavior is not always considered. Purely descriptive procedures need to be supplemented with some type of experimentation. For instance, one could not immediately satisfy a child's apparent "requests" by temporarily withholding food or other favors, or deliberately "misinterpret" the child's messages.

In trying to determine whether a child is able to engage in means-end behaviors, a variety of toys can be used that require a child to perform various motor actions, such as pushing a lever to make a light flash. It is also important to see whether the child searches for objects that are invisible or uses objects as tools to accomplish a certain effect.

To assess whether some of the communicative problems may be attributed to a modality-specific processing problem, some experimental, i.e, "diagnostic teaching," methods are usually needed. While obvious modality preferences and the use of nonverbal means of communication provide some information, more specific information needs to be obtained. To determine whether representational problems are modality-specific, one can compare the rate at which signed versus spoken versus written/pictorial labels are acquired. The use of alternative labels can also be taught in reference to various semantic relations. Notions of sameness, negation, and causality could be marked by abstract-shaped plastic symbols, analogous to the work of Premack (1971, 1976a, 1976b; Premack and Premack, 1974) and Taylor (1976). If those were acquired more rapidly than speech labels this might suggest that the transience of conventional codes (e.g., speech) may have been an obstacle to overall communicative and cognitive development. In these cases it might be preferable to explore the use of a nontransient coding system.

Single, unmodified conventional assessment techniques rarely produce an overall picture of a child's abilities, nor do they provide a basis for curriculum development. Only cumulative assessments allow comparisons among the various aspects of speech, language, communication, and cognition that are impaired. The assessment process should therefore be continuous and be guided by new observations and findings in the classroom and at home. Careful reevaluation of teaching objectives on the basis of such findings will often lead to the selection of new or modified teaching objectives as well as different teaching procedures. Assessment and curriculum design are, therefore, inseparably interlinked (Ruder, 1978). Programming and curriculum design should be monitored by a continuous evaluation of teaching outcome.

TEACHING COMMUNICATION SKILLS

As discussed in Chapter 4, despite apparent grammatical advances, many autistic children fail to use speech, gestures, and the like, as a means to an end. Therefore, emphasis should always be placed on the use of grammatical constructs for purposes of interaction rather than on the isolated production of such constructs. For children who are largely noncommunicative, it is important that speech, signs, or whatever code is used not be separated from their referents, but rather be presented within a functional communicative context. It is crucial that attention be paid to the functions of utterances to be taught. The following section discusses functional concerns and explains their relation to the management of severe behavior problems so prevalent in autism. A later section deals with the ways in which functional communication skills are taught.

Functional Concerns

Current language intervention practices often seem more preoccupied with structural than with functional concerns. For instance, labeling responses, such as "That's a _____," are often the target of initial teaching efforts. But it is questionable whether these are the most appropriate targets, particularly when presented within the context of pictures that are largely meaningless. Both developmental as well as functional criticisms can be made against such practices.

As far as normal development goes, it has been demonstrated (Halliday, 1973, 1975; Bates et al., 1976) that requests, or so-called "instrumentals," are typically the first "speech acts" to be acquired by children (for a further discussion, see Chapter 4). Nevertheless, as pointed out by Leonard (1978), many language programs start with the teaching of object labels (e.g., "That is a _____"). While this may be appropriate for those children who have problems with the linguistic coding of communicative intentions, the same does not apply to children who are largely noncommunicative. In the latter cases the teaching of requests might be more in line with what is known about normal development.

From a functional perspective, further arguments can be raised aginst an early emphasis on labels. First, it is sensible to teach a child speech that can be put to use. On the basis of a criterion of functionality one could argue against the relevance of descriptive statements for many autistic children because they are not inclined to approach adults with phrases such as "This is a horse." A child who does not come up to an adult to nonverbally draw the adult's attention to objects (as children often do normally around 9–12 months) cannot be expected to use taught labels spontaneously. "Spontaneous" use of taught labels would thus be limited to those occasions in which questions such as "What is that?" are specifically addressed to the child. It may be more useful to teach the child to initiate questions such as "What is that?" when presented with unfamiliar objects or with items that he can name (for a more detailed description of such a program, see Guess, Sailor, and Baer, 1976).

Second, utterances that name or identify, such as statements like "That is a _____," are largely under the control of antecedent stimuli, that is, actions or things that were just observed. Because of this property they have been referred to in the operant literature as *tacts* in contrast to utterances classified as *mands* (Skinner, 1957). The latter term refers to those utterances that serve as a means to an end, that is, are controlled by their outcome (for a more detailed discussion of such operant views, see MacCorquadale, 1970, and Segal, 1975). Similar distinctions were made by Premack (1971) with respect to the terms *interrogation* and *identification.* It should be realized that tacts are generally maintained by subtle forms of social reinforcement, such as occasional smiles, changes of body posture, and head nods. Since autistic children are not known for their responsiveness to such forms of social reinforcement, it is questionable whether the teaching of tacts would provide for the spontaneous and generalized use of the speech taught. Spontaneous use may be more easily promoted when those speech forms that provide for an immediate and unambiguous payoff are taught. This may be accomplished through teaching students how to obtain things that are of direct relevance to them. The teaching of requests may thus be the most appropriate starting point. The appropriate expression of needs or desires may facilitate the child's interaction with his environment and thus indirectly serve to alleviate the severe behavioral problems commonly encountered in autism. These severe behavioral problems, combined with the severe communicative deficits of autistic children, are usually the greatest obstacles for those who try to teach autistic children.

As far as the management of behavioral problems is concerned, a thorough discussion of these issues lies beyond the scope of this book. But is should be pointed out that treatment priorities are usually determined by the magnitude of behavioral problems encountered. For instance, it would be difficult to teach imitation skills to a child who cannot be kept in his seat or fails to make eye contact. Therefore, initial treatment emphasis is often placed on appropriate sitting and attending skills (for a review of operant approaches used to establish these skills, see Chapter 6). Futhermore, guidelines for the use of behavioral techniques for classroom management have become available (Kozloff, 1974; Donnellan-Walsh et al., 1976). The management of behavioral problems has to a large extent relied on the use of aversive techniques, which create a multitude of problems particularly in relation to classroom use. However, the use of nonpunitive methods of behavioral management has recently been explored (LaVigna and Donnellan-Walsh, 1976). These techniques, it is hoped, will improve our ability to work effectively with those children who are severely communicatively and behaviorally impaired. The teaching of functional communication skills may be a further aid in the management of behavioral problems. For instance, "speech acts" that provide a child with increased means of control and with a series of socially appropriate skills may to a large extent reduce the behavioral problems. In addition, behavioral problems are often reduced when children are presented with age-appropriate tasks or with teaching programs that are designed to teach in an errorless or virtually errorless manner (Terrace, 1963). Because the establishment of communicative intent is so crucial and appropriate programs are not readily found, the following three subsections are devoted to this matter.

Teaching Objectives

A first concern in program design pertains to the selection of things to be requested, that is, to the identification of appropriate behavioral goals. Given that most autistic children do not seem to be "tuned in" to social stimuli and appear rather limited with respect to the scope of their overall repertoire, teachers and clinicians are generally limited in their choices. But careful observation of and interaction with autistic children will provide clues. Some children may like not only food but also some type of physical stimulation (e.g., being tickled,hugged, tossed, turned, or pulled in a wagon). Others may be enthralled with colored lights, xylophones, music boxes, record players, and so on. Still others may like soft, furry tennis balls, pieces of shoelace, or tree twigs. Because these latter objects might serve as an invitation to an entire range of off-task behaviors, they do not always constitute a first choice. On the other hand, self-stimulatory behaviors might be placed within the context of more appropriate behavior, for example, a give and take interaction, through the introduction of one of these objects. In such a context, the child would have to learn to ask for the object wanted as well as hand it back when asked for it (a response that may need some prompting). Table 4 provides a checklist of factors to be considered in program design.

Alternative Systems of Communication

A second concern in program design lies within the selection of those behaviors that will be required from the child as a means of obtaining food, tickles, toys, or any other privileges. Because the objective lies within the rapid establishment of communicative intent, it is important that functional rather than structural concerns prevail. For instances, if a child does not vocalize or hardly does so, speech may not be the mode of choice, since hand movements are more readily prompted. On the other hand, if a child has been observed to produce speech-like sounds occasionally, such sounds may be put into a communicative context and gradually shaped into closer approximations of adult speech. For instance, an "ee"-like sound may be shaped into "eat," if a child is at all able to vocalize upon command or do so imitatively. One of the most crucial concerns here is whether the child is able to exert voluntary control over his vocalizations. All too often children are required to use spontaneous speech once they have been noted to say something occasionally in an appropriate context. Because such utterances may be largely of a delayed echolalic nature (see Chapters 2 and 3) devoid from communicative intent (see Chapter 4), one should be careful to not accuse the child of a deliberate refusal to cooperate. Distinctions should always be made between those behaviors that are, and those that are not,

Table 4.   Checklist on selecting teaching procedures and program design

1. **Are appropriate instructions and materials being supplied?**
    1.1   Are the instructions concise?
    1.2   Are the instructions given when proper attention is ensured?
    1.3   Are the instructions relevant to the task?
    1.4   Are chances of attention being directed toward irrelevant stimuli being minimized?
    1.5   Are the prompts (i.e., extra help supplied) designed to maximize teaching effectiveness and to minimize chances of erratic attention to irrelevant stimuli?
2. **Are the student's behaviors being properly consequated in order to maximize learning?**
    2.1   Are the consequences supplied relevant to the child?
    2.2   Are the consequences delivered in an immediate and unambiguous manner?
    2.3   Can the student be expected to maintain the behavior in his natural environment once the behavior is learned?
    2.4   Is the rate of payoff for appropriate behavior sufficiently high and not outrated by the frequency of negative consequences?
3. **Are the behaviors expected from the student sufficiently specified?**
    3.1   Are the behaviors expected from the student specified in operational terms?
    3.2   Are success and failure criteria specified so that new objectives can be added or teaching techniques altered at the appropriate times?
    3.3   Can the student be expected to learn the behavior in the time allotted?

under voluntary control. Therefore questions as to whether a child is or is not able to do something should carefully specify the conditions under which that behavior is supposed to occur. Meaningful speech may not be easily taught to children who are as yet unable to imitate speech despite an extensive echolalic repertoire. Those children who tend to reproduce words or phrases some time after their occurrence may not always be able to do so immediately because they are seemingly unable to imitate upon command. In those instances, one could try to teach verbal imitation skills as described by Lovaas (1977; Lovaas et al., 1966) and Kozloff (1974), but this should not delay the establishment of communicative intent.

If stumbling blocks are encountered in the teaching of speech, various other options are left (see discussion in Chapter 6). Several factors need to be considered to decide whether a child should be taught to sign or to use pictures, written word cards, or arbitrary pieces of plastic. As pointed out in the previous chapter, simple answers cannot be given when it comes to the selection of the most appropriate system of communication. The main issues to be considered are summarized in Table 5.

Decisions should be based on a careful weighing of costs and benefits. In doing so, attempts should be made to match the child's level of development and learning characteristics as closely as possible with the perceptual and motor characteristics of the system selected. In this respect, it should be realized that many autistic children reportedly do better when presented with tasks that involve nontransient, visuo-spatial stimuli rather than transient stimuli. Even when the use of pictures, plastic symbols, or written words may not constitute the final teaching objective, they may still be useful in the initial phases of treatment when communicative intent still needs to be established. The basics of communication may be taught more readily in the context of the simplest hand movements; pointing may suffice for these purposes. Nontransient codes may thus serve to teach the idea of communication to children who have failed to grasp the concept of communication in the context of normal social interaction.

Plastic symbols and written words, as well as pictures, may be used as a grammar-practicing device in support of spoken and signed words because they can be used as a visuo-spatial "crutch" in the acquisition of temporal sequences of speech or signs. Use of one particular system of communication can therefore be combined with the use of another system or can serve as a basis for a second system.

Since no absolute criteria can be offered with regard to the selection of the most appropriate system, careful evaluation and reevaluation

Table 5.   Issues in selecting a system of communication

1. **Child characteristics**
   1.1   Age
   1.2   Level of conceptual development
   1.3   Level of social development
   1.4   Use of preverbal performatives (gestures, smiles)
   1.5   Receptive language skills (auditory versus contextual)
2. **Code characteristics**
   2.1   Sense modality involved
   2.2   Patterning dimension
   2.3   Coding potential
   2.4   Response complexity
3. **Learning characteristics**
   3.1   Modality preference
   3.2   Visual discrimination skills
   3.3   Verbal imitation skills
   3.4   Nonverbal imitation skills
   3.5   Overselectivity
4. **Opportunities for use**
   4.1   Home environment
   4.2   Classroom environment
   4.3   Peer interaction
   4.4   General acceptability
   4.5   Practicality

should continuously be made on the basis of data collected. In order to validate a particular choice experimentally, it may be helpful to make systematic comparisons of the rate with which single as well as discriminatory responses are acquired as a function of the type of code used (e.g., visual versus auditory, transient versus nontransient). The suitability of a particular system can then be evaluated by 1) the number of trials that are needed to teach single as well as discriminative responses, and 2) the percentage of correct responses. It may, for instance, be found that a particular system allows a child to respond errorlessly, which may reduce the likelihood of off-task behaviors and thereby reduce the occurrence of behavioral problems.

Teaching Procedures

Once decisions have been made with regard to what the child is supposed to do in order to "request," that is, once responses and consequences are specified, decisions have to be made about teaching procedures. To indicate that the child is supposed to respond the teacher might ask, "What do you want?" or simply focus the child's attention on the consequences to be presented. After such a cue (discriminative stimulus or instruction) is presented, the child will usually be prompted through the required response. This means that the teacher will physically guide the child through the response, present an imitative model, or provide some other type of cue that triggers the correct response. Reinforcement, that is, gratification of the request, is then to follow contingent upon completion of the response. To illustrate this sequence with an example, a teacher holds up a peanut, after which he or she moves the child's hand to produce the appropriate sign. As soon as the sign is completed, the peanut is given to the child, along with verbal praise. Subsequently, the teacher records whether the response was correct and how much of a prompt was required. This will provide the basis for gradual prompt fading. A second trial is then initiated, followed by a third, and so on. This teacher sequence is summarized in Table 6.

To ensure that the sequence of events is presented in a clear-cut manner, it is important that the teacher's actions be concise and unambiguous. If this is not the case, the child may never be able to make the connection between the behavior and its consequence. Many noncommunicative autistic children have failed to learn that their actions can serve as a tool to accomplish something. Therefore, the relationship between response and consequence should be made as salient as possible. When prompted correct responses have been obtained consistently, it is time for the prompt to be faded systematically; that is, the amount of help supplied by the teacher or therapist should be systematically reduced. The child can be considered to have learned the behavior as

Table 6. Outline of teaching sequence (single trial)

Instruction	Prompt	Response	Consequation	Intertrial interval
(discriminative stimulus) The teacher presents the child with the occasion for the response (e.g., by asking "What do you want?" or by showing an object to be labeled or matched with another object or pictures).	(extra help supplied to obtain a correct response) The teacher guides the child through target responses or provides an imitative model or some other clue.	(behavior to be taught) The teacher decides whether the response exhibited meets the previously specified criterion.	(immediate feedback provided by the teacher) The teacher reinforces correct responses and ignores or consequates incorrect responses differentially.	(pause) The teacher records data and rearranges teaching materials to get ready for next trial.

soon as a series of unprompted responses are consistently given in response to the stimulus (instructional cue or discriminative stimulus) presented.

At this point, a second form of requesting behavior needs to be introduced so that discriminatory rather than single responses are required. For instance, a child may be taught to ask for juice as well as a peanut. For this purpose, correct responses are again prompted upon the presentation of the instructional stimulus (in many cases, the mere sight of juice). But requests for juice are now interspersed with requests for peanuts as soon as some consistent "juice" responses have been obtained. During the initial phases of training, the choice may not be completely up to the child. The teacher may still need to decide what is going to be requested, and focus the child's attention accordingly (e.g., point to the juice). In later phases of teaching, two or more objects or pictorial representations of actions (e.g., a photograph of the child hugging his teacher) or some type of question may be presented to the child. A pointing response is now required, accompanied by the appropriate verbal request.

Discriminations of this type which are immediately relevant to the child tend to be acquired more readily than discriminative responses that are not reinforced by different consequences (for experimental verification of this issue, see Saunders and Sailor, 1979). In addition, discriminative responses may be further facilitated through the teaching of negative requests. Teaching the child to protest actively against things he does not like or want may help in gaining control over behavioral problems. By teaching a child to express notions such as "no" and "stop," the child acquires further means to act upon his environment more effectively.

Once discriminative requests are taught, the stage is set for further expansion of the roots of language. Additional language functions and word combinations are introduced. At this point, various language programs may be useful provided that the spoken, signed, or written words, plastic symbols, and so on, are not divorced from their referent, that is, that the communicative symbol is presented in context. Some suggestions for further program design with respect to the specific language needs of autistic children are discussed below.

EXPANDING THE ROOTS OF LANGUAGE

Treatment programs should be designed for each child on the basis of careful assessment of developmental level and learning strategies to ensure the best match between program and child. A program that works with one child may not work with another child. Nevertheless, programs for individual children share common elements and can be drawn from programs designed for a variety of language problems. However, adaptations have to be made if these programs are to be used with autistic and autistic-like children, particularly given the pervasive problems with the semantic and pragmatic aspects of language. For example, the teaching of labels for objects in response to the question "What is this?" will be meaningless if that child is unable to match those objects nonverbally. If the child is unable to match different objects that belong to the same class, he will probably fail to generalize labels taught in reference to objects of that class. In other words, the child must relearn the label for every new object introduced (e.g., for every different cup). Nevertheless, the same child may learn to label in a requesting sense, asking for a favorite object or activity over and over. Simple requests for differential action seem to precede the acquistion of more abstract labels (Schuler, 1979) and can be taught at the same time that the child learns to perform nonverbal matching and sorting tasks.

The correct reproduction of words and phrases may never move beyond sophisticated but meaningless echolalia if the reproduction is not made in the context of interaction. For some children, the focus of treatment might be placed on the communicative use of a limited set of rote phrases, such as "Hi," "Bye-bye," and "Tickle please," rather than on the teaching of grammatical rules. Since the acquisition of a cognitively based complex linguistic system may not be a realistic teaching objective, a limited set of simple requests and interactive language functions may be all that is pursued. But, in all cases, it is important that the integration of linguistic, social, and cognitive skills be attempted. Teaching isolated articulatory, morphological, or syntactic skills is often an invitation to rote and meaningless echolalia.

The following discussion presents some suggestions for the design of language-teaching programs. Aspects of speech, language, communication and cognition are discussed separately, analogous to the rationale established throughout the first chapters of this volume.

Speech

Intelligibility versus Communicative Intent Meaningful usage and communicative intent are of primary importance. Nevertheless, if the intelligibility of speech or signs produced is poor, improvement of speech articulation skills, or more refined hand movements may require special attention. In many cases, the articulatory movements by themselves may not be as crucial as their timing. Problems with intonation seem more prevalent than problems with articulation.

Teaching Imitation Skills Verbal and manual imitation skills may be established as a phase of teaching. Behavioral procedures may be effectively used for such purposes. Teaching verbal imitation skills requires that more and more refined discriminations be made in terms of when to vocalize and in what manner. The training should also lead to increased voluntary control of the vocalizations produced.

Articulation Training When motor production skills remain consistently poor, some articulation drills may be useful. In terms of spontaneous use, differential reinforcement techniques may be used, so that closer and closer approximation are reinforced while lesser achievements are systematically ignored.

Linking Speech to Body Movements Further improvement may come through systematic efforts to interlink articulation skills and other forms of body action rhythmically. For instance, children have been taught to clap or jump in synchrony with syllabic structure. Since many children have difficulties with even the simplest coordination of single syllables with simple body movements, initial teaching efforts rely on prompting. Most children have to be guided manually through body movements, i.e., clapping or tapping in conjunction with monosyllabic vocalizations. Once such unprompted coordinated actions can be carried out, more complex vocalizations can be added. This may be accomplished in a game-like fashion in the context of group interaction. Children may be asked to jump, clap each other's hands, or make other body movements in conjunction with nursery rhymes or with words for objects or actions in the immediate environment. In many cases, such activities improve overall intelligibility and intonational quality.

Language

Researchers must carefully examine both syntactic and semantic considerations when designing language intervention programs. In terms of syntax, many children are able to reproduce rather complex sentences but are unable to generate even the simplest sentences on their own. Therefore, single words (or two-word combinations) may be all the child is able to produce on his own.

Teaching toward Syntactic Productivity Complex sentences often seem processed as a single string of sounds and not as hierarchical constructs. If so, phrases like "May I please go to the playground" are not conducive to further syntactic growth. An autistic child would not readily come up with similar phrases, such as "May I please go to the bathroom" or "Would you give me my puzzle, please?" Single words, however, could be expanded systematically into two-word utterances, which might highlight the idea of constituency. For instance, *more* or *want* can be combined with variety of object or action labels in an attempt to establish the notion of a grammatical category (*more* + X, a class of wanted things).

Using Pictures as Referents   In terms of semantics, it is important that speech, signs, or whatever code is used be placed in meaningful context. Whereas it is a common practice to teach particular sentence structures in response to a series of pictorial representations of actions and events, this task may not be suitable to the needs of the autistic child. Such practices may teach the autistic child to reproduce phrases in response to irrelevant stimuli. A child may learn, for instance, to say "The cat is running" in response to a curl in the cat's tail, or even to a stain or wrinkle that is part of the picture. Pictures should only be used if the child has demonstrated that he can match real-life objects with their three-dimensional representations and pictorially portrayed actions with real-life actions.

Body Actions as Referents   Since the autistic focus of attention is often different from that of others, extra efforts should be made to ensure that labels are associated with their proper referents. To maximize chances that attention is being paid to relevant stimuli, the teacher might use the student's own body actions or those of his peers as a referent. For example, the child could be given the instruction "Go jump" and then asked to describe his own body action. Similarly, he could be asked to label the body actions of peers as they carry out given instructions. (Imitative instructions may be used with children who fail to understand spoken, signed, written, or pictorial instructions.)

Teaching Semantic Categories   In order for a child to learn about actions, as well as about actors and recipients of actions, it may be helpful to have the child label actions carried out by various individuals. Toys and puppets may help. For instance, a teacher might ask a child to tell her what is happening when she makes a toy car hit a block ("The car is hitting the block"). Similarly the teacher might ask the child to act out instructions to increase receptive skills. In both cases, the child must attend to the referents of the grammatical structures presented. This is more easily accomplished when turns are being taken, requiring the active participation of the student. By having the child describe actions carried out by the teacher or by the child ("Susan touches the ball" versus "Jimmy touches the ball"), chances for the integration of syntactic and semantic skills are optimized.

Communication

One of the most striking deficiencies of autistic children lies in their communication. Frequently, their language skills are not used for communication and interaction, but are instead an end in themselves. Speech, signs, or any coding system that is being taught should be used as a means to an end. Meaningful language can be pursued by teaching a series of requests of immediate relevance to the child. But in order to develop communication skills fully, the child must see the other person as a means to an end and as an end in itself, someone with whom to maintain social rapport.

Ensuring the Listener's Attention   The listener's attention must be ensured before questions, requests, and so on, are initiated. First, the child may be required to sign or say a simple word. As a next step, he may be required to make eye contact before addressing the listener. Similarly, the child may be asked to call the other person's name in order to get his attention. Systematic refinements can be added to simulate more normal conversations and interactions.

Autistic children are not skillful at giving instructions to others when presented with tasks such as "Tell so-and-so to . . ." or "Ask so-and-so to . . . ." The following activities may help teach those skills.

Giving Instructions to Others   Children may be taught to ask other children to carry out simple instructions such as "Ask Bobby to clap his hands." These cases may emphasize how important it is that the other child's attention is ensured.

Giving Messages to Others   A child may be asked to "Tell John that it is lunchtime." In doing so, one child learns to find proper ways of obtaining the other child's attention. Correct performance on such tasks relies heavily on verbal prompts.

Learning to Ask Questions   While it is important that labels be learned for objects and actions, it is more important that a child learn to ask for the names of things. This leads to the spontaneous generation of questions such as "What's that?" or "What's that for?" An example of such systematic programming can be found in Guess, Sailor, and Baer (1976).

Learning to Make Phone Calls   Toy phones are a helpful tool for increasing communicative skills. Simple dialogues can be acted out between student and teacher and between student and peers. Subsequently, the child can be instructed to relay particular messages.

Learning to Go Shopping   Role playing as well as supervised "life" practice increases communicative skills. It may be helpful to set up a classroom store where students buy the ingredients for lunches or for classroom cooking projects in exchange for earned tokens. Other children may be involved as volunteers.

Using Role-Play Activities   In order to increase the overall expressiveness of speech, it may be useful to have children express different feelings and emotions in the context of role-play. Children may be asked to say something in an angry or happy manner, for example. Such exercises can be expanded into mini-theater. Again, other students (i.e., peer models) should be encouraged.

Learning to Play Games   Appropriate leisure-time skills are often lacking in autistic children. Many children are unable to involve themselves in appropriate play. To increase these skills it may be useful to teach children the logistics of simple board and dice games. Initially, most children will need to be prompted through such activities; prompts can then be faded, and some appropriate speech may occur. Number concepts, shape and color discrimination, and reading skills can easily be incorporated.

Cognition

Many autistic children are unable to derive features from wholes and to abstract general rather than specific and context-tied rules. In other words, they do not see similarities. This difficulty may be the basis for problems with the generalization of newly acquired behaviors. It is as yet unclear how much teaching may contribute to cognitive gains, but the following activities may be of help.

Matching Objects on the Basis of Sameness or Similarity   It is not uncommon for autistic children to be unable to match identical objects. More problems are encountered when such children expected to match similar or functionally related objects. Similarly, they are often unable to match objects with their three dimensional representations. Those skills should be taught before attempting to attach verbal labels to the same objects.

Matching on the Basis of Isolated Properties   Objects can be matched on the basis of perceptual properties, including characteristics of color, size, transparency, and weight, among others. In addition, objects can be matched on the basis of their functional, as opposed to perceptual, relatedness. Children may learn to match according to a particular rule and, more importantly, to shift rules dependent upon instructions or context. In order to accomplish this task a child may be presented with several objects to be sorted in various ways. The child may be required to match on the basis of color or shape. Ultimately, the child may learn that objects can be sorted on the basis of a variety of ordering principles. These activities increase independent work skills because the students learn sorting tasks that require increasing amounts of time and attention. (The criteria for reinforcement may thus be systematically increased.)

Using Labels in Reference to Matching Principles   In using sorting and matching tasks, decisions must be made in terms of whether verbal instructions should be given or whether teaching should proceed in a completely nonverbal manner. If labels are to be avoided, teaching must rely on manual and imitative prompts and on differential reinforcement. If labels are to be introduced, it is often preferable to use nontransient labels that can be attached to the sorting tasks at hand. Written words or arbitrary symbols can help mark sameness or difference, as well as object properties. In some cases, this may be preferable to the use of speech or signs.

In addition to sameness and differences, notions such as conditionality can be taught. A child could be taught that he is supposed to make a matching response in condition A but not in condition B. (For further reference, see Premack, 1976a, 1976b; Taylor, 1976.)

Pattern Completion   Another activity conducive to a child's capacity to derive and apply rules is pattern completion. The student is presented with tasks that require him to analyze the patterning principle, for example, a blue and yellow alternation, a circle and square alternation, or more complex combinations. Ultimately, the student should learn to compose patterns on his own and be reinforced for alternate rather than identical ways of patterning. Initially, however, many children will have difficulties even with one simple alternation pattern.

Teaching Generalization   In terms of generalization, an autistic child may need numerous instances of a general rule if generalization is to occur. Teaching generalization skills may require that teaching be carried out in a variety of settings, including school, clinic, and home.

In order to promote generalization, it is important that teaching be conducted in a range of contexts. The presence of stimuli irrelevant to the subject matter taught may be distracting because the behaviors taught may become under the control of that stimulus. This objection applies to cues that may be presented inadvertently, as may happen when a teacher's hand is held out in a certain way while teaching.

CONCLUDING COMMENTS

The suggestions that have been discussed in this chapter should be viewed merely as a starting point for the development of innovative programs designed to teach language and language-related skills. So far, there are no comprehensive programs available to teach communication skills to autistic children. It is difficult to determine whether functional communication skills can, in fact, be taught or whether emphasis should be placed on alternative curricular areas. Successes have been recorded in teaching speech and signs, but most autistic children are limited in their ability to use communication spontaneously for social interaction. In other words, speech or signing is rarely used as a means to interact with another person. To quote Lorna Wing (1978), "We often seem to be able to teach these children to communicate, but we don't seem able to teach the joy of communication."

Some of these limitations may be attributed to the preliminary and crude nature of teaching methods. Greater success may be obtained if the focus of treatment is placed on the pragmatic aspects of communication, i.e., on the use of speech and signs as a vehicle of communication. But most importantly, one should keep in mind that all teaching efforts should incorporate the home as well as the classroom and other settings relevant to the child. Because of the pervasiveness of the problem, it is essential that joint efforts be undertaken to create an all-inclusive treatment environment and that ideas, failures, and successes be shared by all.

references

Aborn, M., and Rubenstein, H. 1956. Word-class distribution in sentences of fixed length. Language 32:666–674.

Alajouanine, T., and Lhermitte, F. 1963. Some problems concerning the agnosias, apraxias, and aphasia. *In* L. Halpern (ed.), Problems of Dynamic Neurology. Department of Nervous Disease, Rothschild Hadassah University Hospital and Hebrew University, Hadassah Medical School, Jerusalem.

Alpern, G. D. 1967. Measurement of "untestable" autistic children. J. Abnorm. Psychol. 72:478–486.

Alpert, C. 1980. Procedures for determining the optimal nonspeech mode with the autistic child. *In* R. L. Schiefelbusch (ed.), Nonspeech Language and Communication: Analysis and Intervention. University Park Press, Baltimore.

Anderson, J. E. 1957. An evaluation of various indices of linguistic development. Child Dev. 8:62–68.

Argyle, M. 1969. Social Interaction. Atherton, New York.

Argyle, M. 1972. Nonverbal communication in human social interaction. *In* R. A. Hinde (ed.), Nonverbal Communication. Cambridge University Press, London.

Anthony, A., Bogle, D., Ingram, T. T. S., and McIsaac, M. W. 1971. Edinburgh Articulation Test. Livingstone, Edinburgh and London.

Ausman, J. O., and Gaddy, M. R. 1974. Reinforcement training for echolalia: Developing a repertoire of appropriate verbal responses in an echolalic girl. Ment. Retard. 12:20–21.

Austin, J. 1962. How to Do Things with Words. Harvard University Press, Cambridge, Mass.

Baer, D. M., and Guess, D. 1971. Receptive training of adjectival inflections in mental retardates. J. Appl. Behav. Anal. 4:129–139.

Baird, R. 1972. On the role of change in imitation-comprehension-production test results. J. Verb. Learn. Verb. Behav. 11:474–477.

Baker, L., Cantwell, D. P., Rutter, M., and Bartak, L. 1976. Language and autism. *In* C. R. Ritvo (ed.), Autism. Spectrum Publications, New York.

Baldwin, J. M. 1895. Mental Development in the Child and the Race. (3rd ed., 1925.) Macmillan Publishing Co., New York.

Baltaxe, C. A. M., and Simmons, J. Q. 1975. Language in childhood psychosis: A review. J. Speech Hear. Dis. 40:439–458.

Baltaxe, C. A. M. 1977. Pragmatic deficits in the language of autistic adolescents. J. Pediatr. Psychol. 2(4):176–180.

Baltaxe, C. A. M., and Simmons, J. Q. 1977. Bedtime soliloquies and linguistic competence in autism. J. Speech Hear. Disord. 42:376–393.

Bartak, L., and Rutter, M. 1974. The use of personal pronouns by autistic children. J. Aut. Child. Schizo. 4:217–222.

Bartak, L., and Rutter, M. 1976. Differences between mentally retarded and normally intelligent autistic children. J. Aut. Child. Schizo. 6:109–120.

Bartak, L., Rutter, M., and Cox, A. 1975. A comparative study of infantile autism and specific developmental receptive language disorder: I. The children. Brit. J. Psychiatry 126:127–145.

Bartolucci, G., and Albers, R. J. 1974. Deictic categories in the language of autistic children. J. Aut. Child. Schizo. 4:131–141.

Bartolucci, G., Pierce, S., Streiner, D., and Eppel, P. T. 1976. Phonological investigation of verbal autistic and mentally retarded subjects. J. Aut. Child. Schizo. 6:303–316.

Bates, E. 1967. The emergence of symbols: Does ontogeny recapitulate phylogeny? Unpublished paper, University of Colorado, Boulder.

Bates, E. 1976. Pragmatics and socio-linguistics in child language. In D. Morehead and A. Morehead (eds.), Normal and Deficient Child Language. University Park Press, Baltimore.

Bates, E. 1979. Intentions, conventions and symbols. In E. Bates, L. Benigni, J. Bretherton, L. Camaioni, and V. Volterra (eds.), The Emergence of Symbols: Cognition and Communication in Infancy. Academic Press, New York.

Bates, E., Benigni, L., Bretherton, J., Camaioni, L., and Volterra, V. 1976. From gesture to first word: On cognitive and social prerequisites. In M. Lewis and L. Rosenbaum (eds.), Origins of Behavior: Communication and Language. John Wiley & Sons, New York.

Bates, E., Benigni, L., Bretherton, J., Camaioni, L., and Volterra, V. 1979. The Emergence of Symbols: Cognition and Communication in Infancy. Academic Press, New York.

Bates, E., Camaioni, L., and Volterra, V. 1975. The acquisition of performatives prior to speech. Merrill-Palmer Q. 21:205–226.

Bellugi, U. 1976. Two tales of sign: Iconic and abstract. Ann. N.Y. Acad. Sci. 280:514–538.

Berit-Hallahmi, B., Catford, J. C., Cooley, R. E., Dull, C. Y., Guiora, A. Z., and Raluszny, M. 1974. Grammatical gender and gender identity development: Cross-cultural and cross-lingual implications. Am. J. Orthopsychiatry 44:424–431.

Bettelheim, B. 1967. The Empty Fortress—Infantile Autism and the Birth of the Self. Free Press, New York.

Blasdell, R., and Jensen, P. 1970. Stress and word position as determinants of imitation in first-language learners. J. Speech Hear. Res. 13:193–202.

Bloom, L. 1970. Language Development: Form and Function in Emerging Grammars. The MIT Press, Cambridge, Mass.

Bloom, L., Hood, L., and Lightbown, P. 1974. Imitation in language development: If, when and why. Cog. Psychol. 6:380–420.

Bogen, J. E. 1969. The other side of the brain. II: An oppositional mind. Bull. Los Angeles Neurolog. Soc. 34:135–162.

Bonvillian, J. D., and Nelson, K. E. 1976. Sign language acquisition in a mute autistic boy. J. Speech Hear. Disord. 339–347.

Bormann, C., and Schuler, A. L. 1978. Discrimination training on the basis of a single acoustic parameter in echolalic autistic adolescents. Unpublished paper, Behavior Development and Learning Center, Camarillo State Hospital, Camarillo, Cal.

Bosch, G. 1970. Infantile Autism. Springer-Verlag, New York.

Boucher, J. 1976. Articulation in early childhood autism. J. Aut. Child. Schizo. 6:297–302.

Boyd, W. 1914. The development of a child's vocabulary. Pedagogical Seminar 21:95–124.

Braine, M. D. S. 1963. The ontogeny of English phrase structure: The first phrases. Language 39:1–14.

Bridger, W. H. 1960. Signaling systems in the development of cognitive functions. In M. A. B. Brazier (ed.), The Central Nervous System and Behavior. Josiah Macy, Jr., Foundation, New York.

Bronowski, J., and Bellugi, U. 1970. Language, name and concept. Science 168:669–673.

Broughton, J. M., and Riegel, K. F. 1977. Developmental psychology and the self. Ann. N. Y. Acad. Sci. 291:149–167.

Brown, J. W. 1975. The problem of repetition: A study of "conduction" aphasia and the "isolation" syndrome. Cortex 11:37–52.

Brown, R. 1968. The development of Wh questions in child speech. J. Verb. Learn. Verb. Behav. 7:279–290.

Brown, R. 1973a. A First Language: The Early Stages. Harvard University Press, Cambridge, Mass.

Brown, R. 1973b. Development of the first language in the human species. Am. Psychol. 28:97–106.

Brown, R., and Fraser, C. 1964. The acquisition of syntax. Monogr. Soc. Res. Child Dev. 29:43–79.

Bruner, J. 1964. The course of cognitive growth. Am. Psychol. 19:9–15.

Bruner, J. 1975a. The ontogenesis of speech acts. J. Child Lang. 2:2–19.

Bruner, J. 1975b. From communication to language—A psychological perspective. Cognition 3:255–289.

Bryson, C. Q. 1972. Short-term memory and cross-modal information processing in autistic children. J. Learn. Disab. 5:81–91.

Bryson, C. Q., and Hingtgen, J. N. 1971. Early childhood psychosis: Infantile autism, childhood schizophrenia and related disorders—An annotated bibliography, 1964–1969. National Institute of Mental Health, DHEW Publication No. (HSM) 71-9069, Rockville, Md.

Buium, N., and Stuecher, H. V. 1974. On some language parameters of autistic children. Lang. Speech 17:353–357.

Bulfinch, T. 1947. Bulfinch's mythology. Thomas Y. Crowell Co., New York.

Campbell, B., and Grieve, R. 1978. Social and attentional aspects of echolalia in highly echolalic mentally retarded persons. Am. J. Ment. Defic. 82:414–416.

Carr, E. G., Binkoff, J. A., Kologinsky, E., and Eddy, M. 1978. Acquisition of sign language by autistic children. I. Expressive labeling. J. Appl. Behav. Anal. 11:489–501.

Carr, E. G., Schreibman, L., and Lovaas, O. I. 1975. Control of echolalic speech in psychotic children. J. Abnorm. Child Psychol. 3:331–351.

Carrier, J. K. 1974a. Application of functional analysis and a nonspeech response mode to teaching language. Developing systematic procedures for training children's language. ASHA Monogr. 18.

Carrier, J. K. 1974b. Non-speech noun usage training with severely and profoundly retarded children. J. Speech Hear. Res. 17:510–518.

Carrier, J. K., and Peak, T. 1975. A Non-speech Language Initiation Program. H & H Enterprises, Lawrence, Kan.

Chase, J. B. 1972. Retrolental Fibroplasia and Autistic Symptomatology. American Foundation for the Blind, New York.

Chess, S. 1959. An Introduction to Child Psychiatry. Grune & Stratton, New York.

Chess, S., Korn, S. J., and Fernandez, P. B. 1971. Psychiatric Disorders of Children with Congenital Rubella. Brunner/Mazel, New York.

Chevalier-Skolnikoff, S. 1976. The ontogeny of primate intelligence and its implications for communicative potential: A preliminary report. Ann. N.Y. Acad. Sci. 280:173–211.

Church, J. 1961. Language and the Discovery of Reality. Random House. New York.

Church, J. 1971. The ontogeny of language. *In* H. Moltz (ed.), The Ontogeny of Vertebrate Behavior. Academic Press, New York.

Churchill, D. W. 1972. The relation of infantile autism and early childhood schizophrenia to developmental language disorders of childhood. J. Aut. Child. Schizo. 2:182–197.

Clancy, H., and McBride, G. 1969. The autistic process and its treatment. J. Child Psychol. Psychiatry 10:233–244.

Clark, E. 1977. From gesture to word: On the natural history of deixis in language acquisition. *In* J. S. Bruner and A. Garton (eds.), Human Growth and Development: Wolfson College Lectures, 1976. Oxford University Press, Oxford.

Clark, E., and Sengul, C. J. 1978. Strategies in the acquisition of deixis. J. Child Lang. 5:457–475.

Clark, R. 1974. Performing without competence. J. Child Lang. 1:1–10.

Clark, R. 1977. What's the use of imitation? J. Child Lang. 4:341–358.

Clarke, A. M., and Clarke, A. D. B. 1965. Mental Deficiency: The Changing Outlook (2nd ed.). Methuen, London.

Colby, K. M. 1973. The rationale for computer-based treatment of language difficulties in nonspeaking autistic children. J. Aut. Child. Schizo. 3:254–260.

Colby, K. M., and Parkison, C. 1977. Handedness in autistic children. J. Aut. Child. Schizo. 7:3–11.

Colby, K. M., and Smith, D. C. 1970. Computer as catalyst in the treatment of nonspeaking autistic children. Stanford Artificial Intelligence Project Memo AIM-120, Stanford University, Stanford, Cal.

Coleman, M. P. (ed.). 1976. The Autistic Syndrome. North-Holland, Amsterdam.

Condon, W. S. 1975. Multiple response to sound in dysfunctional children. J. Aut. Child. Schizo. 5:37–56.

Condon, W. S., and Sander, L. W. 1974. Synchrony demonstrated between movements of the neonate and adult speech. Child Dev. 45:456–462.

Corrigan, R. 1976. Patterns of individual communication and cognitive development. Unpublished doctoral dissertation, University of Denver, Denver.

Cox, A., Rutter, M., Newman, S., and Bartak, L. 1975. A comparative study of infantile autism and specific developmental receptive language disorder. II. Parental characteristics. Brit. J. Psychiatry 126:146–159.

Creak, M. 1963. Childhood psychosis: A review of 100 cases. Brit. J. Psychiatry 109:84–111.

Creak, M. 1972. Reflections on communication and autistic children. J. Aut. Child. Schizo. 2:1–8.

Creedon, M. P. 1973. Language development in non-verbal autistic children using a simultaneous communication system. Paper presented at a meeting of the Society for Research in Child Development, Philadelphia.

Creedon, M. P. 1975. Appropriate Behavior through Communication. Publication of the Michael Reese Medical Center, Dysfunctioning Child Center, Chicago.

Creedon, M. P. 1976. The David School: A simultaneous communication model. Paper presented at a meeting of the National Society of Autistic Children, Oak Brook, Ill.

Critchley, M. 1967. Aphasiological nomenclature and definitions. Cortex 3:3–25.

Crowder, R. G., and Morton, J. 1969. Precategorical acoustic storage (PAS). Perception and Psychophysics 5:365–373.

Crystal, D. 1969. Prosodic Systems and Intonation in English. Cambridge University Press, London.

Cunningham, M. A. 1968. A comparison of the language of psychotic and nonpsychotic children who are mentally retarded. J. Child Psychiatry 9:229–244.

Cunningham, M. A., and Dixon, C. 1961. A study of the language of an autistic child. J. Child. Psychol. Psychiatry 2:193–202.

Curcio, F. 1978. Sensorimotor functioning and communication in mute autistic children. J. Aut. Child. Schizo. 3:281–292.

Dalgleish, B. 1975. Cognitive processing and linguistic reference in autistic children. J. Aut. Child. Schizo. 5:353–361.

Day, R. S. 1973a. Digit-span memory in language-bound and stimulus-bound subjects. Haskins Laboratories Status Report on Speech Research SR-34: 127–139.

Day, R. S. 1973b. On learning "secret languages." Haskins Laboratories Status Report on Speech Research SR-34:141–150.

DeLaguna, J. A. 1963 [1927]. Speech: Its Functions and Development. Indiana University Press, Bloomington. [First published Yale University Press, New Haven, Conn., 1927].

DeMyer, M. K. 1975. The nature of the neuropsychological disability in autistic children. J. Aut. Child. Schizo. 5:109–128.

DeMyer, M. K. 1976. Motor, perceptual-motor and intellectual disabilities of autistic children. In L. Wing (ed.), Early Childhood Autism. Pergamon Press, London.

DeMyer, M. K., Barton, S., Alpern, G. D., Kimberlin, C., Allen, J., Yang, E., and Steele, R. 1974. The measured intelligence of autistic children. J. Aut. Child. Schizo. 4:42–60.

DeMyer, M. K., Barton, S., DeMyer, E., Norton, J. A., Allen, J., and Steele, R. 1973. Prognosis in autism: A follow-up study. J. Aut. Child. Schizo. 3:199–216.

Denny-Brown, D. 1963. The physiological basis of perception and speech. In L. Halpern (ed.), Problems of Dynamic Neurology. Department of Nervous Disease, Rothschild Hadassah University Hospital and Hebrew University, Hadassah Medical School, Jerusalem.

Despert, J. L. 1946. Discussion—L. Kanner, Irrelevant and metaphoric language in early infantile autism. Am. J. Psychiatry 103:242–246.

Despert, J. L. 1951. Some considerations relating to the genesis of autistic behavior in children. Am. J. Orthopsychiatry 21:335–343.

DeVilliers, J. G., and DeVilliers, P. A. 1974. Competence and performance in child language: Are children really competent to judge? J. Child Lang. 1:11–22.

DeVilliers, J. G., and Naughton, J. M. 1974. Teaching a symbol language to autistic children. J. Consult. Clin. Psychol. 42:111–117.

DeVries, R. 1970. The development of role-taking as reflected by behavior of bright, average and retarded children in a social guessing game. Child Dev. 41:759–770.

Dewey, M. 1976. The mildly handicapped young person. Proceedings from the British National Society for Autistic Children, September, York University.

Dewey, M., and Everard, M. 1974. The near-normal autistic adolescent. J. Aut. Child. Schizo. 4:348–355.

Dewey, M., and Everard, M. 1975. The autistic adult in the community. Proceedings of the National Society for Autistic Children Annual Conference, June, San Diego, Cal.

Donnellan-Walsh, A., Gossage, L. D., LaVigna, G. W., Schuler, A. L., and Traphagen, J. D. 1976. Teaching Makes a Difference. State Department of Education, Sacramento, Cal.

Dore, J. A. 1974. A pragmatic description of early language development. J. Psycholing. Res. 3:343–350.

Dore, J. 1975. Holophrases, speech acts and language universals. J. Child Lang. 2:21–41.

Dromard, J. A. 1906. A psychological and clinical study of echopraxia. J. Nerv. Ment. Dis. 33:546–547.

Edelheit, H. 1971. The relationship of language development to problem-solving ability. J. Am. Psychoanal. Assoc. 19:145–155.

Eimas, P. D. 1969. Multiple-cue discrimination learning in children. Psycholog. Rec. 19:412–424.

Eisenberg, L. 1956. The autistic child in adolescence. Am. J. Psychiatry 112:607–612.

Eisenberg, L. 1957. The course of childhood schizophrenia. Am. Med. Assoc. Arch. Neurol. Psychiatry 78:69–83.

Elliott, D. E., and Needleman, R. M. 1976. The syndrome of hyperlexia. Brain Lang. 3:339–349.

Epstein, S. 1973. The self-concept revisited. Am. Psychol. 28:404–416.

Erikson, E. H. 1964. Insight and Responsibility. W. W. Norton & Co., New York.

Ervin-Tripp, S. 1964. Imitation and structural change in children's language. In E. H. Lenneberg (ed.), New Directions in the Study of Language, pp. 163–189. The MIT Press, Cambridge, Mass.

Ervin-Tripp, S. 1970. Discourse agreement: How children answer questions. In F. R. Hayes (ed.), Cognition and the Development of Language. John Wiley & Sons, New York.

Fay, W. H. 1966. Childhood echolalia in delayed, psychotic and neuropathologic speech patterns. Folia Phoniatrica 18:68–71.

Fay, W. H. 1967a. Childhood echolalia: A group study of late abatement. Folia Phoniatrica 19:297–306.

Fay, W. H. 1967b. Mitigated echolalia of children. J. Speech Hear. Res. 10:305–310.

Fay, W. H. 1969. On the basis of autistic echolalia. J. Commun. Disord. 2:38–47.

Fay, W. H. 1971. On normal and autistic pronouns. J. Speech Hear. Disord. 36:242–249.

Fay, W. H. 1972. The challenge of personal pronouns. J. Learn. Disabil. 5:299–305.

Fay, W. H. 1973. On the echolalia of the blind and of the autistic child. J. Speech Hear. Disord. 38:478–489.

Fay, W. H. 1975. Occurrence of children's echoic responses according to inter-locutory question types. J. Speech Hear. Res. 18:336–345.

Fay, W. H., and Anderson, D. E. 1979. Echoic responses to the PPVT: A developmental study. Paper presented at the annual meeting of the American Speech and Hearing Association, November, Chicago.

Fay, W. H., and Butler, B. V. 1968. Echolalia IQ, and the developmental dichotomy of speech and language systems. J. Speech Hear. Res. 11:365–371.

Fay, W. H., and Butler, B. V. 1971. Echo-reaction as an approach to semantic resolution. J. Speech Hear. Res. 14:645–651.

Fay, W. H., and Coleman, R. O. 1977. A human sound transducer/reproducer: Temporal capabilities of a profoundly echolalic child. Brain Lang. 4:396–402.

Fay, W. H., and Hatch, V. 1965. Symptomatic echopraxia. Am. J. Occupat. Ther. 19:189–191.

Feldman, C. F. 1977. Two functions of language. Harv. Educ. Rev. 47:282–293.

Fernald, C. D. 1972. Control of grammar in imitation, comprehension and production: Problems of replication. J. Verb. Learn. Verb. Behav. 11:606–613.

Fish, B., Shapiro, T., and Campbell, M. 1966. Long-term prognosis and the response of schizophrenic children to drug therapy: A controlled study of trifluoperazine. Am. J. Psychiatry 123:32–39.

Flavell, J., Botkin, P., Fry, C., Wright, J., and Jarvis, P. 1968. The Development of Role Taking and Communication Skills in Children. John Wiley & Sons, New York.

Fletcher, E. C. 1976. The intonation patterns of autistic children compared to that of normal children. Paper presented at the annual meeting of the American Speech and Hearing Association, November, Houston.

Fouts, K. S. 1976. Discussion paper: Comparison of sign language projects and implications for language origins. Ann. N.Y. Acad. Sci. 280:584–591.

Fraiberg, S. 1971. Intervention in infancy: A program for blind infants. J. Child Psychiatry 10:381–405.

Fraser, C., Bellugi, U., and Brown, R. 1963. Control of grammar in imitation, comprehension and production. J. Verb. Learn. Verb. Behav. 2:121–135.

Freeman, B. J., Ritvo, E., and Miller, R. 1975. An operant procedure to teach an echolalic, autistic child to answer questions appropriately. J. Aut. Child. Schizo. 5:169–176.

Freud, S. 1965. New Introductory Lectures on Psychoanalysis. (Trans. and ed. by James Strachey.) W. W. Norton & Co., New York.

Frings, H., and Frings, M. 1964. Animal Communication. Blaisdell, New York.

Frith, U. 1969. Emphasis and meaning in recall in normal and autistic children. Lang. Speech 12:29–38.

Frith, U. 1970. Studies in pattern detection. II. Reproduction and production of color sequences. J. Exp. Child Psychol. 10:120–135.

Frith, U. 1971. Spontaneous patterns produced by autistic, normal and subnormal children. In M. Rutter (ed.), Infantile Autism: Concepts, Characteristics and Treatment. Churchill Livingstone, Edinburgh and London.

Fröschels, E. 1932. Psychological Elements in Speech. Expression, Boston.

Furneaux B. 1966. The autistic child. Brit. J. Disord. Commun. 1:85–90.

Fulwiler, R. L., and Fouts, R. S. 1976. Acquisition of American Sign Language by a non-communicating autistic child. J. Aut. Child. Schizo. 6:43–51.

Gardner, R. A., and Gardner, B. T. 1969. Teaching sign language to a chimpanzee. Science 165:644–672.

Gardner, R. A., and Gardner, B. T. 1975. Early signs of language in child and chimpanzee. Science 187:752–753.

Geschwind, N. 1965. Disconnexion syndromes in animals and man (Part 2). Brain 88:585–644.

Geschwind, N., Quadfasel, F. A., and Segarra, J. M. 1968. Isolation of the speech area. Neuropsychologia 6:327–340.

Glucksberg, S., and Danks, J. H. 1975. Experimental Psycholinguistics: An Introduction. John Wiley & Sons, New York.

Gold, M. W. 1973. Research on the vocational habilitation of the retarded: The present, the future. In M. R. Ellis (ed.), International Review of Research in Mental Retardation. Vol. 6. Academic Press, New York.

Goldfarb, W. 1961. Childhood Schizophrenia. Harvard University Press, Cambridge, Mass.

Goldfarb, W., Braunstein, P., and Lorge, I. 1956. A study of speech patterns in a group of schizophrenic children. Am. J. Orthopsychiatry 26:544–555.

Goldfarb, W., Goldfarb, N. Braunstein, P., and Scholl, H. 1972. Speech and language faults of schizophrenic children. J. Aut. Child. Schizo. 2:219–233.

Goldstein, K. 1959. Abnormal mental conditions in infancy. J. Nerv. Ment. Dis. 128:538–557.

Goodenough, F. L. 1938. The use of pronouns by young children: A note on the development of self-awareness. J. Gen. Psychol. 52:333–346.

Gray, B. B., and Ryan, B. P. 1974. A Language Program for the Nonlanguage Child. Research Press, Champaign, Ill.

Greenfield, P., and Smith, J. 1976. The Structure of Communication in Early Language Development. Academic Press, New York.

Griffith, R., and Ritvo, E. 1967. Echolalia: Concerning the dynamics of the syndrome. J. Am. Acad. Child Psychiatry 6:184–193.

Guess, D., Keogh, W., and Sailor, W. 1978. Generalization of speech and language behavior: Measurement and training tactics. In R. L. Schiefelbusch (ed.), Bases of Language Intervention. University Park Press, Baltimore.

Guess, D., Sailor, W., and Baer, D. M. 1976. Language development programs for severely handicapped children. In N. Haring and L. Brown (eds.), Teaching the Severely Handicapped. Vol. I. Grune & Stratton, New York.

Guess, D., Sailor, W., Keogh, W. J., and Baer, D. M. 1975. Language development programs for severely handicapped children. In N. Haring, N. E. Sontag, and L. Brown (eds.), Teaching Severely and Profoundly Handicapped Children. Grune & Stratton, New York.

Guess, D., Sailor, W., Rutherford, G., and Baer, D. M. 1968. An experimental analysis of linguistic development: The productive use of the plural phoneme. J. Appl. Behav. Anal. 1:297–306.

Hale, G. A., and Morgan, J. S. 1973. Developmental trends in children's compound selection. J. Exp. Child Psychol. 15:302–314.

Halliday, M. A. K. 1973. Explorations in the Functions of Language. Edward Arnold, London.

Halliday, M. A. K. 1975. Learning How to Mean: Explorations in the Development of Language. Edward Arnold, London.

Hargrave, E., and Swisher, L. 1975. Modifying the verbal expression of a child with autistic behaviors. J. Aut. Child. Schizo. 5:147–154.

Harris, D., and Vanderheiden, G. 1980. Augmentative communication techniques for nonvocal severely physically handicapped children and adults. In R. L. Schiefelbusch (ed.), Nonspeech Language and Communication: Analysis and Intervention. University Park Press, Baltimore.

Hartung, J. 1970. A review of functional speech in autistic children. J. Speech Hear. Disord. 35:203–217.

Hayes, K. B., and Hayes, C. 1952. Imitation in a home raised chimpanzee. J. Comp. Physiolog. Psychol. 45:405–459.

Hebb, D. O. 1949. The Organization of Behavior. John Wiley & Sons, New York.

Hebb, D. O., Lambert, W. E., and Tucker, G. R. 1971. Language, thought and experience. Mod. Lang. J. 55:212–222.

Hermelin, B. 1971. Rules and language. In M. Rutter (ed.), Infantile Autism: Concepts, Characteristics and Treatment. Churchill Livingstone, London.

Hermelin, B. 1976. Coding and the sense modalities. *In* L. Wing (ed.), Early Childhood Autism. Pergamon Press, London.

Hermelin, B., and Frith, U. 1971. Psychological studies of childhood autism: Can autistic children make sense of what they see and hear? J. Spec. Educ. 5:107–117.

Hermelin, B., and O'Connor, N. 1968. Measures of the occipital alpha rhythm in normal, subnormal and autistic children. Brit. J. Psychiatry 114:603–610.

Hermelin, B., and O'Connor, N. 1970. Psychological Experiments with Autistic Children. Pergamon, London.

Hewett, F. M. 1965. Teaching speech to an autistic child through operant conditioning. Am. J. Orthopsychiatry 35:927–936.

Hockett, C. F. 1963. The problem of universals in language. *In* J. H. Greenberg (ed.), Universals of Language. The MIT Press, Cambridge, Mass.

Hollis, J. H., and Carrier, J. K. 1975. Research implications for communicative deficiencies. Except. Child. 41:405–412.

Hollis, J. H., and Carrier, J. K. 1978. Intervention strategies for nonspeech children. *In* R. L. Schiefelbusch (ed.), Language Intervention Strategies. University Park Press, Baltimore.

Hollis, J. H., and Schiefelbusch, R. L. 1979. A general system for language analysis. *In* R. L. Schiefelbusch and J. H. Hollis (eds.), Language Intervention from Ape to Child. University Park Press, Baltimore.

Huttenlocher, P., and Huttenlocher, J. 1973. A study of children with hyperlexia. Neurology 23:1107–1116.

Ingram, D. 1971. Toward a theory of person deixis. Papers in Linguistics (Linguistic Research, Inc.) 4:37–53.

Jakobson, R. 1968. Child Language, Aphasia and Phonological Universals. Mouton, The Hague.

Jeffrey, W. E., and Cohen, L. B. 1965. Response tendencies of children in a two-choice situation. J. Exp.. Psychol. 2:248–259.

Jesperson, O. 1964. Language: Its Nature, Development and Origin. W. W. Norton & Co., New York.

Jeucksberg, S., and Danks, J. H. 1975. Experimental Psycholinguistics: An Introduction. John Wiley & Sons, New York.

Johnston, M. K. 1968. Echolalia and automatism in speech: A case report. *In* H. N. Sloane, Jr., and B. D. MacAulay (eds.), Operant Procedures in Remedial Speech and Language Training. Houghton Miffin Co., Boston.

Kanner, L. 1943. Autistic disturbances of affective contact. Nerv. Child 2:217–250.

Kanner, L. 1946. Irrelevant and metaphorical language in early infantile autism. Am. J. Psychiatry 103:242–246.

Kanner, L. 1948. Child Psychiatry (2nd ed.), Charles C Thomas, Springfield, Ill.

Kanner, L. 1949. Problems of nosology and psychodynamics of early infantile autism. Am. J. Orthopsychiatry 19:416–426.

Kanner, L. 1951. The conception of wholes and parts in early infantile autism. Am. J. Psychiatry 108:23–26.

Kanner, L. 1958. The specificity of early infantile autism. Zeitschrift fur Kinderpsychiatrie, 25:108–113.

Kanner, L. 1971. Follow-up study of eleven autistic children originally reported in 1943. J. Aut. Child. Schizo. 1:119–145.

Keeler, W. R. 1958. Autistic patterns and defective communication in blind children with retrolental fibroplasia. *In* P. H. Hoch and J. Zubin (eds.), Psychopathology of Communication. Grune & Stratton, New York.

Keenan, E., and Schieffelin, B. T. 1976. Topic as a discourse notion: A study of topic in the conversation of children and adults. *In* C. Li (ed.), Subject and Topic. Academic Press, New York.

Keenan, E. 1974. Conversational competence in children. J. Child Lang. 1:163–183.

Kimura, D., and Archibald, Y. 1974. Motor functions of the left hemisphere. Brain 97:337–351.

Klima, E. S. 1975. Sound and its absence in the linguistic symbol. *In* J. Kavanaugh and J. Cutting (eds.), The Role of Speech in Language. The MIT Press, Cambridge, Mass.

Koegel, R. L., and Covert, A. 1972. The relationship of self-stimulation to learning in autistic children. J. Appl. Behav. Anal. 5:381–387.

Koegel, R. L., and Rincover, A. 1977. Research on the difference between generalization and maintenance in extra-therapy responding. J. Appl. Behav. Anal. 10:1–12.

Koegel, R. L., and Schreibman, L. 1976. Identification of consistent responding to auditory stimuli by a functionally "deaf" autistic child. J. Aut. Child. Schizo. 6:147–156.

Koegel, R. L., and Schreibman, L. 1977. Teaching autistic children to respond to simultaneous multiple cues. J. Exp. Child Psychol. 24:299–311.

Koegel, R. L., and Wilhelm, H. 1973. Selective responding to multiple visual cues by autistic children. J. Exp. Child Psychol. 15:442–454.

Konstantareas, M. M., and Leibovitz, S. F. 1977. Auditory-visual vs. visual communication training with autistic children. Paper presented at the annual meeting of the American Speech and Hearing Association, November, Chicago.

Kozloff, M. A. 1974. Educating Children with Learning and Behavior Problems. John Wiley & Sons, New York.

Krauss, R. M., and Glucksberg, S. 1969. The development of communication/competence as a function of age. Child Dev. 40:255–266.

Krauss, R. M., and Glucksberg, S. 1977. Social and nonsocial speech. Sci. Am. 236(2):100–105.

Lancaster, J. B. 1968. Primate communication systems and the emergence of human language. *In* P. C. Jay (ed.), Primates: Studies in Adaptation and Vocabulary. Holt, Rinehart & Winston, New York.

Langer, S. K. 1942. Philosophy in a New Key. Harvard University Press, Cambridge, Mass.

Lassman, F. M., Fisch, R. O., Vetter, D. K., and LaBenz, E. S. 1980. Early Correlates of Speech, Language, and Hearing. PSG Publishing Co., Littleton, Mass.

LaVigna, G. W. 1977. Communication training in mute, autistic adolescents using the written word. J. Aut. Child. Schizo. 7:135–149.

LaVigna, G. W. The behavioral treatment of autism. *In* P. O. Liberman (ed.), Psychiatric Clinics Symposium on Behavior Therapy. W. B. Saunders, Philadelphia. In press.

LaVigna, J. W., and Donnellan-Walsh, A. 1976. Alternatives to the use of punishment in the control of undesired behavior. Paper presented at the 10th Annual Meeting of the Association for the Advancement of Behavior Therapy, December, New York.

Lebrun, Y., Rubio, S., Jongen, E., and Demol, O. 1971. On echolalia, echo-answer and contamination. Acta Neurol. Belgium 71:301–308.

Leland, L. Bormann, G., Schuler, A., and LaVigna, G. 1977. Stimulus overselectivity as a function of repeated exposure to the training stimuli. Unpublished paper, Behavior Development and Learning Center, Camarillo State Hospital, Camarillo, Cal.

Leonard, L. B. 1976. Meaning in Child Language. Grune & Stratton, New York.

Leonard, L. B. 1978. Cognitive factors in early linguistic development. In R. L. Schiefelbusch (ed.), Bases of Language Intervention. University Park Press, Baltimore.

Leonard, L. B., Bolders, J. G., and Miller, J. A. 1976. An examination of the semantic relations reflected in the language use of normal and language disordered children. J. Speech Hear. Res. 19:371–392.

Leopold, W. F. 1949/1970. Speech Development of a Bilingual Child. Vol. III. AMS Press, New York.

Levy-Agresti, J., and Sperry, R. W. 1968. Differential perceptual capacities in major and minor hemispheres. Proceed. Nat. Acad. Sci. 61:1151.

Lieberman, P. 1975. On the origins of language. Macmillan Publishing Co., New York.

Linden, E. 1974. Apes, Men, and Language. Penguin Books, New York.

Lockyer, L., and Rutter, M. A. 1969. A five to fifteen year follow-up study of infantile psychosis. III. Psychological aspects. Brit. J. Psychiatry 115:865–882.

Lockyer, L., and Rutter, M. A. 1970. A five to fifteen year follow-up study of infantile psychosis. IV. Patterns of cognitive ability. Brit. J. Soc. Clin. Psychol. 9:152–163.

Lotter, V. 1967. Epidemiology of autistic conditions in young children. II. Some characteristics of parents and children. Soc. Psychiatry 1:163–181.

Lovaas, O. I. 1977. The Autistic Child: Language Development through Behavior Modification. Irvington, New York.

Lovaas, O. I., Berberich, J. B., Perloff, B. F., and Schaeffer, B. 1966. Acquisition of imitative speech by schizophrenic children. Science 151:705–707.

Lovaas, O. I., Schreibman, J. P., Koegel, R. L., and Rehm, R. 1971. Selective responding by autistic children to multiple sensory input. J. Abnorm. Psychol. 71:211–222.

Lovaas, O. I., Simmons, J. Q., Koegel, R. L., and Stevens-Long, J. 1973. Some generalization and follow-up measures on autistic children in behavior therapy. J. Appl. Behav. Anal. 6:131–166.

Lovaas, O. I., Varni, J. W., Koegel, R. L., and Lorsch, N. 1977. Some observations on the nonextinguishability of children's speech. Child Dev. 48:1121–1127.

Lovell, K., and Dixon, E. M. 1967. The growth of the control of grammar in imitation, comprehension and production. J. Child Psychol. Psychiatry 8:31–39.

Lowell, M. 1976. Audiology assessment. In E. R. Ritvo (ed.), Autism. Spectrum Publications, New York.

Luria, A. R. 1966. Higher Cortical Functions in Man. Basic Books, New York.

Lutzker, J. R., and Sherman, J. A. 1974. Producing generative sentence usage by imitation and reinforcement procedures. J. Appl. Behav. Anal. 7:447–460.

Lyons, J. 1972. Human language. In R. A. Hinde (ed.), Nonverbal Communication. Cambridge University Press, London.

McCarthy, D. 1954. Language development in children. In L. Carmicheal (ed.), Manual of Child Psychology. John Wiley & Sons, New York.

MacCorquadale, K. 1970. On Chomsky's review of Skinner's *Verbal Behavior*. J. Exp. Anal. Behav. 13:83–99.

MacKay, D. M. 1966. Cerebral organization and the conscious control of action. *In* J. E. Eccles (ed.), Brain and Conscious Experience. Springer-Verlag, New York.

MacKay, D. M. 1969. Information, Mechanism and Meaning. The MIT Press, Cambridge, Mass.

MacKay, D. M. 1972. Formal analysis of communicative processes. *In* R. A. Hinde (ed.), Non-verbal Communication. Cambridge University Press, London.

McLean, L. P., and McLean, J. E. 1974. A language training program for non-verbal autistic children. J. Speech Hear. Disord. 39:186–194.

Mahler, M. S., Furer, M., and Settlage, C. 1959. Severe emotional disturbances in childhood: Psychoses. *In* S. Arieti (ed.), American Handbook of Psychiatry. Basic Books, New York.

Malinowski, B. 1949. The problem of meaning in primitive languages. *In* C. K. Ogden and I. A. Richards (eds.), The Meaning of Meaning. Harcourt, Brace, New York.

Maratsos, M. P. 1973a. The effects of stress on the understanding of pronominal co-reference in children. J. Psycholing. Res. 2:1–8.

Maratsos, M. P. 1973b. Nonegocentric communication abilities in preschool children. Child Dev. 44:697–700.

Marler, P. 1970. Birdsong and speech development: Could there be parallels? Am. Sci. 58:669–673.

Marshall, N. R., and Hegrenes, J. R. 1970. Programmed communication therapy for autistic mentally retarded children. J. Speech Hear. Dis. 35:70–83.

Martin, J. G. 1972. Rhythmic (hierarchical) versus serial structure in speech and other behavior. Psycholog. Rev. 79:487–509.

Massie, H. M. 1977. The early natural history of childhood psychosis. J. Am. Acad. Child Psychiatry 16:29–45.

Massie, H. M. 1978. Blind ratings of mother-infant interaction in home-movies of prepsychotic and normal infants. Am. J. Psychiatry 57:1371–1374.

Meneegan, C., and Dreiguss, F. 1972. Hyperlexia. Neurology 22:1105–1111.

Menyuk, P. 1969. Sentences Children Use. The MIT Press, Cambridge, Mass.

Menyuk, P., and Looney, P. L. 1972. A problem of language disorder: Length versus structure. J. Speech Hear. Res. 15:264–279.

Menzel, E. W. 1977. Communication of object-locations in a group of young chimpanzees. *In* P. Hamburg and J. Goodall (eds.), Behavior of the Great Apes. Holt, Rinehart & Winston, New York.

Menzel, E. W., and Johnson, M. K. 1976. Communication and cognitive organization in humans and other animals. Ann. N.Y. Acad. Sci. (Origins of Speech and Language) 280:131–142.

Miller, A., and Miller, E. E. 1973. Cognitive developmental training with elevated boards and sign language. J. Aut. Child. Schizo. 3:65–85.

Mittler, P. 1966. The psychological assessment of autistic children. *In* J. Wing (ed.), Early Childhood Autism. Pergamon Press, London.

Moerk, E. L. 1977. Processes and products of imitation: Additional evidence that imitation is progressive. J. Psycholing. Res. 6:187–202.

Morris, D. 1977. Manwatching: A Field Guide to Human Behavior. Harvey M. Abrams, New York.

Moses, P. J. 1954. The Voice of Neurosis. Grune & Stratton, New York.

Myklebust, H. R. 1957. Babbling and echolalia in language theory. J. Speech Hear. Disord. 22:356–360.

Nakanishi, Y., and Owada, K. 1973. Echoic utterances of children between the ages of one and three years. J. Verb. Learn. Verb. Behav. 12:658–665.

Neisser, V. 1967. Cognitive Psychology. Appleton-Century-Crofts, New York.

Nelson, K. 1973. Structure and strategy in learning to talk. Monogr. Soc. Res. Child Dev. 38(1–2 Serial No. 149).

Nelson, K. 1975. Individual differences in early semantic and syntactic development. Ann. N.Y. Acad. Sci. 263:132–139.

Nelson, K. Early Speech in Its Communicative Context. Yale University Press, New Haven, Conn. In press.

Newport, E. 1976. Motherese: The speech of mothers to young children. In N. J. Castellan, D. B. Pisoni, and G. R. Potts (eds.), Cognitive Theory: Vol. II. Lawrence Earlbaum Associates, Hillsdale, N.J.

Newsom, C. D., Carr, E. G., and Lovaas, O. I. 1977. The experimental analysis and modification of autistic behavior. In R. S. Davidson (ed.), Modification of Behavior Pathology. Gardner Press, New York.

Ney, P. G., Palvesky, A. E., and Markley, J. 1971. Relative effectiveness of operant conditioning and play therapy in childhood schizophrenia. J. Aut. Child. Schizo. 1:337–343.

Nurss, J. E., and Day, D. E. 1971. Imitation, comprehension, and production of grammatical structures. J. Verb. Learn. Verb. Behav. 10:68–74.

O'Connor, N. 1976. The psychopathology of cognitive deficit. Brit. J. Psychiatry 128:36–43.

O'Gorman, J. G. 1970. The Nature of Childhood Autism (3rd ed.). Appleton-Century-Crofts, New York.

Orne, M. T. 1973. Communication by the total experimental situation: Why it is important, how it is evaluated and its significance for the ecological validity of findings. In P. Pliner, L. Kramer, and T. Alloway (eds.), Communication and Affect. Academic Press, New York.

Ornitz, E. M. 1973. Childhood autism—A review of clinical and experimental literature. Cal. Med. 118:21–47.

Ornitz, E. M., Guthrie, D., and Farley, A. H. 1977. The early development of autistic children. J. Aut. Child. Schizo. 7:207–229.

Ornitz, E. M., and Ritvo, E. R. 1976. The syndrome of autism: A critical review. Am. J. Psychiatry 133:609–620.

Palyo, W. J., Cooke, T. P., Schuler, A. L., and Apolloni, T. 1979. Modifying echolalic speech in preschool children: Training and generalization. Am. J. Mental Defic. 83:480–489.

Panagos, J. M. 1975. Probing comprehension of wh questions in the echolalic child. J. S. Afr. Speech Hear. Assoc. 22:23–29.

Petretic, P. A., and Tweney, R. D. 1977. Does comprehension precede production? The development of children's responses to telegraphic sentences of varying grammatical adequacy. J. Child Lang. 4:201–209.

Philips, G. M., and Dyer, C. 1977. Late onset echolalia in autism and allied disorders. Brit. J. Disord. Commun. 12:47–59.

Piaget, J. 1926. The Language and Thought of the Child (1955 ed.). Meridian Books, New York.

Pick, A. 1924. On the pathology of echographia. Brain 47:417–429.

Pike, K. L. 1967. Language in Relation to a Unitheory of Human Behavior (2nd ed.). Mouton, The Hague.

Porshnev, B. F. 1964. Rechepadrazhenie (ekholaliya) kak stupen formiro vtoroi signal noi sistemy [Speech imitation—echolalia—as stage in the development of the second signal system]. Voprosy Psikhologii 10:11–19. [Translated in Soviet Psychol. Psychiatry, 1965, 3:3–9.]

Premack, A. J., and Premack, D. 1972. Teaching language to an ape. Sci. Am. 227:92–99.

Premack, D. 1970. A functional analysis of language. J. Anal. Exp. Behav. 14:107–125.

Premack, D. 1971. Language in chimpanzees. Science 172:808–822.

Premack, D. 1976a. Language and intelligence in ape and man. Am. Sci. 64:674.

Premack, D. 1976b. Language in Apes and Men. Lawrence Erlbaum Associates, Hillsday, N.J.

Premack, D., and Premack, A. J. 1974. Teaching visual language to apes and language-deficient persons. In R. L. Schiefelbusch and L. L. Lloyd (eds.), Language Perspectives—Acquisition, Retardation, and Intervention, pp. 347–376. University Park Press, Baltimore.

Prizant, B. M., and Duchan, Y. F. 1978. Pragmatic and communicative acts of autistic children. Short course presented at the New York State Speech and Hearing Association meeting, April, New York.

Pronovost, W. 1961. The speech behavior and language communication of autistic children. J. Chron. Dis. 13:228–233.

Pronovost, W., Wakstein, M. P., and Wakstein, D. J. 1966. A longitudinal study of speech behavior and language comprehension of fourteen children diagnosed atypical or autistic. Expect. Child 33:19–26.

Prutting, C. A., and Connolly, J. E. 1976. Imitation: A closer look. J. Speech Hear. Disord. 41:412–422.

Ramer, A. L. H. 1976. The function of imitation in child language. J. Speech Hear. Res. 19:700–717.

Ratusnik, C. M., and Ratusnik, D. L. 1974. A comprehensive communication approach for a ten year old nonverbal child. Am. J. Orthopsychiatry 44:396–403.

Rees, N. S. 1972. The role of babbling in the child's acquisition of language. Brit. J. Disord. Commun. 7:17–23.

Rees, N. S. 1975. Imitation and language development: Issues and clinical implications. J. Speech Hear. Disord. 40:339–350.

Rees, N. S. 1978. Pragmatics of language: Applications to normal and disordered language development. In R. L. Schiefelbusch (ed.), Bases of Language Intervention, pp. 191–268. University Park Press, Baltimore.

Reynolds, B. S., Newsom, C. D., and Lovaas, O. I. 1974. Auditory overselectivity in autistic children. J. Abnorm. Child Psychol. 2:153–163.

Ricks, D. M. 1975a. The beginning of verbal communication in normal and autistic children. M.D. thesis, London, 1972. Reported in D. M. Ricks and L. Wing, Language, communication and the use of symbols in normal and autistic children. J. Aut. Child. Schizo. 5:191–220.

Ricks, D. M. 1975b. Vocal communication in pre-verbal normal and autistic children. In N. O'Connor (ed.), Language, Cognitive Deficits and Retardation. Butterworths, London.

Ricks, D. M., and Wing, L. 1975. Language, communication and the use of symbols in normal and autistic children. J. Aut. Child. Schizo. 5:191–220. [Also in Wing, L. (ed.). 1976. Early Childhood Autism (2nd ed.). Pergamon Press, Oxford.]

Rimland, B. 1964. Infantile Autism. Appleton-Century-Crofts, New York.

Rimland, B. 1971. The differentiation of childhood psychoses: An analysis of checklists for 2,218 psychotic children. J. Aut. Child. Schizo. 1:161–174.

Rincover, A., and Koegel, R. L. 1975. Setting generality and stimulus control in autistic children. J. Appl. Behav. Anal. 8:235–246.

Rincover, A., and Koegel, R. L. 1977. Research on the education of autistic children. Recent advances and future directions. In B. Lakey and A. Kazdin (eds.), Advances in Child Clinical Psychology. Plenum, New York.

Risley, T., and Wolf, M. 1967. Establishing functional speech in echolalic children. Behav. Res. Ther. 5:73–88. [Also in Sloane, H. N., and MacAuley, B. D. (eds.). 1968. Operant Procedures in Remedial Speech and Language Training. Houghton Mifflin Co., Boston.]

Ritvo, E. R., and Freeman, B. J. 1977 (April). Proposed definition of the syndrome of autism by the National Society for Autistic Children and the American Psychiatric Association DSM III Committee.

Rodique, E. 1957. The analysis of a three-year-old mute schizophrenic. In M. Klein, P. Heimann, and R. E. Money-Kyrle (eds.), New Directions in Psycho-analysis. Basic Books, New York.

Ross, A. O. 1976. Psychological Aspects of Learning Disabilities and Reading Disorders. McGraw-Hill Book Co., New York.

Ruder, K. F. 1978. Planning and programming for language intervention. In R. L. Schiefelbusch (ed.), Bases of Language Intervention. University Park Press, Baltimore.

Rumbaugh, D. 1977. Language Learning by a Chimpanzee: The LANA Project. Academic Press, New York.

Rumbaugh, D. M., and Gill, T. V. 1976. The mastery of language-type skills by the chimpanzee. Ann. N.Y. Acad. Sci. 280:563–578.

Rumbaugh, D. M., Gill, T. V., and VonGlaserfeld, E. C. 1973. Reading and sentence completion by a chimpanzee. Science 182:731–733.

Rumbaugh, D. M., Savage-Rumbaugh, E. S., Gill, T. V., and Warner, H. 1979. The chimpanzee as an animal model in language research. In R. L. Schiefelbusch and J. H. Hollis (eds.), Language Intervention from Ape to Child. University Park Press, Baltimore.

Ruttenberg, B. A., and Wolf, E. G. 1967. Evaluating the communication of the autistic child. J. Speech Hear. Disord. 32:314–324.

Rutter, M. 1968. Concepts of autism. J. Child Psychol. Psychiatry 9:1–25.

Rutter, M. 1974. The development of infantile autism. Psycholog. Med. 4:147–163.

Rutter, M., and Bartak, L. 1971. Causes of infantile autism. J. Aut. Child. Schizo. 1:20–32.

Rutter, M., Bartak, L., and Newman, S. 1971. Autism: A central disorder of cognition and language. In M. Rutter (ed.), Infantile Autism: Concept, Characteristics and Treatment. Churchill-Livingstone, Edinburgh.

Rutter, M., Greenfeld, D., and Lockyer, L. 1967. A five to fifteen year follow-up study of infantile psychosis. II. Social and behavioral outcome. Brit. J. Psychiatry 113:1169–1182.

Rutter, M., and Lockyer, L. 1967. A five to fifteen year follow-up study of infantile psychosis. I. Description of sample. Brit. J. Psychiatry 113:1169–1182.

Ryan, J. 1977. Early language development: Towards a communicational analysis. In P. M. Richards (ed.), The Integration of a Child into a Social World. Cambridge University Press, Cambridge.

Sachs, J., and Truswell, L. 1978. Comprehension of two-word instructions by children in the one-word stage. J. Child Lang. 5:17–24.

Sapir, E. 1921. Language. Harcourt, Brace and World, New York.

Saunders, R. R., and Sailor, W. 1979. A comparison of three strategies of reinforcement on two-choice learning problems with severely retarded children. AAESPH Rev. 4:323–334.

Saxman, J. H., and Fay, W. H. 1970. Latency of echoic verbal responses by three-year-old children. J. Speech Hear. Res. 13:232–238.

Scaife, M., and Bruner, J. S. 1975. The capacity for joint visual attention in the infant. Nature 253(No. 5489):265–266.

Schaeffer, B., Kollinzas, G., Musil, A., and MacDowell, P. 1975. Signed speech: A new treatment for autism. Unpublished paper, University of Oregon, Eugene.

Scheerer, J. H., Rothmann, E., and Goldstein, K. 1945. A case of "Idiot Savant": An experimental study of personality organization. Psycholog. Monogr. 58(4):1–63.

Schell, R. E., Stark, J., and Giddon, J. J. 1967. Development of language behavior in an autistic child. J. Speech Hear. Disord.

Schiefelbusch, R. L. (ed.), 1980. Nonspeech Language and Communication: Analysis and Intervention. University Park Press, Baltimore.

Schiefelbusch, R. L., and Hollis, J. H. (eds.). 1979. Language Intervention from Ape to Child. University Park Press, Baltimore.

Schneider, D. E. 1938. The clinical syndromes of echolalia, echopraxia, grasping and sucking: Their significance in the disorganization of the personality. J. Nerv. Ment. Dis. 88:18–35, 200–216.

Schopler, E., Boehm, S., and Kinsbourne, M. 1971. Effects of treatment structure on development in autistic children. Arch. Gen. Psychiatry 24:415.

Schover, L. R., and Newsom, C. D. 1976. Overselectivity, developmental level and overtraining in autistic and normal children. J. Abnorm. Child Psychol. 4:289–297.

Schreibman, L. 1975. Effects of within-stimulus and extra-stimulus prompting on discrimination learning in autistic children. J. Appl. Behav. Anal. 8:91–112.

Schreibman, L., Koegel, R. L. and Craig, M. S. 1977. Reducing stimulus overselectivity in autistic children. J. Abnorm. Child Psychol. 5:425–436.

Schreibman, L., and Lovaas, O. I. 1973. Over-selective responses to social stimuli by autistic children. J. Abnorm. Child Psychol. 1:152–168.

Schuler, A. L. 1976. Speech and Language in Autism: Characteristics and treatment. Miniseminar at the annual meeting of the American Speech and Hearing Association, November, Houston.

Schuler, A. L. 1979a. Echolalia: Issues and clinical applications. J. Speech Hear. Disord. 44:411–434.

Schuler, A. L. 1979b. Communicative, conceptual and representational abilities in a mute autistic adolescent: A serial versus a simultaneous mode of processing. Unpublished doctoral dissertation, University of California Santa Barbara.

Schuler, A. L., and Bormann, C. 1977. Tactile-visual matching abilities in verbal and non-verbal autistic subjects. Unpublished paper, Behavior Development and Learning Center, Camarillo State Hospital, Camarillo, Cal.

Schuler, A. L., and Bormann, C. 1978. The non-verbal assessment of conceptual abilities in autistic adolescents. Unpublished paper, Behavior Development and Learning Center, Camarillo State Hospital, Camarillo, Cal.

Schuler, A. L., Fletcher, E. C., and Davis-Welsh, J. D. 1977. Language development in childhood autism: A case study. Paper presented at the annual meeting of the American Speech and Hearing Association, November, Chicago.

Schuler, A. L., LaVigna, G., Bormann, G., and Grumet, B. 1978. A systematic comparison of the acquisition of written, spoken, and signed words in mute autistic adolescents. Paper presented to the annual Los Angeles State University Conference on Childhood Autism, Los Angeles.

Schumaker, J., and Sherman, J. A. 1970. Training generative verb usage by imitation and reinforcement procedures. J. Appl. Behav. Anal. 3:273–287.

Schusterman, R. J. 1964. Strategies of normal and mentally retarded children under conditions of uncertain outcome. Am. J. Ment. Defic. 69:66–79.

Searle, J. R. 1969. Speech Acts. Cambridge University Press, New York.

Segal, E. F. 1975. Psycholinguistics discovers the operant: A review of Roger Brown's *A First Language: The Early Stages*. J. Exp. Anal. Behav. 23:149–158.

Serifica, F. 1971. Object concept in deviant children. Am. J. Orthopsychiatry 41:473–482.

Shapiro, T., Roberts, A., and Fish, B. 1970. Imitation and echoing in young schizophrenic children. J. Am. Acad. Child Psychiatry 9:548–565.

Shipley, E. F., and Shipley, T. E. 1969. Quaker children's use of thee: A rational analysis. J. Verb. Learn. Verb. Behav. 8:112–117.

Shipley, E. F., Smith, C., and Gleitman, L. 1969. A study of the acquisition of language: Free response to commands. Language 45:322–342.

Siegel, G. M. 1969. Vocal conditioning in infants. J. Speech Hear. Disord. 34:3–19.

Silberberg, M., and Silberberg, M. 1967. Hyperlexia: Specific word recognition skills in young children. Except. Child. 34:41–42.

Simmons, J. Q., and Baltaxe, C. 1975. Language patterns of adolescent autistics. J. Aut. Child. Schizo. 5:333–351.

Simon, C. T. 1957. The development of speech. *In* L. Travis (ed.), Handbook of Speech Pathology. Appleton-Century-Crofts, New York.

Simon, N. 1975. Echolalic speech in childhood autism. Arch. Gen. Psychiatry 32:1439–1446.

Skinner, B. F. 1957. Verbal Behavior. Appleton-Century-Crofts, New York.

Snyder, L. S. 1975. Pragmatics in language disabled children: Their prelinguistic and early verbal performatives and presuppositions. Unpublished doctoral dissertation, University of Colorado, Boulder.

Sperry, R. W., Gazzaniga, M. S., and Bogen, J. E. 1969. The neocortical commissures: Syndrome of hemisphere deconnection. Handbook of Clinical Neurology, Vol. IV, Chapter 14. North Holland Publishing Co., Amsterdam.

Stengel, E. 1947. A clinical and psychological study of echo-reactions. J. Ment. Sci. 93:598–612.

Stengel, E. 1964. Speech disorders and mental disorders. *In* A.V.S. de Reuck and M. O'Connor (eds.), Disorders of Language. Little, Brown & Co., Boston.

Stokoe, W. 1972. Semiotics and Human Sign Language. Mouton, The Hague.

Stubbs, E. G. 1976. Autistic children exhibit undetectable hemagglutination-inhibition antibody titers despite rubella vaccination. J. Aut. Child. Schizo. 6:269–274.

Studdert-Kennedy, M. 1975. The preception of speech. *In* T. A. Sebeok (ed.), Current Trends in Linguistics XII. Mouton, The Hague.

Sugarman, S. 1973. A description of communicative development in the prelanguage child. Unpublished honors thesis, Hampshire College, Amherst, Mass.

Sulzbacher, S. J., and Costello, J. M. 1970. A behavioral strategy for language training of a child with autistic behaviors. J. Speech Hear. Disord. 35:256–276.

Taylor, J. (ed.). 1958. Selected Writing of John Hughlings Jackson. Basic Books, New York.

Taylor, J. E. 1976. An approach to teaching cognitive skills underlying language development. In L. Wing (ed.), Early Childhood Autism: Clinical, Educational and Social Aspects (2nd ed.). Pergamon Press, Oxford.

Terrace, H. S. 1963. Discrimination learning with and without "errors." J. Exp. Anal. Behav. 6:1–27.

Thorndike, E. L. 1931 (1966). Human Learning. The MIT Press, Cambridge, Mass. [First printing, 1931.]

Tramontana, J., and Shivers, O. 1971. Behavior modification with an echolalic child: A case note. Psycholog. Rep. 29:1034.

Tubbs, V. K. 1966. The type of linguistic disability in psychotic children. J. Ment. Defic. Res. 10:230–240.

Turner, E. A., and Rommetveit, R. 1967. The acquisition of sentence voice and reversibility. Child Dev. 38:649–660.

Voeltz, L. M. 1977. Rule mediation and echolalia in autistic children: Phonological evidence. Paper presented at the annual meeting of the American Speech and Hearing Association, November, Chicago.

Vygotsky, L. 1962. Thought and Language. The MIT Press, Cambridge, Mass.

Wade, O. C. 1976. Their fingers do the talking. Psychol. Today. June.

Waugh, N. C., and Norman, D. A. 1965. Primary memory. Psycholog. Rev. 72:89–104.

Webster, C. D., McPherson, H., Sloman, L., Evans, M. A., and Kuchor, E. 1973. Communicating with an autistic boy by gestures. J. Aut. Child. Schizo. 3:337–346.

Weir, R. H. 1962. Language in the Crib. Mouton, The Hague.

Wetherby, B., and Striefel, S. 1978. Application of a miniature linguistic system or matrix-training procedures. In R. L. Schiefelbusch (ed.), Language Intervention Strategies. University Park Press, Baltimore.

Whitehurst, G. J., and Vasta, R. 1975. Is language acquired through imitation? J. Psycholing. Res. 4:37–39.

Williams, F., and Naremore, R. C. 1969. On the functional analysis of social class differences in modes of speech. Speech Monogr. 36:77–102.

Wing, J. K. 1976. Kanner's syndrome: A historic introduction. In L. Wing (ed.), Early Childhood Autism: Clinical, Educational and Social Aspects (2nd ed.). Pergamon Press, Oxford.

Wing, L. 1969. The handicaps of autistic children—A comparative study. J. Child Psychol. Psychiatry 10:1–40.

Wing, L. 1974. Autistic Children. Citadel Press, Secaucus, N.J.

Wing, L. 1978. Language, communication and cognition. A symposium chaired at the annual Los Angeles State University Conference on Autism, Los Angeles.

Wing, L., Gould, J., Yeates, J. R., and Brierly, L. M. 1977. Symbolic play in severely mentally retarded and in autistic children. J. Child Psychol. Psychiatry 18:167–178.

Wolf, M. M., Risley, T., and Mees, H. 1964. Application of operant conditioning procedures to the behavior problems of an autistic child. Behav. Res. Ther. 1:305–312.

Wolff, S., and Chess, S. 1965. An analysis of the language of fourteen schizophrenic children. J. Child Psychol. Psychiatry 6:29–41.

Woodworth, R. S., and Schlosberg, H. 1954. Experimental Psychology (rev. ed.). Henry Holt, New York.

Wyllie, J. 1894. The Disorders of Speech. Oliver and Boyd, Edinburgh.

Young, F. M. 1942. Development as indicated by a study of pronouns. J. Gene. Psychol. 61:125–134.

Yule, W., and Berger, M. 1975. Communication, language and behavior modification. In C. C. Kiernan and F. P. Woodford (eds.), Behavior Modification with the Severely Retarded. Elsevier, Amsterdam.

Zipf, G. K. 1949. Human Behavior and the Principle of Least Effort. (1965 ed.). Hafner, New York.

index

Abstract concepts, 6, 122–123, 133
Adolescents and adults, language development, 80–83
Alternative systems of communication, 148–158
  computer programs, 158
  plastic symbols, 149–151, 155–157
  signs and signing, 148–155
  teaching communication skills, 177–180
  teaching non-oral systems, 153–158
  written word training, 157–158
Aphasia, 17, 21, 132
  echolalia, 53, 62
Articulation, 47–49, 184
  echolalia, 47–49
Assessment of language functioning, 167–174
Attentional idiosyncrasies, 127–128
Autism, 3–18
  attitudes toward, 3, 9
  causes, 3, 7, 154
  characteristics, 3
  early infantile autism, 3–6, 14
  early interpretations, 7–9
  incidence, 16–17
  language and diagnosis, 9, 13–17
  language disorder, 9–13, 99–110
  as symbolic disorder, 129–130
  syndrome, 9–13, 136
    definition, 15–16
    follow-up studies, 11–12
    investigations of, 9–13
    language aspects, 4–7
    symptoms, 6, 15–16
  terminology, 14, 134
Automaticity of behavior, 90–91

Babbling by autistic children, 23, 101
Behavior
  anomalies in autism, 104–105, 134, 136
  automaticity, 90–91
  deficiencies in autism, 108–111
  disorders of social behavior, 108–109
  lack of means-end, 104–105, 127–128, 172–173
Behavior modification therapy, 12, 139–149
  control procedures, 140
  description and review, 140–145
  discrimination training, 144
  language-training programs, 144–147
  prompting and prompt fading, 141–143
  reduction of disruptive behavior, 140
  reinforcements, 139–140, 144
  speech training, 140–145
  verbal imitation drills, 140–142, 145–146
Blindness, 16, 38–39
  autistic echolalia, 38–41
Body language, 91–92, 106
  linking speech to, 184
  as referents, 185

Chimpanzees, teaching language to, 90, 95, 100, 129, 148–153, 155
Coding of intentions and meanings, 91–92
Cognitive/language disorders, 12, 115–136
  cognitive abilities, 115–126
    evidence from other sources, 120–126
    evidence from testing, 116–120
  components of "language-mindedness," 126–131
  definition of cognition, 115
  developmental discontinuity, 115–116, 168–169
  information processing, 120–121
  interaction of linguistic and cognitive deficits, 11, 126–131
  linguistic, cognitive, and social development, 131–135

Communication
  acquisition of skills, 93–99
  alternative systems of, 148–158
    teaching non-oral systems,
      153–158
  in autism, 99–110
    communicative competence,
      105–110
    functions of speech, 99–105
    language deficit, 99
  automaticity of behavior, 90–91
  behavioral problems and, 89,
    108–109
  coding of intentions and meanings,
    91–92
  conversational clumsiness, 107–108,
    111
  deficits, 98–99
  definition, 90
  early utterances, 96–97
  early vocalizations, 95–96
  egocentric or private speech,
    104–105
  features of, 89–93
  intentional and nonintentional,
    91–92, 110, 177–180
  interaction of cognitive, linguistic,
    and social development,
    131–135
  learning to communicate, 93–99
  mother-child interaction, 98
  nonverbal, 89, 91, 94, 101–102
  prelanguage skills, 94–95
  social context of speech, 98, 103
  speaker-listener interactions,
    106–107
  speech sounds, 89
Communicative intent, 91–92, 110
  echolalia and, 53–63
  teaching, 177–180, 183
Comprehension deficits, 55, 131
Conceptual abilities, 127–128
  tests of, 118–119
Conversational skills, 107–108, 111,
  131

Deafness, 13, 16, 22
Developmental problems, 126–135
  discontinuity, 115–116, 168–169

linguistic competence, 37–38
  normal vs. autistic, 132–133
  stagnation, 134
Diagnosis of childhood autism, 13–17
  behavioral limitations, 15–16
  checklist method, 14–15
  Diagnostic Form E-2, 14–15
  differential, 16–17, 134, 170
  language and, 13–17
Directions, misunderstanding, 82, 186
Discrimination learning, 124–125
  reinforcements, 144
Down's syndrome, 122

Early infantile autism, 3–6
  severe language impairment, 99–110
  terminology, 14
Echolalia, 3–5, 7, 10, 25–41
  adult symptoms, 32
  affirmation by repetition, 54
  articulation and, 47–49
  blind children, 38–41
  characteristics, 27–31
  classification of, 53
  and communicative intent, 53–63
  comprehension deficits, 55, 74–75
  definition, 25–27
  delayed, 56–59, 89
  developmental echoing, 26–31
  illnesses associated with, 32
  imitations and echoes, 28–30, 53
  immediate and delayed, 53–59
    differences between, 57–58
  intervention program, 38
  latencies between trigger and echo,
    34
  linguistic competence and, 37–38,
    57
  mitigated, 59–63
  non-autistic, 31–34
  pathology, 37–38
  post-echoic language, 74–75
  relationship to understanding,
    35–36
  research needs, 28–29
  schizophrenic children, 35–36
  teaching verbal imitation skills,
    141–143
  vocal delivery and, 41–49
Eye movements, 91–92, 139–140, 186

Facial expressions, 3, 49, 91, 106
  communicative value, 91–92
"First words," 4, 24, 77–78, 95–97
Follow-up studies, 7–8, 11–12, 18

Gender, confusion with, 81, 83
Generalization, 3, 76, 78, 121, 164,
    187
  lack of, 125, 146–148
  limited abilities in, 5–6
  teaching, 188
Gestural behavior, 71, 91–92, 106
Grammatical construction, 80
  teaching, 147, 159, 163–164

"Idiot savant," 6, 78
Imaginary activity, 129
Imitation, 133
  role in language development,
    28–30
  teaching skills, 183
  verbal imitation skills, 140–144
Information processing, 120–121
Instructions, following, 82, 186
Intelligence of autistic children, 6, 16,
    24
Intervention strategies, 12, 18, 134,
    139–164
  alternative systems of communica-
    tion, 148–158
    computer programs, 158
    plastic symbols, 149–151,
      155–157
    signs and signing, 148–155,
      177–180
    teaching non-oral systems,
      153–158
    written word training, 157–158
  behavioral approaches, 139–149
  discussion of, 158–162
  divergent approaches, 162–163
  guidelines for, 167–189
  implications, 162–164
  reinforcing consequences, 163
  teaching communication skills,
    174–189
Intonational irregularities, 146
  autistic deficiencies, 44–45, 107, 146
  emotional factors and, 43–44

  emphasis and final word, 47
  interactions with syntax and seman-
    tics, 46
  voice quality and, 42–47
Introversion, 7

Labels and labeling, 75–76, 172–173
  intervention techniques, 143,
    146–147, 175
  symbolic, 128
Language, 53–85
  abnormalities of grammatical con-
    struction, 79–80
  adolescent and adult, 80–83
  analyses and surveys, 82
  analyzing and coding experiences,
    84
  autistic pronouns and deixis, 63–74
    non-autistic pronominal develop-
      ment, 65–70
    pronominal reversal and avoid-
      ance, 70–74
    self-differentiation, 64–65
  communicative intent, 53–63, 127
  deictic deficiencies, 66–67, 73
  delayed and deviant development,
    14, 18
  disorders, 3, 12–13, 18, 99, 132, 135
  echolalia and communicative intent,
    53–63
  failure to generalize meaning, 78
  first associations, 78–79
  grammatical abnormalities, 79–80,
    163–164
  impairment in early childhood
    autism, 99–110
  interaction of cognitive, linguistic,
    and social development,
    131–135
  intervention techniques, 146–147,
    163–164
  invented words, 80
  labeling, 75–76, 172–173
  means-end behavior, 127–128
  object naming, 84
  post-echoic, 74–85
    adolescent and adult language,
      80–83
    language cast in concrete, 77–80
    from sound to sense, 75–77

Language—*continued*
    pragmatic aspects, 93–94, 97–99
    as prognostic factor, 8
    referents, 84, 174, 185
    relationship between cognitive and
        linguistic skills, 127–131
    remediation and, 77
    repetitions of utterances, 9
    skills needed, 126–131
        teaching, 184–185
    symptoms, 4–7
    syntactic and semantic considera-
        tions, 184
    teaching chimpanzees, 148–153
    teaching procedures, 184–185
    yes concept, 5, 79, 82
Learning problems of autistic chil-
    dren, 124–125
Left-handedness, 126
Linguistic competence, 105–110
    delayed echolalia and, 57
    from sound to sense, 75–77
"Literalness," excessive, 3, 5, 14–15,
    129

"*Mands*" and "*tacts*," 103–104,
    175–176
Matching objects, 187–188
Memories, rote, 4, 7, 11, 72
Mental capacities of autistic children,
    116
Mental retardation, 16, 17
"Metaphoric language," 5–7, 14–15,
    57
Monotonous speaking manner, 43,
    105
Mutism or muteness, 3, 21–25
    deafness and, 22
    diagnosis, 14
    elective, 4, 23–24
    "first words," 24
    functional, 21
    noise hypersensitivity and, 22
    semi-mute, 21
    total, 21

Objects
    identification, 144
    matching, 187–188
    relation to, 3, 6, 84

Operant learning techniques, 12, 102,
    139
    see also Behavior modification
        therapy

Parents of autistic children, 3, 13
Patterns, detection of, 120, 188
Personality organization, 6, 59
Pitch inflections, 10, 41–43, 97
Plagiarism, 61
Plastic symbols, 159–160, 178–179
    alternative method of communica-
        tion, 149–151
    teaching non-oral systems of com-
        munication, 155–158
Play behavior, 121–122
    abnormalities of symbolic, 59,
        121–122
    learning to play games, 187
Pointing behavior, 68, 71
Prepositions, difficulties with, 81
Prognosis, 8, 12, 61–62
Prompting techniques, 141–143
Pronominal difficulties, 4–5, 7, 63–74,
        84–85, 133–134
    autistic children, 63–74
    and deixis, 63–74
    ego, 66
    intervention procedures, 73–74
    linguistic deixis, 68
    non-autistic pronominal develop-
        ment, 65–70
    pronominal development, 63–65
    relative comprehension, 67–68
    "reversal" and "avoidance," 1, 7,
        62–63, 70–74, 160
    self-differentiation and, 64–65
    you/me dichotomy, 68–70
Pronominal reversals, 1, 7, 62–63,
    70–74, 160
Psychological functioning, 10–11

Questions, responses to, 79

Reading skills, 6, 157
Referents, 84, 174, 185
Reinforcement, 139–140
    social, 147, 176

Remedial efforts, *see* Intervention techniques
Repetition of utterances, 3-4, 9, 122 *see also* Echolalia
Representational inabilities, 130, 133-134
Requests, communication problems, 108-110
Role-playing activities, 186

Sameness, insistence on, 127
Schizophrenia, childhood, 3, 17, 26
Self-differentiation problems, 64-65, 134
Self-identity, origin of, 65
Sensitivity, lack of, 72
Sentence formation, 4-5, 93
Signs and signing, 148, 160
    teaching autistic children, 153-158
Sitting skills, 139-140, 142-143, 176
Skills in autistic children, 126-127
    spatial and temporal, 126-127
Social awareness, absence of, 7, 72
Social development, 169-170
    interaction of cognitive and linguistic development and, 131-135
Special education, 10, 13
Speech, Language, and Hearing (SLH) Examination, 32-33
    Verbal Comprehension subtest, 35
Speech behavior, 9-10, 21-50, 90
    autistic peculiarities, 105-110
    characteristics of articulation, 47-49
    delayed onset of speech, 24-25
    echolalia, 25-41
        autistic, 34-41
        developmental echoing, 26-31
        non-autistic, 31-34
    egocentric or private, 104
    functions, 99-105
        classification of, 96-97, 101
    intelligibility versus communicative intent, 183
    interaction of cognitive, linguistic, and social development, 131-135
    intervention techniques, 140-145, 183-184
    speech imitation skills, 140-142
    intonation, 41-42

language comprehension and, 9-11, 87-111, 187
    mechanistic and flat in affect, 43, 105, 111
    muteness, 21-25
    sensory stimulation, 99
    teaching programs, 140-145, 183-184
    verbal imitation skills, 140-144
    vocal delivery, 41-49
    voice quality and intonation, 42-47
Speech disorders, 13
Speech pathology, 10, 13
Spelling, 6
Stimuli
    inability to interpret meaningfully, 11
    overselectivity, 123-124, 135, 155, 159
    sensory, 99
Symbolization, 133
    deficiencies, 126-128
    labeling, 128-129
Symptoms, autistic language, 4-6, 15-16

Teaching language skills, 174-188
    alternative systems of communication, 177-180
    assessment and curriculum design, 167-174
    cognition, 187-188
        generalization, 188
        matching objects, 187-188
    communications, 185-187
        design of language-teaching programs, 182-188
        ensuring listener's attention, 186
        expanding roots of language, 182-188
    functional concerns, 175-176
    grammar-practicing devices, 179, 183
    language, 184-185
    limitations, 188-189
    management of behavioral problems and, 176
    matching program and child, 182-183
    objectives, 167-169, 177

Teaching language skills—*continued*
  procedures, 180–182
    discriminative responses, 182
    responses and consequences,
      180–182
    selection of objectives, 167–169,
      177–178
    speech, 183–184
    verbal imitation skills, 140–144, 178
Temper tantrums and screaming, 131,
  134
  intervention techniques, 139–140
Terminology, 14, 134
Tests and testing, 13, 135
  autistic and mentally retarded chil-
    dren, 117
  conceptual abilities, 118–120
  Edinburg Articulation Test, 48
  Illinois Test of Psycholinguistic
    Abilities, 13
  match-to-sample, 118–119
  nonverbal conceptual, 127
  Northwestern Syntax Screening
    Test, 13
  Peabody Picture Vocabulary Test,
    13, 48, 63
  performance of autistic children,
    116–120
  problems associated with, 169
  prognostic value of IQ tests,
    117–118
  validity of, 116, 118
Therapy, language-oriented, 8
  see also Intervention strategies
Tools, use of, 133

Verbal peculiarities, 6
Visuo-spatial abilities, 120, 126
Vocal delivery, 41–49
  characteristics of articulation, 47–49
  segmental and nonsegmental, 41
  voice quality and intonation, 42–47
Vocalizations, 95–96, 100, 163
  self-stimulatory, 101–104

Withdrawal behaviors, 3, 118
Written word training, 157–158

Yes concept, 5, 79, 82
Yes/no questions, 129